Lecture Notes
in Business Information Processing   15

Series Editors

Wil van der Aalst
Eindhoven Technical University, The Netherlands

John Mylopoulos
University of Trento, Italy

Norman M. Sadeh
Carnegie Mellon University, Pittsburgh, PA, USA

Michael J. Shaw
University of Illinois, Urbana-Champaign, IL, USA

Clemens Szyperski
Microsoft Research, Redmond, WA, USA

Janis Stirna   Anne Persson (Eds.)

The Practice of Enterprise Modeling

First IFIP WG 8.1 Working Conference, PoEM 2008
Stockholm, Sweden, November 12-13, 2008
Proceedings

 Springer

Volume Editors

Janis Stirna
Royal Institute of Technology and Stockholm University
Department of Computer and Systems Sciences
FORUM 100, 16440 Kista, Sweden
E-mail: js@dsv.su.se

Anne Persson
University of Skövde
School of Humanities and Informatics
P.O. Box 408, 54128 Skövde, Sweden
E-mail: anne.persson@his.se

Library of Congress Control Number: 2008938156

ACM Computing Classification (1998): J.1, H.4, K.6.1

ISSN   1865-1348
ISBN-10   3-540-89217-6 Springer Berlin Heidelberg New York
ISBN-13   978-3-540-89217-5 Springer Berlin Heidelberg New York

Springer is a part of Springer Science+Business Media

springer.com

© IFIP International Federation for Information Processing, Hofstrasse 3, A-2361 Laxenburg, Austria 2008
Printed in Germany

Typesetting: Camera-ready by author, data conversion by Scientific Publishing Services, Chennai, India
Printed on acid-free paper   SPIN: 12566938   06/3180   5 4 3 2 1 0

Preface

Enterprise modeling (EM) has gained substantial popularity both in the academic community and among practitioners. A variety of EM methods, approaches, and tools are developed and offered on the market. In practice they are used for various purposes such as business strategy development, process restructuring, as well as business and IT architecture alignment and governance.

PoEM 2008, the First IFIP WG 8.1 Working Conference on The Practice of Enterprise Modeling, took place in Stockholm, Sweden. It is the first conference aiming to establish a dedicated forum where the use of EM in practice is addressed by bringing together researchers, users, and practitioners. The goals of PoEM 2008 were to develop a better understanding of the practice of EM, to contribute to improved EM practice, as well as to share knowledge and experiences.

The theme of PoEM 2008 was EM in different application contexts, e.g., software development, including agile development, as well as business development, governance, and change. We focused on the following topics: evaluation of EM methods from a practice perspective, the process of modeling and guidelines for modeling, management of EM projects, use of EM in different contexts, facilitation and group dynamics, the competency of modelers and modeling teams, model and process quality aspects, reuse of enterprise models, modeling languages, the use of EM in different contexts, tools and workbenches, enterprise model management, success factors in EM, teaching the practice, EM and agile development, enterprise knowledge architectures, standardization issues and reference models, method engineering in EM, concordance between EM and information systems development.

The focus area of PoEM 2008 attracted 34 submissions from 16 countries, out of which the Program Committee selected 17 high-quality papers. The resulting program reflects the fact that the topic of EM encompasses human and organizational issues as well as technical aspects of information systems engineering. The program also featured a keynote by Björn Nilsson, one of Sweden's most experienced EM practitioners. To stimulate open exchange of ideas PoEM 2008 also included two joint brainstorming sessions on the emerging challenges of EM.

We devote a special thanks to the members of the International Program Committee for promoting the conference and for providing excellent reviews of the submitted papers. Their dedicated work was vital for putting together a high-quality working conference. A special thanks goes to the University of Skövde, Jönköping University, and the Royal Institute of Technology for supporting the organization of the conference.

The PoEM 2008 organizers would also like to thank the conference sponsor – Fraunhofer Institute for Software and Systems Engineering (ISST), Germany.

July 2008

Janis Stirna
Anne Persson

Organization

General Chair

Janis Bubenko Jr.   Royal Institute of Technology, Sweden

Program Committee Co-chairs

Janis Stirna   Jönköping University, Sweden
Anne Persson   University of Skövde, Sweden

Organizing Chair

Lena Aggestam   University of Skövde, Sweden

Program Committee

Akhilesh Bajaj	University of Tulsa, USA
Marko Bajec	University of Ljubljana, Slovenia
Rimantas Butleris	Kaunas University of Technology, Lithuania
Wolfgang Deiters	Fraunhofer ISST, Germany
Eric Dubois	CRP Henri Tudor, Luxembourg
Xavier Franch	Universitat Politècnica de Catalunya, Spain
Paolo Giorgini	University of Trento, Italy
Remigijus Gustas	Karlstad University, Sweden
Terry Halpin	Neumont University, USA
Lennart Holmberg	Kongsberg Automotive AB, Sweden
Stijn Hoppenbrouwers	Radboud University Nijmegen, The Netherlands
Jarl Höglund	Allmentor AB, Sweden
Paul Johannesson	Royal Institute of Technology, Sweden
Maria Jönsson	Tele 2 AB, Sweden
Håvard Jørgensen	Active Knowledge Modeling AS, Norway
Evangelia Kavakli	University of the Aegean, Greece
Marite Kirikova	Riga Technical University, Latvia
John Krogstie	Norwegian University of Science and Technology, Norway
Marc Lankhorst	Telematica Instituut, The Netherlands
Michel Leonard	Université de Genève, Switzerland
Peri Loucopoulos	Loughborough University, UK
Graham McLeod	Inspired, South Africa
Christer Nellborn	Nellborn Management Consulting AB, Sweden

Björn Nilsson	Anatés AB, Luxembourg
Selmin Nurcan	Université Paris 1 Panthéon Sorbonne, France
Andreas Opdahl	University of Bergen, Norway
Oscar Pastor	Valencia University of Technology, Spain
Naveen Prakash	GCET, India
Erik Proper	Radboud University Nijmegen, The Netherlands
Jolita Ralyte	Université de Genève, Switzerland
Sudha Ram	University of Arizona, USA
Colette Rolland	Université Paris 1 Panthéon Sorbonne, France
Michael Rosemann	Queensland University of Technology, Australia
Sanda Ruza	Ernst &Young SIA, Latvia
Camille Salinesi	Université Paris 1 Panthéon Sorbonne, France
Kurt Sandkuhl	Jönköping Technical University, Sweden
Ulf Seigerroth	Jönköping International Business School, Sweden
Keng Siau	University of Nebraska-Lincoln, USA
Guttorm Sindre	Norwegian University of Science and Technology, Norway
Pnina Soffer	University of Haifa, Israel
Olegas Vasilecas	Vilnius Gediminas Technical University, Lithuania
Christer Wåhlander	Visuera Integration AB, Sweden
Eric Yu	University of Toronto, Canada

External Reviewers

Kestutis Kapocius
Algirdas Laukaitis
Magnus Lundqvist
Jan Neuhaus
Moses Niwe
Aidas Smaizys
Christer Thörn
Manfred Wojciechowski

Table of Contents

Knowledge and Enterprise Architecture Modeling

Enterprise Modeling Approaches I

Process Modeling

Network and Value Modeling

Enterprise Modeling II

Enterprise Modeling Research Directions

The Early Phases of Enterprise Knowledge Modelling: Practices and Experiences from Scaffolding and Scoping

Kurt Sandkuhl[1] and Frank Lillehagen[2]

[1] School of Engineering at Jönköping University,
P.O. Box 1026, 55111 Jönköping, Sweden
Kurt.Sandkuhl@jth.hj.se
[2] Active Knowledge Modeling AS,
P.O. Box 376, 1326 Lysaker, Norway
f.lillehagen@akmodeling.com

Abstract. Enterprise modelling concepts, methods or technologies have been found useful for a variety of application areas and purposes. The experience report presented in this paper is from the area of enterprise knowledge modelling with an application case in automotive supplier industries. The purpose of the overall modelling process is to create an active knowledge model. The scope of the paper are the early phases of the enterprise knowledge modelling process, called scaffolding phase and scoping phase. An important observation is the need for continuous and intertwined development of meta-model, model, modelling process and modelling team.

Keywords: Enterprise knowledge modelling, practice report, active knowledge modelling.

1 Introduction

During the last 20 years, enterprise modelling concepts, methods or technologies have been found useful for a variety of application areas and purposes, like understanding and improving the business processes in an organization, capturing requirements in software system development, visualizing document and information flow, preparing strategic decisions in IT governance, analyzing fraud risks, evaluating business value of IT investments, orchestrating the project validation, and many more.

As a consequence, researchers and practitioners from many different disciplines have been contributing to development of enterprise modelling practices, including information system development, software engineering, enterprise engineering or organizational development.

The experience report presented in this paper is from the area of enterprise knowledge modelling with an application case in automotive supplier industries. The objective of the research work performed was to develop and evaluate a model-based collaboration infrastructure for use in distributed product design. In this context, modelling of the relevant part of the application case was initiated. The purpose of the modelling process was to create an active knowledge model, i.e. an enterprise

J. Stirna and A. Persson (Eds.): PoEM 2008, LNBIP 15, pp. 1–14, 2008.

knowledge model, which supports execution of work tasks and is adaptable to the user's local demands (cf. section 2.2). The scope of the paper is the early phases of the enterprise knowledge modelling process, called scaffolding phase and scoping phase. These phases were selected for the experience report as they resulted in experiences and work practices of potential interest for enterprise modelling in general.

The paper is structured into four more chapters: Chapter 2 will summarize the background for our work including the industrial case considered, the area of active knowledge modelling and the modelling approach used. Chapter 3 will present the practice of scaffolding and scoping. Chapter 4 discusses limits and potentials of the scaffolding practices. Chapter 5 summarizes the achievements.

2 Background

The experience report presented in this paper is based on an industrial case, which is introduced in section 2.1. Furthermore, a short introduction to the specifics of active knowledge modelling will be given (section 2.2) and the modelling approach used will be presented (section 2.3).

2.1 Industrial Case

The experiences presented are based on work in the EU-FP6 project MAPPER[1] (Model-adapted Process and Product Engineering). MAPPER had a runtime from autumn 2005 to spring 2008 and aimed at enabling fast and flexible manufacturing in networked enterprises by providing methodology, infrastructure and reusable services for participative engineering.

The industrial case considered in this paper was a use case in the MAPPER project and focuses on distributed product development and multi-project lifecycles in a networked organization with different subsidiaries of an automotive supplier. The main partner is the business area "interior" of a first tier automotive supplier with the main product development sites in Scandinavia. The interior area mainly includes seat comfort products like seat heater, seat ventilation, climate control, lumber support and head restraint. During the MAPPER project, the focus was on the advanced engineering unit, where product development tasks are concentrating on pre-development of new concepts and new materials.

Development of products includes elicitation of system requirements based on customer requirements, development of functional, design of logical and technical architecture, co-design of material, electrical and mechanical components, integration testing and production planning including production logistics, floor planning and product line planning. The process is geographically distributed involving engineers and specialists at several locations of the automotive supplier and sub-supplier for specific tasks. A large percentage of seat comfort components can be considered as product families, i.e. various versions of the components exist and have to be maintained and further developed for different product models and different customers. In this context, flexible product development in networks with changing partners on customer and sub-supplier side is of crucial importance.

---

[1] See [1] for more information about MAPPER.

The purpose of the enterprise knowledge modelling in this use case was to capture the relevant product knowledge and process knowledge required for supporting collaborative engineering at different sites of the automotive supplier. The knowledge model was expected to contribute to solving a number of challenges:

- To support fast integration of geographically distributed collaboration partners
- To enable flexible development processes, combining pre-defined processes for coordinated development tasks and ad-hoc process changes.
- To coordinate a large number of parallel product development activities

2.2 Enterprise Knowledge Modelling and Active Knowledge Models

Enterprise knowledge modelling is applying and extending approaches, concepts and technologies from enterprise modelling and enterprise architecture for knowledge representation and knowledge-based solutions. In general terms, enterprise modelling is addressing the systematic analysis and modelling of processes, organization structures, products structures, IT-systems or any other perspective relevant for the modelling purpose. Enterprise models can be applied for various reasons, like visualization of current processes and structures in an enterprise, process improvement and optimization, introduction of new IT solutions or analysis purposes. [9] provides a detailed account of enterprise modelling and integration approaches including reference models.

The field of enterprise architectures received a growing attention during the last years in the context of IT-governance or corporate governance. Main intention is to visualize the architecture of IT-application and infrastructure in an enterprise including the supported processes or organization units. Such enterprise architecture models are closely related to enterprise models, as they to a significant extent have to cover the same aspects (e.g. processes and organization structures). However, enterprise architectures focus on providing a basis for analyzing current IT architectures in enterprises and providing a basis for (strategic) planning of future developments. [10] discusses in particular the connection between enterprise architecture and IT governance.

Enterprise knowledge modelling combines and extends approaches and techniques from enterprise modelling and enterprise architectures. The knowledge needed for performing a certain task in an enterprise or for acting in a certain role has to include the context of the individual, which requires including all relevant perspectives in the same model. Using the knowledge is applying different reflective views on the knowledge model. *Enterprise knowledge modelling* aims at capturing reusable knowledge of processes and products in knowledge architectures supporting work execution [2]. These architectures form the basis for model-based solutions, which often are represented as active knowledge models [3]. [4] identifies characteristics of active models vs. passive models and emphasize that "the model must be dynamic, users must be supported in changing the model to fit their local reality, enabling tailoring of the system's behaviour".

In MAPPER, these active knowledge models included the POPS* perspectives [5]:

- the process perspective (P) captures the work processes and tasks in the networked enterprise,

- the organization perspective (O) includes all roles involved in the processes and their skills and competence profiles,
- the product perspective (P) focuses on components, configuration possibilities and dependencies of the product under consideration,
- the systems perspective (S) includes the IT systems supporting work processes and product development,
- further perspectives (*) depend on the requirements of the enterprise under consideration and can include business objectives, customer requirements regarding the products or key success factors.

These perspectives are mutually reflective, i.e. each perspective influences content and meaning of the other perspectives, which is captured in relationships and dependencies between the elements of the perspectives. The active knowledge model developed in MAPPER can be executed in the MAPPER infrastructure, which for example includes a basic work flow engine and model-configured role-specific work places for capturing product knowledge.

2.3 Enterprise Knowledge Modelling with C3S3P

Enterprise knowledge modelling in the industrial case was performed according to the C3S3P methodology. C3S3P is based on work in several EU projects from the area of networked and extended enterprises. An extended enterprise is a dynamic networked organization, which is created ad-hoc to reach a certain objective using the resources of the participating cooperating enterprises. In order to support solutions development for extended enterprises, the EXTERNAL project developed a methodology for extended enterprise modelling [6], which initially was named SGAMSIDOER. This methodology was further developed towards a complete customer delivery process denoted C3S3P, which was used in the ATHENA[2] and MAPPER projects.

C3S3P distinguishes between seven phases called Concept study, Scaffolding, Scoping, Solution modelling, Platform integration, Piloting in real projects and Performance monitoring and management. The C3S3P phases roughly include the following:

- Concept Study: pre-studies are performed to investigate whether EM is a suitable and accepted way of developing executable solutions for the networked enterprise
- Scaffolding[3] aims at creating shared knowledge and understanding among the participants of the project about the scope and challenges of the project.
- Scoping: creation of models supporting the networked enterprise for a defined scope including all relevant dimensions required, like process, product, organization or IT-systems
- Solutions Modelling: refining the scoping model by integration personnel, product structures, document templates and IT systems required for using the enterprise model in an actual project

---

[2] http://www.athena-ip.org/

[3] The term scaffolding indicates the intention of this phase to create a firm structure supporting the development of a solution without making this structure a part of the solution – like in construction projects where the scaffold supports the construction of a building.

- Platform Configuration: configure the solution models for use in the networked or extended enterprise by connecting the enterprise model to the platform used (see [1] for details on the MAPPER platform)
- Platform Delivery: encompasses the roll-out of model-configured solutions
- Performance Improvement by capturing indicators for process and product quality and using adequate management instruments.

The work performed in MAPPER included two cycles of using C3S3P. The first cycle focused on capturing organizational knowledge and best practices for networked manufacturing enterprises. The second cycle focused on integration of product knowledge into the best practices. The practices presented in the following chapter are primarily taken from the first cycle and focus on scaffolding and scoping. The scaffolding phase of the second C3S3P cycle was considerably shorter than in the first cycle, as a lot of shared understanding of the problem domain already had been created.

3 Practice of Scaffolding and Scoping

The objective of this chapter is describe the way of working during scaffolding and scoping, including practices applied, some illustrative examples of the models produced and an overall structure of the early phases of this enterprise knowledge modelling process.

3.1 Scaffolding Phase

Before starting the scaffolding phase, a concept study was performed, which aimed at creating a shared understanding of the task at hand, the product design terminology used, and the organizational context at the automotive supplier. During this study, the automotive supplier basically gave a detailed introduction into aspects like what are seat comfort products and components, and how are they developed and manufactured. This introduction included visits at the engineering labs, manufacturing plant and test facilities.

Preparation Steps

At the beginning of the scaffolding phase, a number of preparation steps had to be taken, which were contributing to a joint understanding of visual knowledge modelling and a prerequisite for the later phases. After having identified all use case team members from the involved MAPPER partners, the team members were offered an introduction and basic training in the METIS[4] tool, which was selected as modelling tool. Furthermore, an agreement was made to start with scaffolding workshops involving all team members and to locate these workshops at the automotive supplier's premises, in order to have quick access to stakeholders and material, which could support modelling. An initial distribution of roles to persons was made, which included the following roles for the modelling process:

---

[4] The METIS tool was recently renamed into Troux Architect. For tool information see www.troux.com

- Manager: the owner of the use case who is responsible for establishing the use case at the use case partner, assigning the right personnel resources, arranging meetings, etc.
- Planner: the person responsible for proposing the way of working and establishing a consensus between all partners, coordinating the different tasks, moderating the meetings, etc.
- Modelling expert: provides expert knowledge in modelling process, methods and tools to the use case team
- Facilitator: is experienced in using the selected modelling process and tool and facilitates model construction and capturing of knowledge in the models
- Coach: supports the modelling process and model development by coaching the modellers
- Modeller: develop the enterprise models in the selected tool during the modelling process
- Domain expert: provide knowledge about the domain under consideration, which is basis for modelling

Modelling
Based on the above preparations, an iterative process started, which at the end resulted in 3 major versions of the scaffolding model. The first actual modelling step

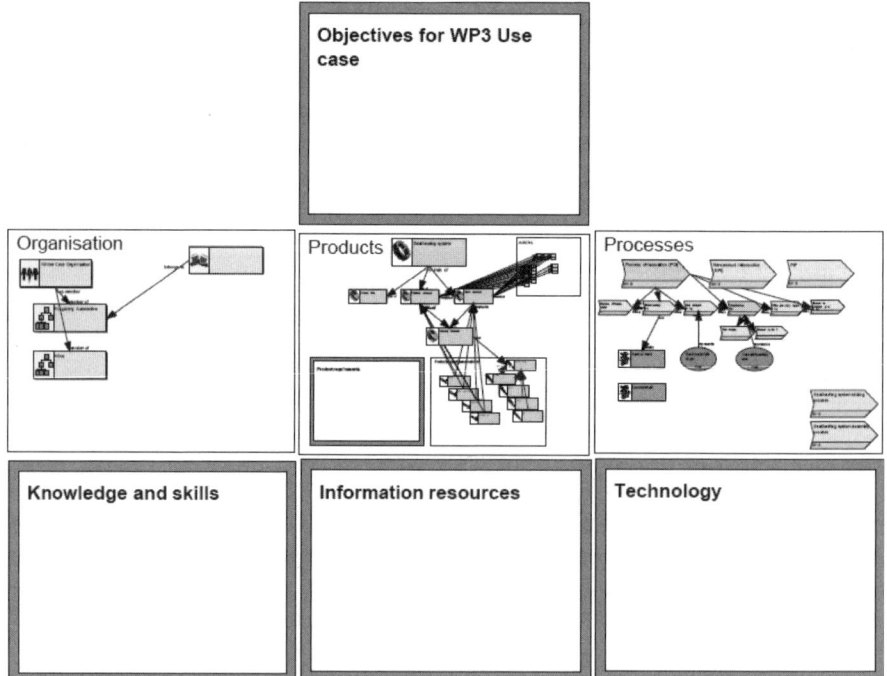

Fig. 1. The first scaffolding model basically identified the required modelling perspectives. Most of the boxes, which are called containers for the sub-models, were empty in this phase.

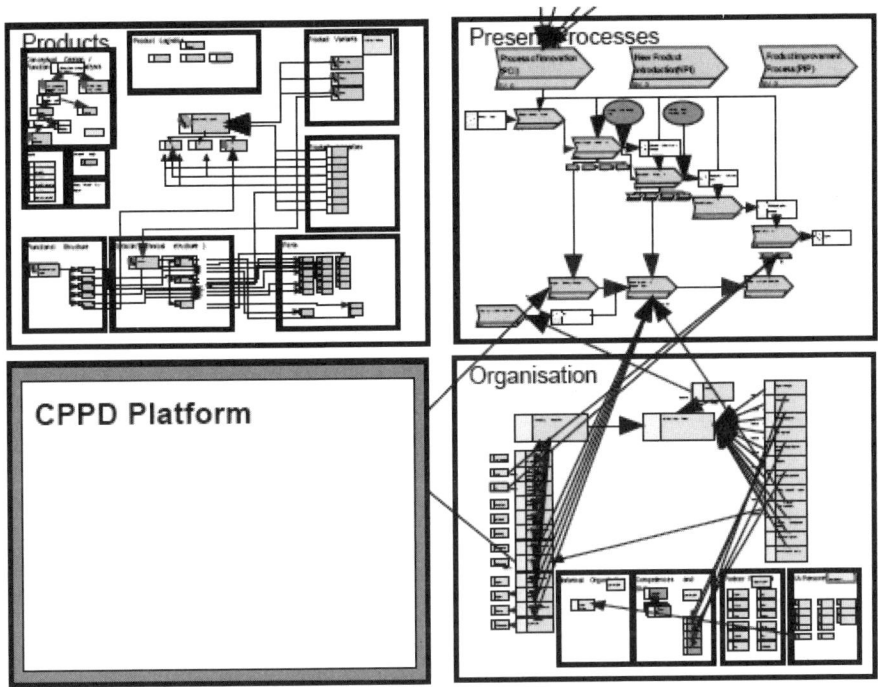

Fig. 2. The 3rd scaffolding model version included more details for each perspective. The figure shows the organization, product and process containers.

in the first iteration was to clearly define the purpose of the model to be developed. Within the scaffolding phase, the purpose was to model the current situation in the use case subject as seen by the different stakeholders from the automotive supplier (R&D manager, engineers with different specialisations, purchaser, customer responsible, etc.) in order to create a joint understanding in the complete use case team. Starting from the POPS* approach, the perspectives were identified that were considered relevant for the modelling purpose. The initial POPS* perspectives Process, Organisation, Product and Systems were during this step supplemented with other perspectives like Objectives, Technical Approaches or Skills. The definition of additional perspectives had to be repeated in all iterations.

The modelling work performed in joint workshops with all use case team members consisted of a combination of presentations with regards to the current situation in the use case subject, discussions for clarifying concepts and creating a joint understanding, and model creation and editing. The modelling work usually was structured by differentiating between sessions focusing on single perspectives, like process or organisation, and sessions aiming at inter-perspective relationships. This way of working turned out to create the necessary balancing between capturing very detailed aspects within the perspectives and more general aspects.

The modelling workshops usually were 2 or even 3 day events. Between two workshops, the coach and modelling expert checked the jointly developed models and details like textual descriptions were added. At the beginning of each consecutive

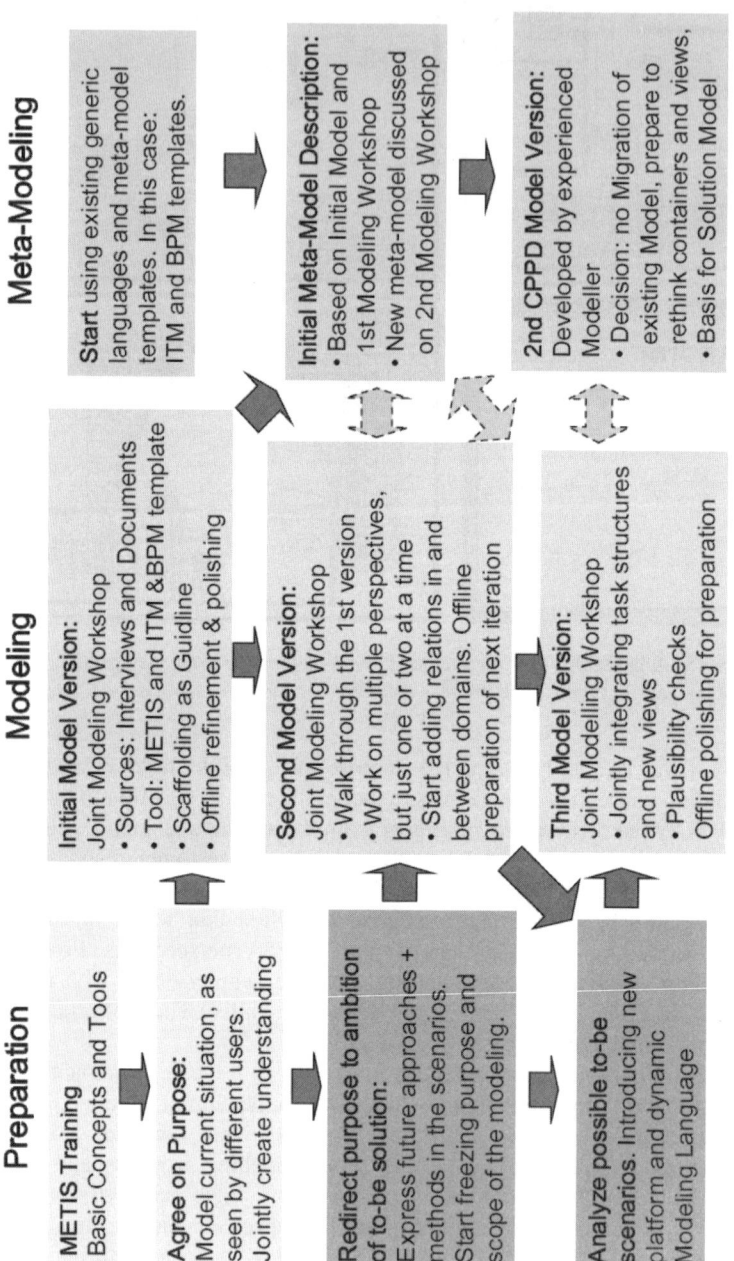

Fig. 3. Work steps in the scaffolding and scoping phase

modelling workshop, a walk through the current model version was the first step in order to make sure that all participants had the same understanding of the status and in order to verify the modifications made between the workshops. After the 3rd model iteration in the scaffolding phase, the scaffolding model was considered detailed enough and sufficiently complete.

Meta Modelling

Besides the actual modelling, development of a suitable meta-model for the purposes of the use case was another important subject. During the scaffolding phase, the work was based on the BPM[5] and ITM[6] meta-models provided by Troux, which are available as templates for the METIS tool. Experience from the modelling workshop showed that these two templates and their respective modelling elements covered a large part of the needs. Missing model elements were mainly identified for the "Product" perspective, as different conceptual views on a product (like geometric, electrical, material or cost view) have to be supported and interconnected in the same model. In order to provide suitable elements, work on a new meta-model was started, which should integrate the required elements of BPM and ITM and add specific constructs for the product view. This meta-modelling activity was initiated by Troux and led to an initial meta-model proposal for Collaborative Product and Process Development (CPPD). After an initial meta-model version, work on CPPD was performed in parallel with development of the scaffolding model and continued even during scoping.

Fig. 3 illustrates the activities in the scaffolding phase, which can be divided into preparation work, modelling and meta-modelling.

3.2 Scoping Phase

The scoping phase used the same tools and roles as the scaffolding phase, but had a different purpose: Focus in the scoping phase was on developing initial versions of solution models that specified the intended future way of working in the use case subject, i.e. the future product development process at the automotive supplier's business area seat comfort. Furthermore, the solution models should be executable in the MAPPER infrastructure, i.e. all modelling perspectives had to be defined on such a level of detail that they contained all model elements required for execution. In comparison to the scaffolding model, the solution model had to fulfil higher demands with respect to completeness and consistency, e.g. the complete process flow or set of required tasks within a process had to be modelled and not just the essential ones illustrating the way of working. Furthermore, much more technical details had to be included, e.g. all collaboration services needed, internal IT-systems and information sources required to support a task had to be specified including their technical interfaces.

Due to the requirements regarding completeness, consistency and level of detail, the way of modelling had to be revised. Jointly working on METIS models in workshops and creating all model elements jointly was no longer appropriate. Instead, we decided to first create textual scenario descriptions for all relevant tasks. These

---

[5] BPM = Business Process Modelling.
[6] ITM = Information Technology Management.

textual descriptions included information about the intended way of working, involved roles, and tools or documents used. They also contained statements explicitly identifying requirements. Based on each scenario description, a model was developed by the coach and modelling expert, which was afterwards presented and discussed with the team members from the automotive supplier. The joint modelling workshops performed during the scoping phase aimed at presenting the current modelling status, and at discussing questions like how to integrate collaboration support on base of the solution model, how to integrate methodology support into the solution model, how model development and meta-model development correspond or how the future distribution of work would look like. Thus, the modelling workshops, which always started with a walk through the current model status, still formed an essential part of the process.

The work during the scoping phase was structured by dividing the design process into 9 main tasks and grouping these 9 tasks into 3 pilot installations. The tasks for the first pilot were given priority and developed first. As a consequence, models for these tasks existed early in the process already in a 2nd or 3rd version, while some of the tasks for pilot 2 and 3 were available only in a first iteration.

The solution modelling phase, i.e. refining the scoping model for use in an actual project, is not in the scope of this paper. Selected aspects of solution modelling as process and an example for the solution model are discussed in [1].

4   Experiences

Many experiences and practices regarding scaffolding and scoping are already included in section 3. This section adds experiences regarding stakeholder participation and the two cycles of C3S3P performed.

As indicated above, participation of stakeholders from different departments of the automotive supplier and from different MAPPER partners has to be considered a key success factor for creating enterprise knowledge models suitable for use in everyday practice. However, we experienced that different levels of participation were adequate for the different modelling phases (see section 2.2 for a description of the phases).

In the initial phase, scaffolding, nearly all stakeholders were participating all the time during the model development process. This included presentations from and discussions with the automotive supplier about the application domain and the use case subject, discussions and joint decisions about perspectives to be included in the model, consideration about the meta-model, joint creation and editing of the models with METIS and textual descriptions of the model elements. In terms of the produced size of models, these model sessions might not have been very productive. But in terms of sharing knowledge and creating a joint understanding of both, the use case subject and the nature and process of modelling, the joint modelling sessions with all stakeholders were extremely valuable. They created a joint ownership of the result. Only between the modelling sessions, there was a "non-participatory" work step, which concerned the consolidation of the model and the meta-model. Introducing the results of this work step to all stakeholders at the beginning of the next modelling session by walking through the model was very useful. This contributed to getting everybody onto the same level of information and supported double-checking of understandability and correctness of the model.

During the second phase, scoping, the way of working was changed and the level participation reduced: before developing METIS models, we developed textual scenario descriptions for the task under consideration. The scenario descriptions were developed with participation of all stakeholders, but the development of models based on the scenario description was done "in private" by the modelling expert. Main reason for this change was the required level of detail of the models. As the objective was to provide executable models, a lot of detailed and partly technical information had to be included. Joint editing of such models was not only perceived very time consuming but also overloading some stakeholders with technical details considered not relevant for them. However, the models produced by the expert were presented to the other stakeholders for validation purposes and in order not to loose the joint ownership of the results.

The work performed in MAPPER included two cycles of using C3S3P. The first cycle focused on capturing organizational knowledge and best practices for networked manufacturing enterprises. The second cycle focused on integration of product knowledge into the best practices. The scaffolding phase of the second C3S3P cycle were considerably shorter than in the first cycle, as a lot of shared understanding of the problem domain already had been created. However, there still was the need to explore the principal design solution, configurable components and parameters of the product area under consideration. The scoping phase to a large extent consisted of identifying the required configurable workplaces, which were created during the solution modelling phase. Platform integration and piloting in real-world projects were not clearly separated due to the tight project schedule. Creation of workplaces for engineers at the use case partner in running projects was the main aim. The performance monitoring phase was not yet performed (see [8] for a more detailed discussion).

For the industrial partner participating in the described case, developing enterprise knowledge models was a new experience. Before the beginning of MAPPER, model-basing for them primarily meant the use of simulation models or geometric models in product design. During the second C3S3P cycle it became very clear that the future use of knowledge models and modelling approaches at the use case partner would depend on establishing changed work practices and on a better understanding in larger parts of the company what potentials and benefits knowledge modelling can contribute. As a consequence, work on social practice design [14] was initiated aiming at creating a knowledge modelling culture.

5 Related Work

In contrast to the wealth of publications discussing concepts, techniques, tools, methodologies or selected aspects of enterprise modelling, there are relatively few experience reports or best practices published. Most relevant for a related work discussion would be work using the same methodology (C3S3P). But this would limit the discussion to only a few publications, which all were already mentioned earlier in this article [6, 7, 8]. Thus, this section will also discuss experiences from neighbouring areas.

[11] state quite similar goals and perspectives in their work on enterprise modelling, which is tightly related to the TOVE[7] project. They aim at "a computational representation of structure, activities, processes, information, people, behaviour, goals, and constraints of a business, government, or other enterprise". Both, the objective of a formal, computational model and the different perspectives captured in such models are very close to the objective of the enterprise knowledge modelling performed in our case and the perspectives of POPS*. However, TOVE puts much more focus on functional completeness, efficiency, minimality or generality, using an ontological approach and representation. From our experience, we would support the importance of these quality criteria, but emphasize the need for a visualization of the enterprise model and all relations between the different perspectives that is easily understood and consistently applied and interpreted in the enterprise. Visual models as used for scaffolding and scoping in MAPPER seem to have an advantage in supporting this goal as compared to ontological representations.

Our experiences regarding role distribution and user participation are supported by other researchers. [12], for example, in their experience report using the EKD enterprise modelling method emphasize the importance of a clearly stated mission (in our case, the agreement between the stakeholders about the purpose of the modelling phase), of team composition and in particular the role of the facilitator, and of adequate tool support. Furthermore, they emphasize the need for combining modelling language and adequate modelling process, which fits to our view that meta-model and modelling process should be adjusted before and during the modelling work.

The scaffolding phase spends considerable time and efforts on identifying the needed perspectives of an enterprise model and on understanding the situation under consideration. Only after several scaffolding iterations, we moved on to the scoping phase, i.e. toward preparing solutions for the identified problems and objectives. The advantage of this approach is a tight integration between the different perspectives from the very beginning, i.e. all perspectives of the scaffolding model were elaborated in sufficient detail and thoroughly related to the other perspectives. We experienced this as very useful for the scoping phase, as it helped to raise awareness for important commonalities or dependencies between perspectives and objects, and for essential relationships within the considered case. This experience we share with [13], even though they address in their work a completely different application field. Their work on ERP systems showed that expressing organizational needs in goal-strategy terms by using a visualization easily understood by the enterprise helps to take a more holistic perspective. The "map" applied in their work includes so diverse perspectives as requirements, system parameters, strategies, or functionality. The experiences reported are that this was very useful in focusing on dependencies and strategically important questions.

6 Summary

The paper presented practices and experiences from the early phases of enterprise knowledge modelling at an automotive supplier. The objective of the model development

---

[7] TOVE = Toronto Virtual Enterprise.

was to support collaborative product design in a networked manufacturing enterprise. The modelling approach used was C3S3P, the scope of the paper included the scaffolding and the scoping phases.

One of the most important observations from the modelling case described is the continuous and intertwined development of several perspectives:

- The meta-model, which evolved from an off-the-shelf template to a specialized meta-model for collaborative product and process development,
- The model as such with the different phases described in chapter 3. It should be noticed that the models resulting from scaffolding and scoping could be considered as both, artefacts on their own rights and transient results between two model phases
- The modelling process was guided by the C3S3P phases, which offers a high degree of freedom in terms of how to implement the phases. The modelling process as such therefore was subject of continuous adaptation based on the progress and evolving necessities in the modelling sessions performed.
- The modelling team and partly the role distribution in the team changed in course of the work, as different domain experts or specialist for knowledge modelling of particular perspectives had to integrated

The recommendation resulting from this observation is to establish during enterprise knowledge modelling, in particular if C3S3P is applied, a methodology adaption task focusing on identifying and tackling the needs for adjustment in the above discussed perspectives. Investigating this evolutionary process and identifying key success factors based on wider empirical grounding and existing work in method development would be an interesting future line of work.

Furthermore, the differences, advantages and disadvantages of C3S3P in comparison to other enterprise modelling methodologies, like EKD [15], should be investigated and exposed. For the case discussed in this paper, C3S3P was predetermined as methodology. Although the experiences with C3S3P were positive, a comparison to other approaches would be valuable.

Acknowledgements

The authors wish to thank the anonymous reviewers of the paper for their valuable comments.

The paper is to a large part based on research carried out in the EU project FP6-IST-NMP 016527 MAPPER "Model-adapted Product and Process Engineering". The authors wish to thank their co-workers when developing the MAPPER enterprise knowledge models. Furthermore, the work was supported by the Swedish Knowledge Foundation with grant #2005-0252 (project infoFLOW).

References

1. Johnsen, S., et al.: Model-based adaptive Product and Process Engineering. In: Rabe, M., Mihok, P. (eds.) Ambient Intelligence Technologies for the Product Lifecycle: Results and Perspectives from European Research. Fraunhofer IRB Verlag (2007)

2. Lillehagen, F., Karlsen, D.: Visual Extended Enterprise Engineering embedding Knowledge Management, Systems Engineering and Work Execution. In: IEMC 1999 - IFIP International Enterprise Modelling Conference, Verdal, Norway (1999)
3. Krogstie, J., Jørgensen, H.D.: Interactive Models for Supporting Networked Organizations. In: Persson, A., Stirna, J. (eds.) CAiSE 2004, LNCS, vol. 3084, pp. 550–563. Springer, Heidelberg (2004)
4. Jørgensen, H.D., Krogstie, J.: Active Models for Dynamic Networked Organisations. In: Dittrich, K.R., Geppert, A., Norrie, M.C. (eds.) CAiSE 2001, LNCS, vol. 2068. Springer, Heidelberg (2001)
5. Lillehagen, F.: The Foundations of AKM Technology. In: Proceedings 10th International Conference on Concurrent Engineering (CE) Conference, Madeira, Portugal (2003)
6. Krogstie, J., Lillehagen, F., Karlsen, D., Ohren, O., Strømseng, K., Thue Lie, F.: Extended Enterprise Methodology. Deliverable 2 in the EXTERNAL project (2000), http://research.dnv.com/external/deliverables.html
7. Carstensen, A., et al.: Integrating Requirement and Solution Modelling: Approach and Experiences. In: EMMSAD 2007, Trondheim, Norway (accepted, June 2007)
8. Stirna, J., Persson, A., Sandkuhl, K.: Participative Enterprise Modelling: Experiences and Recommendations. In: Krogstie, J., Opdahl, A.L., Sindre, G. (eds.) CAiSE 2007 and WES 2007. LNCS, vol. 4495, pp. 546–560. Springer, Heidelberg (2007)
9. Vernadat, F.: Enterprise Modelling and Integration: principles and applications. Chapman & Hall, London (1996)
10. Niemann, K.: From Enterprise Architecture to IT Governance. Vieweg Verlag, Wiesbaden (2006)
11. Fox, M., Gruninger, M.: Enterprise Modelling. AI Magazine 19(3) (1998)
12. Stirna, J., Persson, A.: EKD – An Enterprise Modelling Approach to Support Creativity and Quality in Information Systems and Business Development. In: Halpin, T., Krogstie, J., Proper, E. (eds.) Innovations in Information Systems Modelling: Methods and Best Practices. IGI Publishing (to appear, 2008)
13. Rolland, C., Prakash, N.: Bridging the Gap Between Organisational Needs and ERP Functionality. Requirements Engineering 5, 180–193 (2000)
14. Jacucci, G., Wagner, I., Tellioglu, H.: Design Games as a Part of Social Practice Design: A Case of Employees Elaborating on Organizational Problems. In: Proceedings of 16th European Conference on Information Systems, Galway, Ireland (June 2008)
15. Bubenko, J., Persson, A., Stirna, J.: User Guide of the Knowledge Management Approach Using Enterprise Knowledge Patterns. In: Deliverable D3, project HyperKnowledge (IST-2000-28401). Royal Institute of Technology, Sweden

Modeling Knowledge Transfer in a Software Maintenance Organization – An Experience Report and Critical Analysis

Golnaz Elahi[1], Eric Yu[2], and Maria Carmela Annosi[3]

[1] Department of Computer Science, University of Toronto, Canada, M5S 1A4
gelahi@cs.toronto.edu
[2] Faculty of Information, University of Toronto, Canada, M5S 3G6
yu@ischool.utoronto.ca
[3] Ericsson Software Research, Marconi SpA, Italy
mariacarmela.annosi@ericsson.com

Abstract. Modeling notations have been introduced to help understand the *why* behind software processes. We ask how are these techniques being used in industrial practices? The first part of this paper reports on the experiences at an industrial software organization, Ericsson Marconi SpA, in applying i* modeling to analyze knowledge transfer effectiveness for software maintenance. The modeling was done in-house without consultation with the i* research community. In the second part of the paper, university researchers analyze the modeling experience in that organization, drawing a comparison with the usage of i* typically envisaged by the research community. We found that the modeling approach used at the industry site employed smaller and simplified models, but were effective for highlighting key issues for the organization and communication. From the case study, we draw some conclusions for the future development of the i* modeling approach.

1 Introduction

Modeling notations have been introduced to help understand the *why* behind software processes [1]. To design effective Enterprise Modeling (EM) languages and methods, it is of importance to study how practitioners apply the methods developed by research communities in real-world practices, what are the properties of the enterprise models developed in practice, and how the EM language and method developed by researchers were understood in practice. While practitioners focus on applying the techniques for practical purposes, results of studies on adoption of EM techniques by practitioners would provide directions for future EM research toward practical proposals for modeling and analysis approaches.

This paper aims to analyze the properties of the enterprise models developed in a real-world instance. To have a basis for comparison, an alternate set of models of the same organization and problem was developed according to the researchers anticipated usage of the modeling technique. We study and compare the size, complexity, understandability, modeling style, appropriate and full use

J. Stirna and A. Persson (Eds.): PoEM 2008, LNBIP 15, pp. 15–29, 2008.
© IFIP International Federation for Information Processing 2008

of the modeling notation capabilities, and deviations from the syntax of the modeling notation for the two sets of models.

The first part of this paper reports the experience of applying an agent- and goal-oriented approach to EM used in the Ericsson Marconi SpA software maintenance organization to model and analyze a number of Knowledge Management (KM) strategies applied in the maintenance team. The KM strategies applied in that organization involves restructuring roles, positions, and their activities within the enterprise. The analysts at Ericsson Marconi SpA modeled and analyzed the KM strategies and policies by using the i* [2] agent- and goal-oriented approach. In this experience, i* modeling technique was used by the in-house analysts at Ericsson without consultation with the i* research community. The i* modeling and analysis were used to help the team members understand and explain the significance and impact of the KM policies they applied.

In the second part of this paper, the models developed at Ericsson Marconi SpA are analyzed to draw conclusions about the use and adoption of EM in practice. In this analysis, researchers develop a new set of models based on their understanding of the KM strategies and organizational settings at Ericsson Marconi SpA. The new set of models developed by researchers is compared with the modeling and analysis approach employed at Ericsson Marconi SpA.

2   Case Study Background

This section explains the organization context at Ericsson Marconi SpA and the reasons, process, and outcomes of applying i* modeling EM at that organization. The Ericsson Corporation applies benchmarking to compare its local design centers which are spread in many countries worldwide. Performance in maintaining the software products under the responsibility of a local design center is often the way to judge the effectiveness and the efficiency of that center. At the Ericsson Marconi SpA local center, a Knowledge Management (KM) project was launched to effectively manage the maintenance activities. The KM efforts involved applying organizational strategies and structures within the maintenance team which are described in more detail in section 3.

The project leader of the KM initiative needed to describe the maintenance processes and explain how and why the KM strategies for knowledge transfer were successful in the maintenance team. Motivated by the desire and need to explain and promote successful KM practices to other groups, the KM project leader and process owner searched for a modeling method suitable for the intended purpose in the EM and process modeling literature. The project leader believed that i* was the only modeling notation that can express and visualize concepts like social interactions and knowledge transfer. She chose the i* modeling framework, while her i* modeling skills and expertise were limited to her own studies in the literature. The i* notation was chosen because she found i* modeling simple, easy to learn, and adaptable in industrial contexts.

The i* modeling notation provides the means to express goals of actors and tasks and resources needed to achieve the goals. The models provide a basis for evaluating different degrees of goal satisfaction among different stakeholders. By making the relations between stakeholders' goals and knowledge transfer instruments explicit, the models can demonstrate how and why the knowledge instruments work or fail. These properties of the i* modeling approach provides a suitable basis for modeling enterprise strategic structure and role dependencies.

3   Enterprise Modeling Experience at Ericsson Marconi SpA

This section describes the KM needs and strategies and the enterprise models developed to analyze and explain the KM strategies at Ericsson Marconi SpA. The experience of EM is described based on the internal reports provided by one of the paper's author at Ericsson Marconi SpA, who was the project leader and process owner that produced the i* models, later consultations with that author, and a short workshop paper analyzing the i* models [3].

The modeling process started with identification of roles, positions, and their dependencies and goals in the Ericsson maintenance team. As the modeling progressed, the model became complex. It was realized that putting all actors and processes into one model was useless, since no conclusion could be deducted from such a complex model. Therefore, an slicing approach was adopted for breaking the maintenance processes into smaller models based on the actors' goals.

The KM strategies and structures that were applied in the maintenance team target three main goals: 1) Expanding individuals' tacit knowledge by focusing on knowledge creation strategies by individuals; 2) Expanding team tacit knowledge by focusing on the social relationships among members of the maintenance organization; 3) Enabling knowledge sharing by applying KM strategies and structures to the knowledge environment.

3.1   Expanding Individuals' Tacit Knowledge: Knowledge Creation Strategies

Individual technical skills and knowledge about the product and system are critical to the maintenance activities. To increase the individual tacit knowledge and reduce the faults' handling costs, some KM strategies were applied in the maintenance team. Half of the maintenance team was put into a core group, which consisted of ten individuals. This group was the focal point of the maintenance team to assure knowledge sharing within cross-functional teams.

The core members need to play two roles: one as a *Maintainer member* and one as a *Subsystem Responsible*, which is a member of development project team and needs to *Attend Product Committee (PC) inspection*. In this way, the variety of correlated activities was guaranteed for the core members. Fig. 1 was developed to describe the activities of the subsystem responsible as an i* model: 1) To attend to the PC reviews as a permanent member in order to guarantee the correct evolution of products; 2) To update the subsystem documents at every project development release.

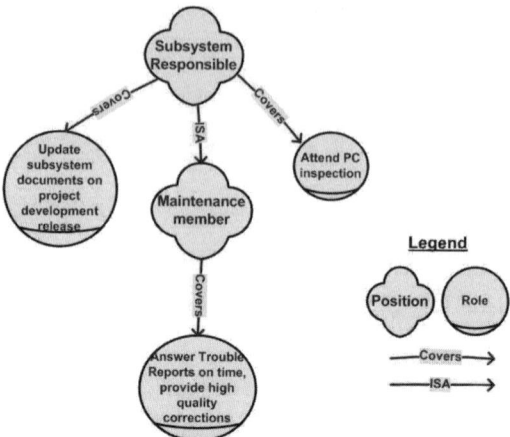

Fig. 1. Roles that belong to the subsystem responsible position. (The legends are added to the original models obtained from Ericsson.

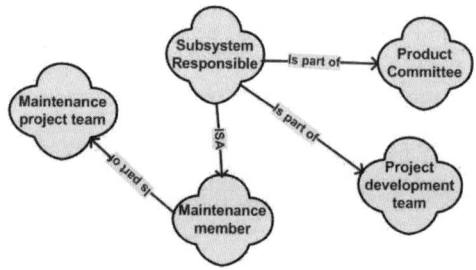

Fig. 2. Relationship between organizational positions

Ensuring Knowledge Transfer among Different Team Positions and Roles. The model in Fig. 2 was developed to describe that the subsystem responsible interacts with different organizational positions by being member of multiple teams. When the core members of the maintenance team work as a maintainer, they gain field experience by facing problems that have been discovered by the internal and external customers, solving faults, and proposing effective solutions at the product level. The maintainer as a subsystem responsible, can gain knowledge at the product level. Then later they have the chance to re-acquaint this knowledge during the evolution of the product under maintenance.

Subsystem responsibles collaborate in the feasibility phase of development project by reviewing all documents under the PC inspection. In this way, the combination of these two roles that the core members play raise the quality of the experience they gain. On the other hand, the PC also takes advantages from the specific background knowledge of the subsystem provided by the subsystem responsibles, which in turn, raises, the level of competence for the inspections.

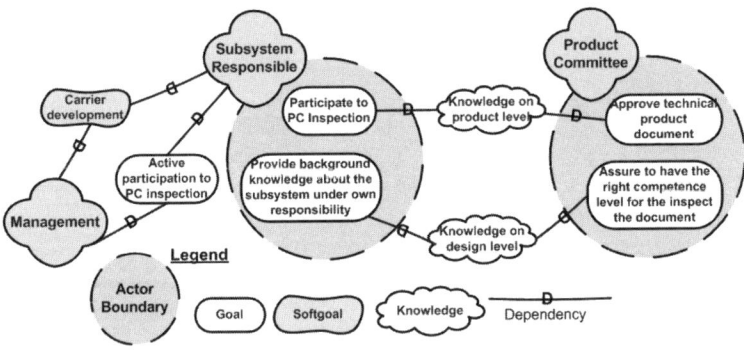

Fig. 3. Knowledge transfer from *Product Committee* members to *Subsystem Responsible* at the product level

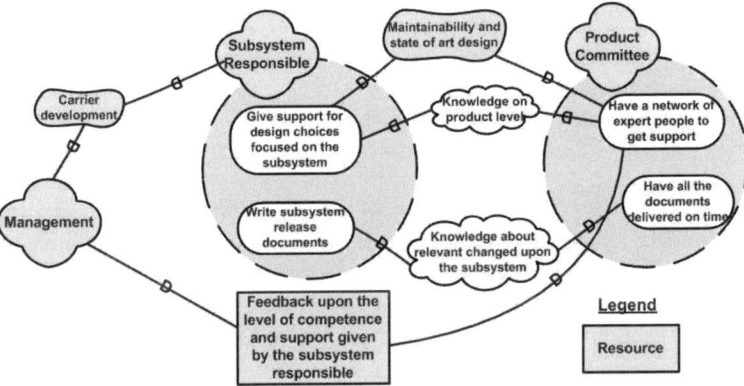

Fig. 4. Knowledge transfer from the project development team to the subsystem responsible at the design level by attending PC meetings

This requires that subsystem responsibles attend the PC for the inspection. In this way the PC inspection becomes an instrument for having an effective knowledge transfer, also in addition to the knowledge transfer by the core maintenance member.

The model in Fig. 3 was developed to illustrate the knowledge dependencies discussed. The *Subsystem Responsibles* are encouraged by the organization to attend the PC inspections. In addition, the *Management* applies some enforcement mechanism, in which the performance of subsystem responsibles is measured and evaluated by the number of attendances at PC inspection. The model in Fig. 4 was developed at Ericsson to illustrate how the new KM structure helps *Subsystem Responsibles* to gain knowledge. Since the *Subsystem Responsibles* are engaged in system development, they need to update all the subsystem release documents to record changes from the last release. To gain knowledge of product at the design level, the organization forces the maintainers to attend PC inspections for all development documents, write the subsystem release

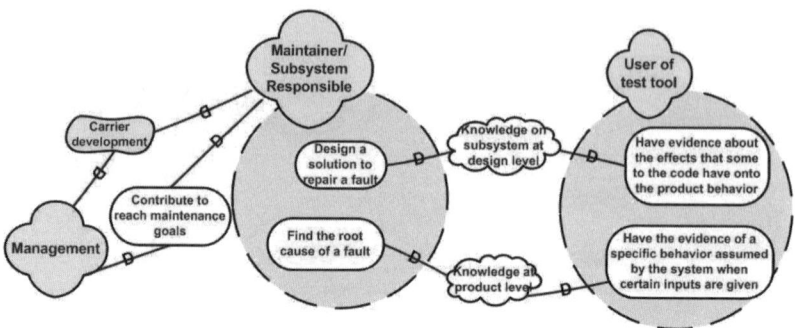

Fig. 5. Gaining knowledge through using the testing tools

documents, and communicate with the development team. The organizational interface between the *Subsystem Responsibles* and the *Project development team* is a way to guarantee an effective knowledge transfer at the design level to the *Subsystem Responsibles*. The model in Fig. 4, developed at Ericsson implicitly illustrates the enforcement mechanism that the management applied to ensure performance of the subsystem responsibles.

Gaining Knowledge Through Use of Testing Tools. The model in Fig. 5 was developed to illustrate how testing tools that simulate the behavior of the system are another source of knowledge for maintainers. Such tools are essentially used for test purposes by the testers. In the maintenance team, those tools are useful means to help maintainers analyze the faults individually. Knowledge creation starts when the maintainers need to simulate a fault. For this purpose, the maintainer launches the testing tools and configures it with the scenario described in the trouble report.

This requires background knowledge about similar faults, testing tools, and product at the system level. Without knowledge at the system level, simulating the fault would be burdened by a sequence of trial attempts without considering any rationale for the fault. Using testing tools, maintainers learn about the effects of the adopted solution on the whole system.

3.2   Expanding Team Tacit Knowledge: Social Relationships Structures

To increase the collaborations, facilitate sharing the experiences among the maintenance team members, and build mutual trust among them, the organization provided means for formal face to face communication among team members. The formal meetings that were set to transfer knowledge include desk checking the solution that fixes the fault reported in the trouble report. The model in Fig. 6 was developed to explain why and how knowledge of team members is expanded by formal desk check of the solution. The desk check is a mandatory step before delivering the corrections and is performed by two maintainers which

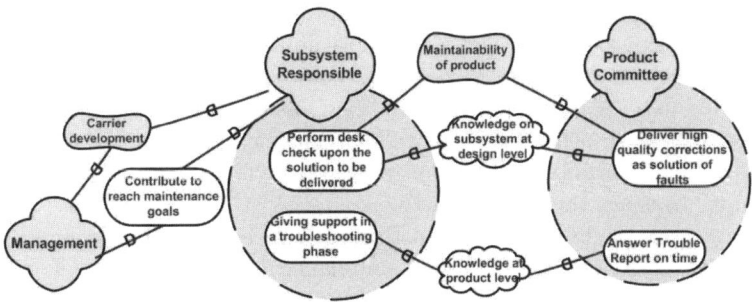

Fig. 6. Expanding knowledge of team members by formal desk check

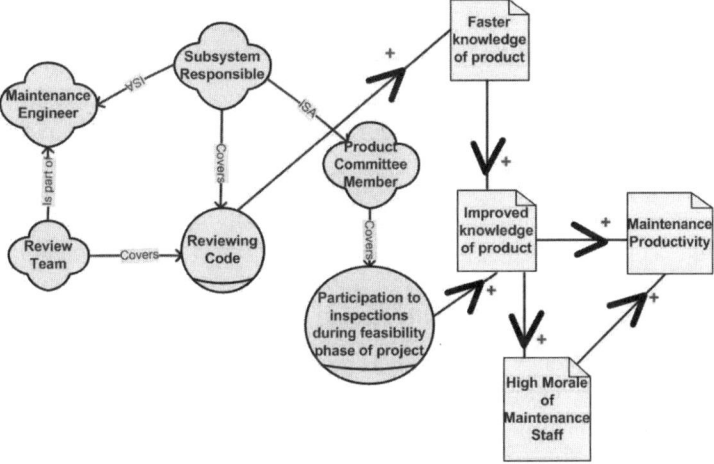

Fig. 7. Social relationships between actors within the maintenance team and the impacts of the relationships on goals of different actors. (The modeler employs a rectangle to model the softgoals, syntactically deviating from i* notation.)

did not fix the trouble. This check aims to find the possible faults of the solution adopted by the other maintainers.

Fig. 7 was developed to explain the social relationships between actors within maintenance team and the impacts of the relationships on goals of various roles and positions. The strong team spirit enables the interactions among the maintenance team members, and this greatly facilitates mentoring purposes. In this way, the team members feel they work more effectively and with higher level of communication.

3.3   Enabling Knowledge Sharing: Strategies for Knowledge Environment

Although a number of knowledge environment strategies were applied to the team environment, the KM project leader and analyst did not develop i* models for expressing the impact of physical facilities and environmental changes that facilitate knowledge sharing. Those strategies aimed to enable knowledge sharing in the organizational environment of the maintenance team. For example, the maintenance team is located within an open space consisting of several cubes, separated from each other by short walls. Team member that are doing similar types of activities are located in the same room. This helps them to have the opportunity to share their experiences.

The enterprise models developed at Ericsson express the relationships between various roles and positions in the maintenance team, the goals of roles and positions, their dependencies, and knowledge acquisitions dependencies. Utilizing the i* modeling and analysis technique helped the KM initiative to systematically represent, capture, and analyze the strategic organizational relationships relevant to knowledge transfer. By capturing and analyzing such strategic relationships, it is possible to make visible the reasons why newly adopted strategies and structures improved knowledge transfer.

4   Critical Analysis of the Ericsson Modeling Experience

This section gives a critical analysis of the modeling experience at Ericsson, drawing a comparison with the usage of i* typically envisaged by the research community.

4.1   Characteristics of the Enterprise Models Developed at Ericsson

The Strategic Dependency (SD) models developed at Ericsson explain the positions and roles at the organization. These models were used to explain additional responsibilities of the core members of the maintenance team. Strategic Rationale (SR) models refines the goal and knowledge dependencies between roles and positions. These models were used to illustrate the motivations behind the collaboration amongst different roles and positions, including knowledge transfer motivations and mechanisms.

The models developed at Ericsson involved adoption of the i* modeling techniques to suit the practitioners' needs. As a result, some models deviate from the i* syntax and modeling style laid out by the researchers University of Toronto (U of T) [2] and [4]. The source for the models was the first hand experience of the modeler and the she was the key users of developed models. Reviewing and analyzing these models, we observed some common properties:

1. The models developed at Ericsson focus on one goal of each actor and a small fragment of the enterprise.
2. Each model focuses on one strategy and its benefit. In this way, each model communicates one single message.
3. The models employ a subset of the i* modeling elements and do not use the full range of the i* notation capabilities. For example, very few contribution links are used in the models, tasks are not included, and resources and softgoals are rarely employed. The most frequently used elements are roles, positions, goals, and dependencies.

4. The models have several deviations from the i* syntax developed at U of T. However, the models communicate the intuitions of the context, and the enterprise structure, people's activities, and goals are semantically understandable.

5. Although the syntax of the i* notation is not accurately followed, the intuitions behind the i* approach for enterprise modeling is understood by the developers of the models. The i* models illustrate the distributed intentionality in the maintenance team and their dependencies.

6. Wherever the developer needed to express a concept that the i* does not express or the developer did not know how to express by using the i* modeling constructs, the developer used an improvised notation.

7. The models are not detailed and extensive. Goals are not refined into tasks and other goals using decomposition and means-end relationships. In this way, only the main important intuitions of a KM strategy are expressed in the models and details are omitted.

4.2 Developing an Alternate Set of Models

In order to further analyze the Ericsson experience, the i* researchers involved in this study developed an alternate set of i* models using the conventional i* modeling syntax which the researchers at U of T developed. The models were developed based on the description that accompanied the models provided by the Ericsson analyst. We compare the models developed by researchers with the models used at Ericsson for practical purposes, to draw conclusions about real-world application of i* modeling as an specific goal-oriented EM technique. Such conclusions help toward improving the practical aspects of the i* Framework, and EM in general. For example, in a previous work, deviations from the i* syntax were studied in [5]. In that study, based on the identified common deviations, suggestions for improving the usability and effectiveness of the i* syntax were proposed. In addition, analysis and comparison of two sets of model provide initial intuitions about how models, modeling process, and model-based analysis are adopted in real-world practices of EM.

Fig. 1 shows the model developed at Ericsson Marconi SpA to explain the roles that a *Subsystem Responsible* plays. This model expresses that a *Subsystem Responsible* is also a *Maintenance member*, which describes the strategy of *double roles* for some members. In this model, the title of roles that the positions play express the tasks and activities that the positions are responsible for. The alternate approach to model this strategy is to structure the responsibilities of a position as tasks and goals of the roles covered by the position. Fig. 8 depicts the new model of the same positions and roles based on the alternate approach used by the researchers.

Fig. 9 gives the new model corresponding the model in Fig. 3. The SR model in Fig. 3 presented the goal and knowledge dependencies among the introduced roles and positions. The model in Fig. 9 shows why and where knowledge of products or subsystems are required and how the roles can obtain this knowledge. For example, the new model captures *why* the *Product Committee* needs

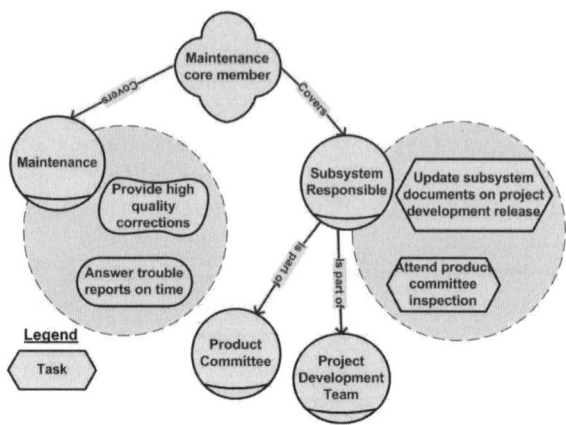

Fig. 8. A refinement of the model presented in Fig. 1 and Fig. 2. This model introduces special position called core member of maintenance team that covers two roles.

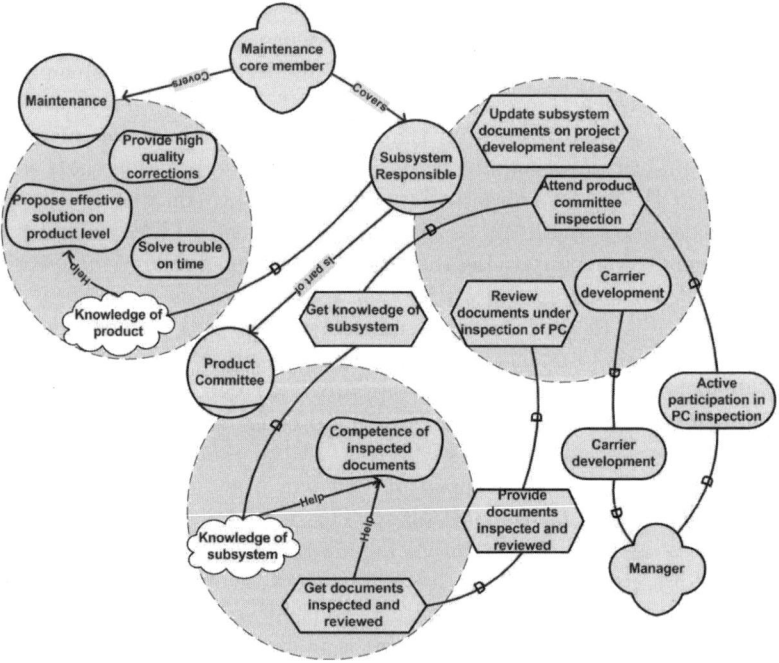

Fig. 9. A new model of knowledge transfer at the product level from Product Committee members to Subsystem Responsible. The model corresponds to the model in Fig. 3.

the *Knowledge of subsystem* in addition to how *Product Committee* can obtain it. The model is incomplete, since some elements such as *Provide high quality corrections* are not related to other elements. The incomplete parts of the models

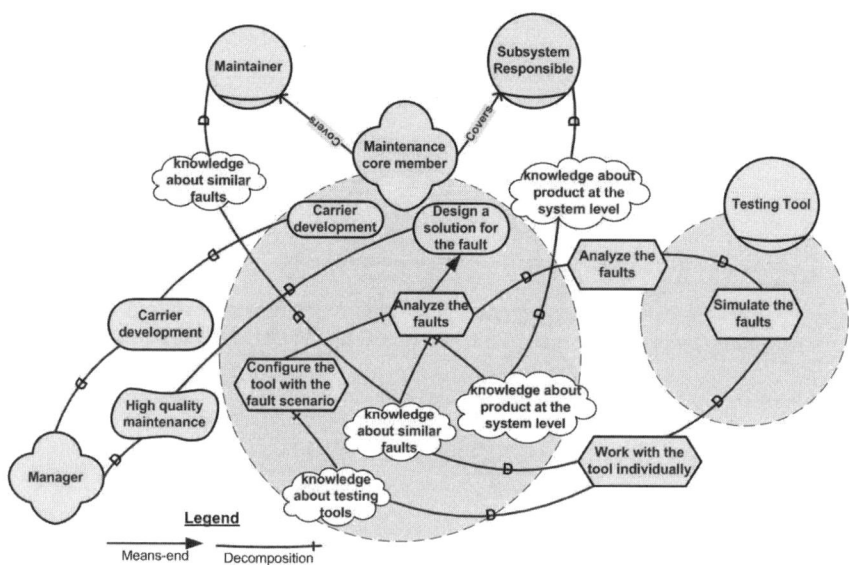

Fig. 10. A new model of knowledge transfer from Product Committee members to subsystem responsible at the product level. The model corresponds to the model in Fig. 5.

are due to the lack of description in the text accompanying the models. Due to space restriction, the new refined models for Fig. 4 and Fig. 6 are omitted.

Fig. 5 shows how maintainers benefit from using the testing tool and what kind of knowledge and experience they can gain. We explain the benefits of using the testing tool in a new model developed by the researchers, shown in Fig. 10. In this model, the required knowledge such as *knowledge about similar faults* and *knowledge about test tools* is modeled as a decomposition of the *Design a solution for the fault* task. In this way, the model expresses why that piece of knowledge is required. Similar to the model in Fig. 5, the knowledge elements are linked to tasks and goals of other actors by dependency links. For example, the *Maintenance core member*'s main goal is *Design a solution for the fault*. To achieve this goal, the *Maintenance core member* can analyze the faults by simulating them on the testing tool, and in order to do this, the maintainer needs to have *knowledge about test tools*. To gain this piece of knowledge the maintainer depends on using the *Testing Tool*.

The model in Fig. 7 was developed at Ericsson to show the strategic relationship in the maintenance team and the impacts of the relationships on goals such as *Maintenance productivity*. This model makes use of a new symbol to represent quality goals. The i* syntax does not allow linking actors to softgoals by contribution links. In addition, instead of actors, goals or tasks of the actors affect other goals. Therefore, we developed a new model, shown in Fig. 11, to express the intuitions of the model in Fig. 7, avoiding the syntactical deviations.

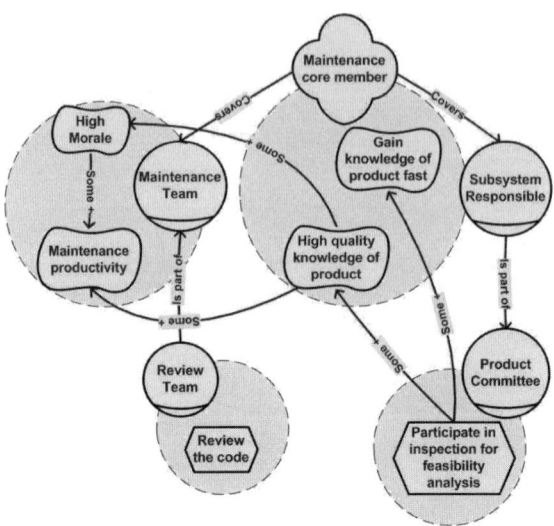

Fig. 11. A new model of the strategic relationships in the maintenance team and the impacts of the relationships on goals of team members. This model corresponds to the model in Fig. 7.

Properties of the Alternate Set of Models. The researchers tend to develop one large and comprehensive model rather than multiple simple models. These models contain more actors and complex relationships. The complexity of new models may stem from the fact that researchers have seen and analyzed the original models; therefore, they added more details to the original models.

While the title of roles in the original models express the tasks or goals of the roles, in the new models, tasks and goals of the roles and positions are i* elements inside the boundary of the actors. Adding this explicit structure increases expressiveness and understandability of the new models, while results in more complicated models. The new models developed by researchers also make use the full range of available i* modeling elements such as tasks and softgoals in addition to goals, and relationships such as contributions, decompositions, and means-end in addition to dependencies.

The models developed at Ericsson are simpler than the models developed by researchers in terms of number of elements, relationship between elements, and variety of i* elements used in the models. Simple models are better for understanding the problem for new users of the i* models. In addition, simpler models, while conveying less information, are easier for communicating the information. On the other hand, simple models, which do not capture details of goals' refinement, task decompositions, and goal contributions, do not provide required basis for reasoning about the goal satisfaction and denial.

Goals in the Ericsson models are not related to any other subgoals or higher goals; therefore, if analysts wanted to evaluate satisfaction or denial of goals, they would have to make judgment based only on external evidence or own knowledge, not making use of the structure of the goal model. On the other hand, the goals in the models developed by the researchers are linked to subgoals, tasks, and higher (soft)goals. Therefore, the analysts can use the structure of the goal model to propagate satisfaction or denial values from leaf to root goals. In sum, the extensive and detailed models trade understandability and easier communication for the ability to perform reasoning using the model structure.

5   Related Work

Modeling and reasoning about enterprise knowledge can guide the organizational transformation. Enterprise Knowledge Modeling [6] is a collection of conceptual modeling techniques for describing different facets of the organizational domain. The relationship between EM and KM are studied in [7], where the authors concluded that EM and KM follow a merged future and both are required as the key contributors to decision making in an enterprise. Although knowledge creation activities are viewed as more important and more difficult to manage, effective knowledge reuse and knowledge transfer, as a pre-requirement for reuse, are more frequent organizational concerns [8].

Strohmaier et al. [9] argue that effectiveness of instruments used for knowledge transfer depend on the stakeholders that participate and share an interest in knowledge transfer and on their acceptance, motivation and goals. Therefore, goal-oriented EM approaches provide a suitable basis for modeling knowledge transfer instruments. For example, based on concerning stakeholders' willingness, goals, and conflicts, the contribution in [9] proposes an agent-oriented modeling approach, based on the i* Framework, for analyzing the effectiveness of knowledge transfer instruments, considering the goals from different interdependent stakeholders.

In another experience of using i* for modeling knowledge transfer in a maintenance organization, Actor Dependency (AD) models of the i* Framework were used in an experience to model and analyze a large scale maintenance organization [10]. The AD model was found to be very useful for capturing the important properties of the organizational context of the maintenance process, and aided in the understanding of the flaws found in this process.

6   Conclusion, Limitations, and Future Work

In this paper, we reported on the experience of applying the i* EM approach in the Ericsson Marconi SpA software maintenance organization to model and analyze their KM strategies. The modeling and analysis practices helped the practitioners to understand the significance and impact of the KM policies they applied, and enabled them to represent, capture, and analyze the strategic organizational relationships relevant to knowledge transfer and explain why they worked well with other teams.

Comparing the models developed at Ericsson with the models that the researchers developed, we concluded that the enterprise models developed in practice are relatively simpler and smaller. While, in this study, the researchers tend to develop one complicated model that illustrates the relation between smaller models, developing multiple models which each addresses one specific concern was more favorable in this experiment. This may stem from the lack of training or experience of the practitioner in developing complicated models. In addition, since the practitioner at Ericsson used the models as a communication and explanation tool, detailed models were not suitable for audiences which were not familiar with i* modeling. Although syntactical deviations from the i* notation in the models developed by the Ericsson practitioner are frequent, the models communicate the intuitions of the KM strategies and policies well. The syntax deviations provide further motivation for modifications to the i* syntax as suggested in [5].

These observations need to be considered in designing and revising EM languages such as i*. This study shows the need for sub models as considered in EKD Frameworks [6] for reducing the complexity of the models. In order to develop sub models to divide the model into smaller consistent models which do not lose any information, slicing and grouping mechanisms are needed.

However, one major limitation of this study is drawing the conclusions based models developed in one single organization and by one modeler. A main threat to the validity of this study is the personal biases of the researchers. In this study, the developer of the alternate set of models and the researcher that analyzed the results are the same people. Therefore, the researcher may be biased for evaluating whether the new models are more understandable and expressive than original ones. In addition, this study and the conclusions about properties of enterprise models in real-world practices rely only on one experience and use of one specific modeling method in one specific experience. The conclusions drawn in this study may be valid only in a situation where the modeler is not trained for using a modeling and analysis method. Conclusions and hypothesis drawn in this study need to be evaluated by analyzing more practical models and also models developed using other EM methods.

Acknowledgment

Financial support from Natural Science and Engineering Research Council of Canada and Bell University Labs is gratefully acknowledged. The authors would like to thank Ericsson Software Research, at Marconi SpA, Italy, for providing the opportunity of the collaboration, and Jennifer Horkoff for useful discussions and comments.

References

1. Yu, E.S.K., Mylopoulos, J.: Understanding Why in Software Process Modelling, Analysis, and Design. In: Proc. of 16th ICSE, pp. 159–168 (1994)
2. Yu, E.: Modeling Strategic Relationships for Process Reengineering, Ph.D thesis, Department of Computer Science, University of Toronto, Canada (1995)

3. Annosi, M.C., De Pascale, A., Gross, D., Yu, E.: Analyzing knowledge transfer in software maintenance organizations using an agent- and goal-oriented analysis technique- an experience report. In: Proc. of 3rd Int. i* Workshop, pp. 5–8 (2008)
4. i* Guidelines, version 3 (2007),
   http://istar.rwth-aachen.de/tiki-index.php?pagerefid=67
5. Horkoff, J., Elahi, G., Yu, E., Abdulhadi, S.: Reflective Analysis of the Syntax and Semantics of the i* Framework. In: Second Workshop on Requirements, Intentions and Goals in Conceptual Modeling (RIGiM 2008) (to appear, 2008)
6. Bubenko, J.A., Persson, A., Stirna, J.: EKD - Enterprise Knowledge Development, User Guide (2001), http://www.dsv.su.se/~js/ekd_user_guide.html
7. Ted Goranson, H., Huhns, M.N., Nell, J.G., Panetto, H., Carbó, G.T., Wunram, M.: A Merged Future for Knowledge Management and Enterprise Modeling. In: ICEIMT, pp. 37–50 (2002)
8. Markus, M.L.: Towards a Theory of Knowledge Reuse: Types of Knowledge Reuse Situations and Factors in Reuse Success. Journal of Management Information Systems 18(1), 57–93 (2001)
9. Strohmaier, M., Yu, E., Horkoff, J., Aranda, J., Easterbrook, S.M.: Analyzing Knowledge Transfer Effectiveness - An Agent-Oriented Approach. In: Proc. of the 40th Hawaii Int. Conf. on System Sciences (2007)
10. Briand, L., Melo, W., Seaman, C., Basili, V.: Characterizing and Assessing a Large-Scale Software Maintenance Organization. In: Proc. of the 17th Int. Conf. on Software Engineering, pp. 24–28 (1995)

An Artifact Model for Projects Conforming to Enterprise Architecture

Ralph Foorthuis[1], Sjaak Brinkkemper[2], and Rik Bos[2]

[1] Statistics Netherlands, Henri Faasdreef 312, 2492 JP The Hague, The Netherlands
RFTS@cbs.nl
[2] Utrecht University, Information and Computing Sciences, Padualaan 14,
3584 CH Utrecht, The Netherlands
S.Brinkkemper@cs.uu.nl, R.Bos@cs.uu.nl

Abstract. This article presents a model for projects that have to adhere to Enterprise Architecture (EA) in order for their results to be aligned with the broader organization. The model features project artifacts (i.e. deliverables such as Software Architecture Documents), their mutual relationships, their relationship with EA, and the processes in which they are created and tested on conformance. We start with applying Activity Theory to show the crucial mediating role that artifacts have in projects and to identify and justify the new EA-related artifacts we introduce. We subsequently incorporate these findings and existing best practices in a standard systems development approach in order to create a practical model that projects can apply for EA conformance. This model features both new, dedicated EA artifacts, and well-known existing artifacts of which we describe the way they should conform to EA. Finally, two action research studies are used to empirically support the model.

Keywords: projects, enterprise architecture, project conformance, analysis and design artifacts, systems development.

1 Introduction

Recent years have yielded a wide array of publications on Enterprise Architecture (EA). However, the topic of projects that have to apply and conform to the high-level solutions and constraints provided by an EA has received little attention in this research area. Nonetheless, project conformance is a highly relevant topic, as EA aims to align projects (and the processes and systems they implement) with the broader organization. Various benefits are claimed as a result of EA [1, 2, 3, 4, 5]. EA should enable local initiatives to contribute to the enterprise's core business objectives in an agile fashion, and facilitate the integration, undoubling and outsourcing of processes and systems. In addition to these benefits for the organization as a whole, EA is claimed to provide projects themselves with value in a number of ways [1, 5, 7, 8]. In this respect, EA is said to improve project success, to reduce project risk, duration and complexity, to speed up project initialization and to reduce their costs. Regardless of whether these claims are valid, the question of how local projects can conform to an overall architecture has recently been identified as an important research area [9, 10].

J. Stirna and A. Persson (Eds.): PoEM 2008, LNBIP 15, pp. 30–46, 2008.

In a previous paper on projects conforming to EA [10] we identified key architectural project artifacts (i.e. deliverables or working products, such as the Software Architecture Document). In addition, we identified best practices for this type of project, and presented them relatively independent from each other [11]. A next step is to take these artifacts and practices to formulate a coherent model for deliverables in projects applying EA prescriptions. Therefore, the research question of this paper is:

> *What artifacts are relevant for projects conforming to EA, how are they related to EA, and how are they created and tested on conformance?*

The goal of this research is twofold. First, our model of the artifacts and their related processes and roles provides organizations with a (semi-)structured approach to carry out projects conforming to higher level architectures. Second, by adopting an Activity Theory perspective in order to understand, identify and justify relevant new project artifacts, we learn more about the nature of projects conforming to EA.

The *projects* referred to in the remainder of this paper are projects containing both a business (re)design component and an IT component. Central to this study is that they are specific, local projects that have to adhere to Enterprise Architecture. Therefore, we do not consider initiatives to implement e.g. enterprise-wide services to be projects here, since these may be seen as part of (or directly related to) the EA itself and are therefore located at another level. See section 2 for more information.

The paper will proceed as follows. In section 2 we will briefly present a framework demonstrating our view on EA and projects. In section 3 we will apply Activity Theory to specify the role of project artifacts, understand projects conforming to EA, and thereby identify and justify important artifact types for this kind of project. In section 4 we present our artifact model. Section 5 describes our empirical research strategy and the results from this participative approach in a national statistical agency. Section 6 is for conclusions and further research.

2   Enterprise Architecture and Project Conformance

We define *Enterprise Architecture* as the high-level set of views and prescriptions that guide the coherent design and implementation of processes, organizational structures, information provision and technology within an organization or other socio-technical system [11]. The *views* typically provide insight into the context and meaning of a system, and its fundamental organization, its components and their interrelationships. As such, views can depict both the as-is and the to-be situation. *Prescriptions* can be principles, models or policy statements. They focus solely on the to-be situation and thus provide generic constraints and direction for both high-level, enterprise-wide endeavors and more detailed local initiatives. As such, they are the means by which the EA guides projects.

Figure 1, adapted from [10] and [11], shows the conformance relationship between projects and Enterprise Architecture. The Project Architecture consists of two parts. The *Project Start Architecture* (PSA) is the collection of prescriptions from an EA that is relevant for the current project, and the early translation of these prescriptions to the specific situation (see also [5]). As a result, the PSA specifies the project's

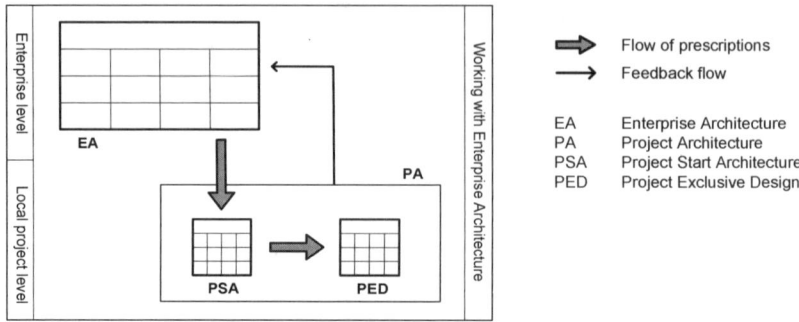

Fig. 1. The Project Conformance Framework

direction and boundaries at the start of the project, and as such stimulates EA awareness amongst project members [11]. Consequently, the fundamental analysis and design artifacts that describe the specific solution that will be created in the project will have to be compliant with the prescriptions in the PSA. This collection of fundamental artifacts is called the *Project Exclusive Design* (PED). The PED can contain artifacts such as a (Business) Vision document, a Domain Model, architecturally significant Use Cases and a Software Architecture Document. The PSA and the artifacts of the PED will be incorporated in our model in section 4.

During or after the creation of the Project Architecture, the project members can provide the enterprise architects with feedback on the EA. With these comments on the prescriptions and views, the EA can be further refined.

Although governmental and commercial organizations have developed approaches for stimulating projects to conform to EA, not much academic research has been done on the topic [11]. Important lessons learned so far include: use a PSA for a first translation of EA prescriptions and to create architectural awareness; review artifacts on EA conformance; use artifact templates to stimulate EA conformance; use one PSA version for the business analysis phase and another for the IT development phase; involve EA architects in the project; provide feedback to the EA architects to refine the EA [2, 5, 11, 8]. We have incorporated this knowledge into our model in section 4.

3 Applying Activity Theory to Projects Conforming to EA

This section will discuss Activity Theory (AT) and apply it to projects conforming to EA. See [15] for a general treatment of AT and [16, 17, 18] for an overview in the context of IS. AT is used in IS research mainly in the fields of Computer Supported Cooperative Work and Human-Computer Interaction. Activity Theory is relevant here for two reasons. First, it demonstrates the meaning and importance of artifacts in a project. This is relevant in this paper, as form the core element of our artifact model. Second, applying AT helps to identify and theoretically justify the new EA-related artifacts that we will use in our model. Section 3.1 describes important elements of Activity Theory. Section 3.2 applies these elements to projects conforming to EA.

3.1 The Elements of Activity Theory

According to [6], an artifact is "something created by humans usually for a practical purpose." Consequently, an artifact can be almost anything, such as a surgical instrument, a chair, a book or even the knowledge in a book. This broad definition is also used in Activity Theory, a theoretical approach in which artifacts have a very important function in *mediating* human activities. Artifacts are seen as tools, rules or the way that labor is divided [18, 19]. According to [15, 16], artifacts mediate between the elements of activities: active *subjects* (actors), *objects* (that need to be transformed to the desired outcome) and the *community* (those who share the object). An artifact can mediate not only between a subject and other elements, but also helps both explicitly and implicitly in tuning the actors involved. Figure 2 shows the structure of an activity. A continuous line represents mediation between the elements of an activity (which is represented by rectangles), whereas a broken line denotes the relation that is being mediated by artifacts (which are represented by ellipses).

Over the years, the artifacts have often been adopted and developed in such a way that they can mediate activities within a community [17]. In a hospital, for example, a surgical instrument (artifact) that is used within an operating room can be seen as a mediator between the surgeon (subject) and the patient being operated (object). This activity hopefully results in a cured patient (outcome). [16] describes the artifact as being both *enabling* (as it embeds the historically collected experience and skills) and *limiting* (as one specific tool does not allow all possible actions). In this example, the artifact is a physical tool. However, artifacts can also be seen as being less tangible, even cognitive in nature. For example, the heuristics, experiences, concepts, methods, roles and also the language and signs used in carrying out a task. In this paper, however, we will take an even narrower view of artifacts, as we focus on the deliverables or work products. Inspired by [21], we define an *artifact* as an intermediate work product that is produced and used during a project, and has the function to capture and convey project information. This can be both information about the desired outcome (specialist artifacts) and about the project itself (project management artifacts). Created during projects, artifacts are subject to version control.

In this article, artifacts are either documents (e.g. Software Architecture Documents) or models (e.g. Use Case Models). We consider the artifacts that are central to our study mainly to be *tools* (because a document such as a Use Case is an analysis

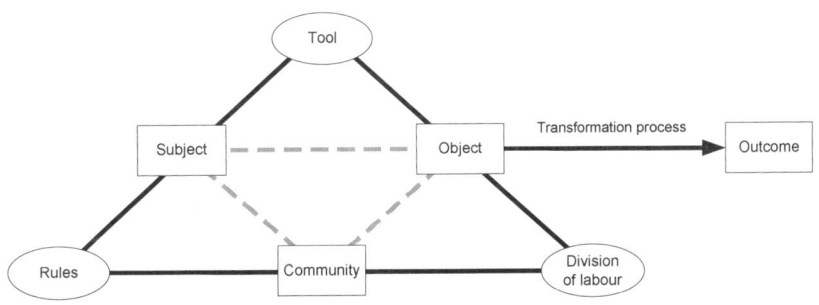

Fig. 2. Mediation between elements of an activity [from 16]

and communication tool used in understanding, building and documenting the desired IT system). However, they are also closely related to AT's *rules* (because creating and using artifacts is bound to the method's rules of the game) and *division of labor* (because an artifact is usually created by a specific project role).

An activity consists of several short-term processes called *actions* [16]. Actions cannot be fully understood without taking into account the broader activity, as they are all instrumental in transforming its shared object into the intended outcome.

To understand the dynamics of activities, three *levels of a collaborative activity* are acknowledged in AT [17, 22]. Because of their hierarchical nature, we consider these levels to be valuable in analyzing the dynamics between the EA-level and the project-level. As such, they can assist in identifying and theoretically justifying crucial EA-related artifacts, which we will incorporate into our model. The lowest level of an activity is the *co-ordinated level* of work, capturing the routine and normal flow of interaction. The actors are individually following their roles, which are embodied in a *script* coordinating the actions. Such a script supplies working instructions, which are coded in explicit rules (e.g. plans, role descriptions) or in implicit, unwritten culture. The actors involved work in isolation, focusing solely on their own actions. The actors could be seen as passive participants instead of active subjects, as the script ensures that they are working in harmony with each other and their environment. It is followed strictly and is not being discussed. [17] gives the example of a hospital kitchen only delivering the food on the basis of standard requests, not taking into account the motives of the involved healthcare professionals.

At the *co-operative level* of work, the actors focus on a *shared object* instead of each focusing blindly and passively on performing their predetermined individual roles. They actively try to find mutually acceptable ways to conceptualize and solve the problem. This requires the actors to go beyond their scripts, balancing their own actions with the actions of others, possibly even influencing them. Although the script itself is not rewritten, it is insufficient in the current situation and active discussion is required to determine how to go beyond it. However, the object being worked on is stable and agreed upon, enabling the participants to relate to each other in the discussion and make corrective adjustments. In the hospital example, if the kitchen staff and the ward's healthcare professionals share the same motive and object (the patient who needs to be cured) we speak of co-operation. The activities of the kitchen would then be determined both by the request and the patient's status. Therefore, if the ward orders the normal dinner for a patient with heart disease, the kitchen staff – knowing the dinner is too fat – can contact the ward to discuss the diet and correct the request.

At the *co-constructive level*, the actors focus on fundamentally reconceptualizing the nature of the interaction between the collaborating participants, and of the organization in which they are situated. Co-construction has two important aspects. First, the actors need to reach an understanding of a *shared object* (i.e. it has to be collectively constructed). This implies a joint and accepted understanding of the problem situation, of its relevance and of the nature of the solution being worked on. Second, one or more *scripts* will be created or heavily revised. Co-construction is typically located at the level of the entire organization since it fundamentally reconceptualizes both the script and the shared object. Therefore, it is a process rarely taking place in the ongoing flow of daily work actions. In the example of [17], the hospital can decide to implement the model of the "Patient Focused Hospital", moving from a model of patient treatment with relatively independent departments to a more holistic model organized around teams of healthcare professionals.

Upward transitions between the three levels are caused by *reflections* on the script or on the object [17]. These reflections can be triggered by a *breakdown* or a *deliberate shift in focus.* [22] and [23] provide two mechanisms that are involved in breakdowns, namely *disturbances* (unintentional deviations in the observable flow of interaction, resulting from an obstacle, difficulty, failure or conflict) and *ruptures* (blocks or gaps in the flow of information between participants and the shared understanding). The reflection can culminate in one or more solutions, causing a downward transition from one level to another that establishes the resolution at the lower level. For example, installing an updated procedure that now takes exceptions into account.

3.2 Applying Activity Theory to Projects

This first part of this section will demonstrate that AT can be meaningfully applied to projects conforming to EA. This shows the important mediating function of artifacts, and as such the relevance of our artifact model in section 4. The second part will use the levels of section 3.1 to identify and justify new EA-related project artifacts.

We consider a business (re)design and IT project that conforms to EA to be a collaborative activity involving both project members and enterprise architects. Figure 3 shows the activity triangle applied to projects. The *subjects* are the project members. In AT this may be an individual, but also a collective [18, 19]. In a project this will depend on whether an artifact is created by one or by more project members. The *object* is the solution that is being worked on (e.g. programming code), and the *outcome* consists of the implemented business processes and information systems.

Examples of *tools* are not only the applied modeling tools, programming languages, editors and compilers [18], but also the artifacts that are central in this paper (deliverables such as Vision and Software Architecture Documents). Examples

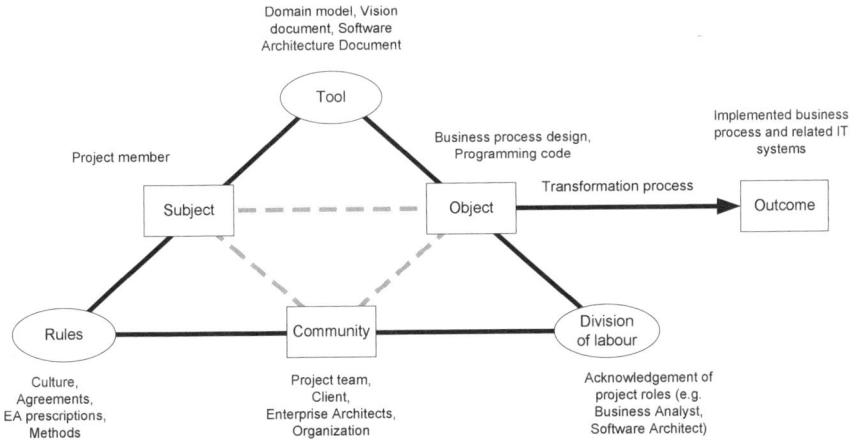

Fig. 3. The structure of an activity applied to projects conforming to EA

of *rules* are systems development methods and formal and informal agreements with project members. Moreover, the Enterprise Architecture is an important provider of rules (i.e. prescriptions). Examples of the *division of labor* are the roles that individuals play, such as the system analyst, software architect and project manager.

The project here is an *activity* consisting of several *actions*. For example, an action may be the process of creating a Use Case artifact. Such an action cannot be fully understood without the frame of reference of the overall activity and its object and motive [16] – creating and delivering a business process and information system.

To fully understand an artifact such as the Software Architecture Document, it should be seen in the context of time in several ways. First, the concept (and template) of this document has been developed over years, eventually using the 4+1 view model of architecture [24]. Second, the artifact itself (or rather, an instantiation of it) is created each time in the course of a project, in several versions. Such a dynamic artifact is different from a stable artifact that does not change during the activity, such as a surgical instrument.

Although we have adopted a limited view on artifacts here, we still acknowledge the crucial mediating role they have in projects. This holds at different mediation levels. First, mediation occurs *between the project and the environment*. Considering the immediate environment, requirement artifacts like Vision documents and Use Cases can be used to create a shared understanding among the client, future end users and enterprise architects. Furthermore, the more distant colleagues in the organization and even entire industry contribute knowledge such as artifact templates, best practices, text books and white papers. They do not share the immediate object, but they do share an abstraction of it. Second, artifacts help mediate *between the actions of project members*. Inside the project, individual project members partly communicate by the artifacts they create and share. A project manager communicates what needs to be done in what project phase by his project plan. A system analyst communicates to the software architect what the high-level requirements for the system are by his Vision document. Third, artifacts also help mediate *the actions of an individual project member*. An artifact's template not only provides structure for the artifact itself, but it also identifies and structures the actions that need to be carried out by its creator. For example, a Vision document contains a Product Position Statement and a features section. These imply two distinct analytical actions for the system analyst to perform, albeit that the results of these actions should be consistent. Furthermore, a template can contain advice for the author, guiding his or her actions.

Below, we will apply the three levels of a collaborative activity to projects conforming to EA in order to identify important areas for EA-related mediation and, as a consequence, for artifacts. In the context of EA, *co-construction* typically implies creating or updating the Enterprise Architecture and its architectural prescriptions. Co-construction is therefore located at the level of the EA, where (an abstraction of) the object is being reconceptualized. In the case of this paper's statistical agency it may be the statistical product (publication) that needs to be created, or the information system that generates this statistical product. In addition to the reconceptualization of the object, one or more written scripts are being created in the form of enterprise-wide high-level design choices and constraints (prescriptions) regarding this object. This can take the form of models or architectural principles such as "Software will be developed in conformance with the organization's programming standards" and "If feasible, statistical products will be created using existing register data instead of self-developed surveys". Consistent with AT, creating an EA is a reflective activity rarely taking place in the ongoing flow of daily project actions. Therefore, to be able to communicate the prescriptions to projects, the EA needs to be captured in one or more artifacts (which we will call the Full EA Documentation in the next section).

Co-operation means actively discussing the script in relation to the shared object, and going beyond the script without fundamentally questioning or reconceptualizing it [22]. From the perspective of this paper, this is the level where project members and enterprise architects meet. In order for project members to correctly apply the EA, they may need to consult the enterprise architects and discuss the prescriptions' meaning, relevance and application in the project context. This may therefore result in an artifact in which the enterprise architects can capture their advice (we will call this the EA Consultancy Report). Even if discussions with enterprise architects are not deemed necessary, project members may well be faced with prescriptions that impact the project so profoundly that they need to be actively discussed inside the project (e.g. the principle prescribing that a statistical product should be created using register data). Having such a fundamental impact, relevant EA prescriptions should be discussed at the beginning of the project, and their initial, intended application and tailoring should be recorded. The resulting set of prescriptions (we will call this the Project Start Architecture) will then function as boundary-setting and direction-providing for the remainder of the project. More discussions are likely to occur when these prescriptions are actually applied during the remaining phases of the project. It is necessary to inform the enterprise architects about the project members' experience with these prescriptions-in-action (we will call this the EA Feedback Report). The feedback can be used to update the EA. Or, to put it in terms of AT, this allows for the activity system to reconstruct itself [23]. In short, the co-operative discussions lead to communication both up to the enterprise architects and down to the project members.

Co-ordination only takes place at the project-level, as enterprise architects are not actively involved at this level. In fact, there is no discussion at all, as project members perform their EA-compliant actions in isolation. The project is able to adhere to architectural prescriptions by individually applying them. Therefore, discussing the script in relation to the shared object is not necessary, neither with the enterprise architects nor with fellow project members. An example at this level is adherence to the architectural principle "Software will be developed in conformance with the organization's programming standards." One such standard might be to apply the UpperCamelCasing naming convention to variable names. It is not difficult to see that project-wide and even organization-wide compliance is possible by individual developers independently following the script – in this case the principle and the standards it refers to. Although enterprise architects are not actively involved in performing EA-compliant actions at the co-ordinated level, they can get indirectly involved. As a script is *prescriptive* and therefore implies conformance, the extent to which the project conforms to EA prescriptions will have to be checked and communicated (resulting in what we will call the EA Conformance Report). Note that testing on EA conformance is not only relevant for co-ordination, but also for co-operation, as both levels apply EA prescriptions.

There are several mechanisms that can trigger the transition to a higher level. A *breakdown* can occur because of a poorly formulated EA prescription (a rupture) or a non-effective EA prescription (a disturbance). An example of a *deliberate shift in focus* is an idea for a new, improved or extended prescription, originating in a project. Enterprise architects have to know if any such transition occurs – yet another indication of how important the EA Feedback Report mentioned above is.

A co-constructive effort might seem removed from the actual task itself (in this case carrying out a project). However, as [17] points out, it is essential to view it as a part of the same activity because it helps to improve performing the task. This is especially apparent at the co-operated level, which implies that EA architects should be actively involved in projects, providing advice and also testing on EA conformance. Furthermore, note that our application of the three levels describes the collaborative activity of *carrying out projects conforming to EA*, not the activity of *creating the EA* (there would be some overlap, but in the latter case the focus of the lowest levels would shift from the project members to the enterprise architects).

Concluding this section we observe that Activity Theory demonstrates the crucial role of artifacts in mediating between processes and helps in identifying and justifying the relevant artifacts for projects conforming to Enterprise Architecture.

4   The Artifact Model

Based on the findings of the previous section, we will present the model for projects conforming to EA here. This model features EA-related artifacts used in or created by projects, the relationships of these artifacts with EA, and the actions in which they are created and tested on conformance.

We will use the Rational Unified Process (RUP) as a base model to extend. RUP is a software engineering process that provides a disciplined approach to assigning tasks and responsibilities in software development, featuring e.g. business modeling, requirements elicitation and technical systems design [21, 24]. We will use RUP for several reasons. First, RUP is the *de facto* standard for software engineering [14]. Consequently, we can take for granted the existing RUP artifacts, and only need to justify the new EA-related artifacts. Second, being a "unified" approach, it features artifacts and techniques also present in other approaches (such as the Vision document, Use Cases and UML). This makes our model relevant for other approaches as well. Third, RUP is also used in the organization in which we did our empirical research, making it possible to experiment with it.

The model is presented visually in Figure 4. In order to present an orderly and understandable diagram, we have included only the fundamental analysis and design artifacts (as contained in the Project Architecture of section 2) and an occasional project management artifact. See also [10] for the artifacts in the Project Architecture. See tables 1 and 2 for a description of the artifacts.

In terms of Activity Theory, the diagram shows the *(sub-)actions* and the *artifacts* used and generated therein. The *subjects* and *division of labor* are also present in the form of the roles that perform the *(sub-)actions*. In terms of the *community*, the

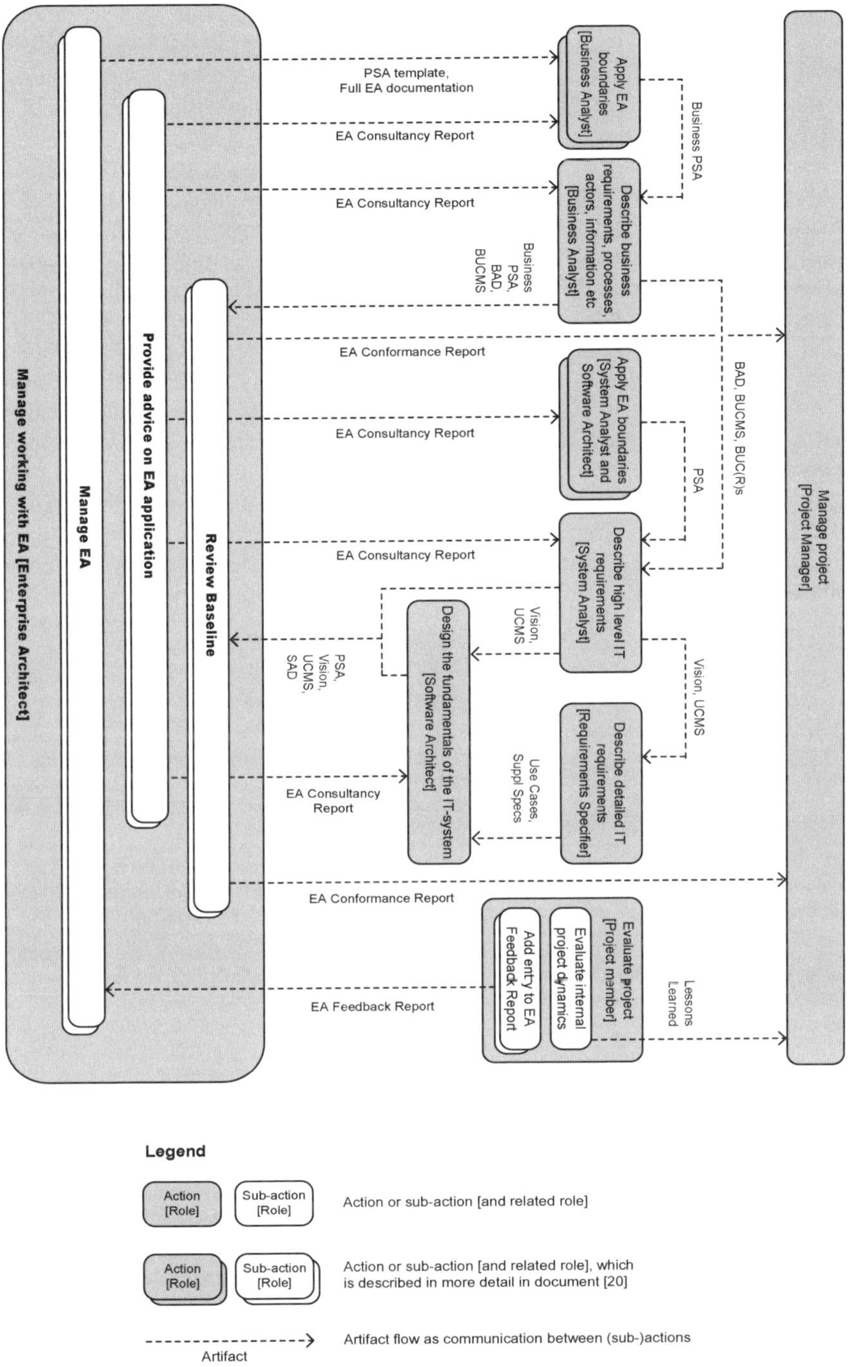

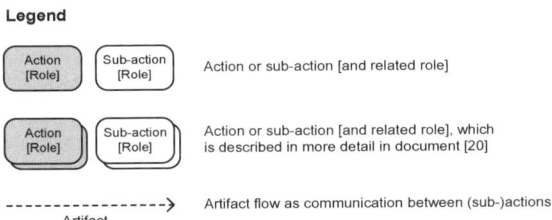

Fig. 4. The artifact model: artifacts and the actions that create and use them in projects

diagram features not only the actions of project members, but also those of the project's environment. These external actions and roles are printed in bold text. The flow of time is implicitly included by reading from left to right, but it should be noted that the length or surface area of the actions is not necessarily indicative of the relative duration or amount of work.

The interaction between actions – and therefore between actors – is specified in terms of artifacts, explicitly representing their mediating function on two of the mediation levels of section 3.2. First, *between the project and the environment*: PSA templates, actual PSAs, EA Consultancy Reports and EA Conformance Reports are used to align the project with the EA and other projects. Also, EA Feedback Reports are used for input to update the EA with knowledge from real-life situations. Finally, several existing RUP artifacts are used here. Second, the mediation *between the actions of project members* is represented: the (Business) PSA communicates to which prescriptions the individual project members and their artifacts should adhere. Other artifacts describe e.g. requirements. The third level, *actions of an individual project member,* can be found in [20] as it is too detailed to discuss here.

Below, the artifacts created by projects are described in more detail. Existing RUP artifacts are defined according to [21, 24]. These existing, well-known project artifacts feature a "Relation to EA" section specifying in what way they will have to conform to EA. Artifacts that are new and exclusive to working with EA are displayed underlined.

Table 1. The artifacts created by the project

Business PSA: The collection of business prescriptions from the EA that is relevant for the specific project, and their initial translation to the project situation. This artifact specifies the boundaries for the business analysis phase of the project, and can be seen as a preliminary version of the PSA artifact (see below). Can also contain a sketch of the intended situation.
PSA: The collection of business and IT prescriptions from the EA that is relevant for the specific project, and their initial translation to the project situation. This artifact specifies the boundaries for both the business and the IT phases of the project. The PSA includes the Business PSA.
BAD: The Business Analysis Document contains the Business Vision document and the Business Architecture Document. The Business Vision describes the business goals and requirements of the project. The Business Architecture Document describes the fundamental aspects of the business from a number of perspectives (e.g. key business processes, organizational structure, delivered products and services, business domain and market). *Relation to EA*: The Business Vision should explicitly state that the future business setting will be consistent with the EA. This can be done in the *Constraints* and *Applicable Standards* sections.
BUCMS: The Business Use Case Model Survey is a model of the business goals and intended functions that identify roles and business deliverables in the production situation. *Relation to EA*: This artifact is well-suited to specify the utilization of the enterprise-wide services delivered (or defined) by the EA, using secondary actors representing these EA services.
BUC(R): A Business Use Case (BUC) is a description of a business process from an external (e.g. customer), value-added point of view. A Business Use Case Realization (BUCR) can be used to describe the business process from an inside (e.g. business worker) perspective. *Relation to EA*: The content should be consistent with PSA (and therefore EA) prescriptions. The way in which EA business services will be used should be (non-technically) described in detail.

Table 1. (*continued*)

Vision: The Vision document is a description of the high-level requirements of the IT system. It captures the essence of the product in terms of needs, features and design constraints. *Relation to EA*: The Vision should explicitly state that the IT system will be consistent with the EA. This can be done, for example, in the *Applicable Standards* and *Assumptions and Dependencies* sections. Also, the role of the Enterprise Architect should be included in the *Stakeholders* section. Finally, the features, which describe the system, should be consistent with the EA.
UCMS: The Use Case Model Survey provides a model of the system's intended functions and its environment. Contains all Use Cases that describe the system and the actors that interact with it. *Relation to EA*: This artifact is well-suited to specify the utilization of the enterprise-wide IT services delivered (or defined) by the EA, using secondary actors representing these EA services.
Use Case: Use Cases describe the detailed functionality of the IT system as tasks that can be carried out with the system. This takes the form of a sequence of actions that the system performs, yielding an observable result of value to the actor initiating the Use Case. *Relation to EA*: The content should be consistent with the EA and PSA. The way in which EA IT services will be used should be (non-technically) described in detail.
Suppl Specs: The Supplementary Specifications artifact describes the requirements of the IT system that can not be easily captured in one specific Use Case. *Relation to EA*: The content should be consistent with PSA (and therefore EA) prescriptions.
SAD: The Software Architecture Document provides a comprehensive architectural overview of the system, describing several software-architectural views, such as the *deployment view*. *Relation to EA*: The content should be consistent with the EA and PSA. The way that the EA's IT services will be used should be technically described.
Lessons Learned: This artifact collects and explicitly states improved practices for future projects (excluding feedback regarding the EA).
EA Feedback Report: This artifact, which does not need to be a lengthy report, provides feedback to the Enterprise Architect about applying the architectural principles, and, for example, using enterprise-wide services delivered by the EA. Any project member who has to adhere to EA while carrying out actions can add entries to this report. The feedback can result in EA prescriptions and views being changed, added, removed, grouped or stated more clearly in the EA.

The table below describes the artifacts delivered by the Enterprise Architect.

Table 2. The artifacts created by the Enterprise Architect role

PSA template: The template that assists the authors in creating the Business PSA and the PSA.
Full EA documentation: The full and official artifacts, which describe the EA in detail.
EA Conformance Report: A report created by the Enterprise Architect in which an artifact baseline of the project is judged against the EA per prescription. (A *baseline* is a set of artifacts which the project pretends is complete and accorded by its immediate stakeholders.) The report can be formal or informal and contains a final judgment and suggested actions for the project.
EA Consultancy Report: A report created by the Enterprise Architect in which the project is given tailor-made advice on the application of EA prescriptions. May or may not be on request.

Several remarks should be made. First, the Enterprise Architect supplies the PSA template and Full EA documentation only to the Business Analyst. However, this does not imply that other project members do not have access to this material, as we assume the Business Analyst will distribute it. Second, it is important to understand that in a real-life project an artifact can be a formal, elegantly written document, but that it can also be a simple e-mail. Moreover, in some cases a written or drawn artifact may not be the only or most effective way of communication. For example, a face-to-face dialogue may sometimes be a better way to communicate advice than an EA Consultancy Report. However, it is often still advisable to also create a physical artifact, as it persists what has been said and may prevent unnecessary discussion afterwards.

Third, in our model we differentiate between the EA itself (the Full EA documentation) and the artifacts based on it. A generic PSA template could be created, however, already containing the EA prescriptions that are relevant for projects [see also 11]. This is interesting, as it blurs the distinction between EA and project template. However, as an EA also comprises prescriptions that are not relevant for projects, we still see the EA as a separate entity.

5   Empirical Support

In Action Research (AR) the researcher participates in a real-world situation to help solve an immediate problem situation while carefully informing theory [25]. To ensure maximum relevance and scientific rigor, we followed the formalized Canonical Action Research (CAR) approach and applied its five principles, as described in [26]. Participating in a project allowed us not only to discover best practices, but also to experiment with them. The CAR was carried out in Statistics Netherlands (SN), the Dutch government agency responsible for producing and publishing undisputed, consistent and relevant statistical information. Late 2006, the EA had been officially approved by SN's top management. None of the authors was actively involved in creating the Enterprise Architecture. See [11] for more information about SN and its EA. The principal researcher participated in two business process redesign projects with an IS component: the CPI (consumer price index) and the Energy statistics. The CPI calculates the average price change of consumer goods and services purchased by Dutch households, and as such influences salaries, pensions and rent levels. The Energy statistics provide information about physical energy flows in relation to energy commodities (e.g. oil and electricity) and energy producers and consumers. In both projects, the principal researcher participated as a business and system analyst. In these projects the business processes, statistical methods and supporting IT systems were being redesigned. Research data were collected by keeping a daily research diary, recording audio and/or taking minutes of discussions and analyzing documents (e.g. EA artifacts and presentations).

During the research we adhered to the five principles of CAR [26]: the Researcher-Client Agreement, the Principle of Theory, the Cyclical Process Model (see below), Change through Action and Learning through Reflection. As artifacts are central to the current paper and we have already described the application of these five principles in our projects in [11], we shall focus here on how the cyclical process model was applied to create project artifacts. The cyclical process model is used in CAR in order to ensure systematic rigor.

As artifacts are central in our study and SN needed a practical approach for creating them when conforming to EA, the action in our CAR consisted of creating several project artifacts. The research therefore featured a large number of small cycles, as every project artifact required several versions. Below, we will describe the five stages of the cyclical process model [25, 26] and the way we applied them.

- *Diagnosing*: Diagnosing refers to the definition of the organization and its problems by the researcher, which directly informs the planning of actions. Therefore, this action is not only performed at the start of the research project, but also as a regular part of each subsequent cycle. In our study, the participating researcher started with an orientation phase, in which the EA was assessed independently. Each CAR project also had an orientation phase in which the domains and its problems were explored by reading documents and interviewing key people. In each subsequent stage the current state of the project was analyzed in order to be able to determine what (aspects of the) artifacts had the highest priority.
- *Action Planning*: In action planning, the actions that should solve or improve the problems are specified using a theoretical framework. At the start of our study this was the framework as described in [10]. In later cycles the (preliminary version of the) artifact model was used for planning. Two main actions that required planning were creating a new version of a specific artifact and a review session to discuss it.
- *Action Taking*: The researcher and practitioners work together to intervene in the organization, causing change in the setting. In the case of our study, action taking meant analyzing input information (such as statistical methodology documents), interviewing stakeholders and writing or visually modeling the artifact. Finally, the artifact had to be distributed to the relevant stakeholders. In the creation process, it was sometimes necessary to (re)define artifacts when no relevant predefined artifacts existed in Statistics Netherlands. For example, neither the PSA nor a specific format (template) for a business analysis artifact existed.
- *Evaluating*: After the action is taken, the researchers and practitioners evaluate the outcome. In our study, therefore, after a new version of an artifact was created it was reviewed by project members, future users or other stakeholders. If all involved agreed that the artifact was finished, it was approved. If not, the shortcomings were captured in the review history, and another cycle would be required.
- *Reflecting*: Specifying learning is usually an ongoing process, as it was in our study. Interesting findings were recorded in the daily research diary and, if needed, changes were made to the current artifact model. Also, an artifact model was tailored specifically for SN (e.g. including statistical method artifacts) and interesting findings were collected in a document to share with the practitioners.

In addition to the projects, the participating researcher was involved in several sessions that Statistics Netherlands organized in order to invent a way in which projects conforming to EA can be carried out. The sessions included enterprise architects, business analysts, system analysts and information managers. As a result, the researcher created a preliminary version of the artifact model for SN, which was discussed, and after several iterations was included in the official documentation. The model presented in this paper evolved from the model in this documentation, based on the subsequent experiences in the AR projects.

Therefore, it is not the case that *Activity Theory* and the *best practices* of [11] were the input for the model of section 4, and that the *empirical research* has the function of testing it. Rather, in the research these three elements were all input for the model simultaneously. In other words, the model resulted from the CAR, instead of being tested by it. Testing the model is therefore a suggestion for further research. The table below gives an overview of the artifacts created in the Energy project.

Table 3. Creation of project artifacts for the Energy project

Artifact	#Instances	#Cycles (#Versions)	Format	Assisted by Enterpr Architect	Reviewed by Enterpr Architect	(Co-) written by researcher	Roles
PID	1	2 (3)	Document				Proj Man
Bus PSA	1	1 (3)	Document			√	Business Analyst
BAD	1	6 (10)	Document		√	√	Business Analyst
LIM	1	6 (18)	Document		√	√	Business Analyst
Stat Method	1	4 (10)	Document				*Statistician*
PSA	1	2 (6)	Document		√	√	Syst Anal Softw Arch
Vision	1	3 (9)	Document				Syst Anal
UCMS	1	4 (9)	Document			√	Syst Anal
Key UCs	3	UC06: 2 (4) UC07: 3 (8) UC12: 1 (5)	Document				Req Spec
SAD	1	1 (18)	Document	√	√		Softw Arch
EA Feedbk	1	1 (1)	E-mail		√	√	All
EA Conformance Rep	1	1 (1)	E-mail	n.a.	n.a.		Enterpr Architect

The number of cycles is operationalized by the number of review sessions related to a unique artifact version (e.g. two review sessions discussing the same version of an artifact counts as one cycle). The number of instances of "Key UCs" is the number of architecturally significant Use Cases identified in the Use Case View section of the SAD. The CPI project was very similar, the main difference being that the researcher also created a Vision document and a key Use Case.

Experimenting with the artifacts in real-life projects also provided us with the knowledge of how to make their contents consistent with the organization's EA. This knowledge was input for the "Relation to EA" sections in the tables of section 4.

As the table's *italics* show, the statistical project featured artifacts not present in the artifact model: the statistical method document and the LIM (Logical Information Model describing statistical datasets). This indicates that our artifact model should be seen as heuristic by nature: it provides guidance, but the model should be checked for validity and possibly be tailored to the specific organization or project situation. One can especially wonder if all of the artifacts in the model are mandatory. In our opinion artifacts should be delivered only if relevant to the situation. This can also be seen from the table, as the Energy project did not produce any Business Use Cases.

The table also shows that an enterprise architect was involved in creating the Software Architecture Document, but no architect actively assisted in creating the business-oriented artifacts. This was due to the fact that the decision to involve enterprise architects more closely in projects was taken by SN's management at a moment that the business analysis phase of the Energy project had already been completed.

More recent projects, depending on their importance, also had an enterprise architect attached to them that was specialized in the business aspects of the EA.

6 Conclusion

Focusing on the real-life application of Enterprise Architecture, this paper features several contributions. First, we have demonstrated that Activity Theory can be usefully applied to projects conforming to EA. This allows us to learn more about the nature and structure of this type of project in relation to EA, and the role of artifacts therein. Second, AT's levels of a collaborative activity have helped us to identify and justify the artifact types that are relevant for projects conforming to EA. Third, this theoretical knowledge has been used to create a model for projects conforming to EA. This model – also based on RUP, best practices identified earlier and empirical action research – provides a practical approach for carrying out projects conforming to EA, and for testing projects on conformance by enterprise architects. Finally, we presented how each individual deliverable in this model, both new and existing, should conform to Enterprise Architecture.

Further research might focus on testing the artifact model in similar and different settings. Furthermore, we have used RUP for our specific model, but, as the dedicated EA artifacts we have introduced are generic in nature, it would also be valuable to incorporate them in other systems development approaches. As we focus on artifacts, this would especially be interesting for 'document-light' agile methods, such as Extreme Programming and Lean Software Development.

As a final remark, we have focused on the artifacts that play a major role in carrying out projects conforming to EA. As a consequence, however, several aspects of carrying out projects have received little or no attention in this paper. For example, leadership styles and risk analysis (see e.g. [12] and [13]), which are important aspects in their own right but might also prove relevant for projects conforming to EA.

Acknowledgements. The authors wish to thank Marc Houben, Frank Hofman, Marlies van Steenbergen, Wiel Bruls and the PoEM 2008 reviewers for their valuable remarks.

References

1. Bucher, T., Fischer, R., Kurpjuweit, S., Winter, R.: Enterprise Architecture Analysis and Application. An Exploratory Study. In: EDOC Workshop TEAR Proceedings (2006)
2. The Open Group: TOGAF. Version 8.1 Enterprise Edition (2003)
3. Lankhorst, M.: Enterprise architecture at work. Modelling, communication and analysis. Springer, Heidelberg (2005)
4. Pulkkinen, M., Hirvonen, A.: EA Planning, Development and Management Process for Agile Enterprise Development. In: Proceedings of the 38th Hawaii International Conference on System Sciences, HICSS (2005)
5. Wagter, R., Berg, M., van den Luijpers, J., van Steenbergen, M.: Dynamic Enterprise Architecture: How to Make It Work. John Wiley & Sons, New Jersey (2005)
6. Merriam-Webster's Online Dictionary (accessed September 3, 2008),
   http://www.merriam-webster.com/dictionary/artifact

7. Capgemini: Enterprise, Business and IT Architecture and the Integrated Architecture Framework (accessed October 27, 2007), http://www.capgemini.com/services/soa/ent_architecture/enterprise_arch/
8. Pulkkinen, M.: Systemic Management of Architectural Decisions in Enterprise Architecture Planning. Four Dimensions and Three Abstraction Levels. In: Proceedings of the 39th Hawaii International Conference on System Sciences, HICSS (2006)
9. Bandara, W., Indulska, M., Chong, S., Sadiq, S.: Major Issues in Business Process Management: An Expert Perspective. In: ECIS 2007 Proceedings (2007)
10. Foorthuis, R.M., Brinkkemper, S.: A Framework for Local Project Architecture in the Context of Enterprise Architecture. Journal of Enterprise Architecture 3(4), 51–63 (2007)
11. Foorthuis, R.M., Brinkkemper, S.: Best Practices for Business and Systems Analysis in Projects Conforming to Enterprise Architecture. Enterprise Modelling and Information Systems Architectures 3(1), 36–47 (2008)
12. Box, S., Platt, K.: Business Process Management: Establishing and Maintaining Project Alignment. Business Process Management Journal 11(4), 370–387 (2005)
13. Project Management Institute: A Guide to the Project Management Body of Knowledge, 3rd edn. Project Management Institute, Inc., Pennsylvania (2004)
14. Ambler, S.W., Nalbone, J., Vizdos, M.J.: The Enterprise Unified Process: Extending the Rational Unified Process. Prentice Hall, Englewood Cliffs (2005)
15. Engeström, Y.: Learning by Expanding: An Activity-Theoretical Approach to Developmental Research, Orienta-Konsultit Oy, Helsinki (1987)
16. Kuutti, K.: Activity Theory as a Potential Framework for Human-Computer Interaction Research. In: Nardi, B. (ed.) Context and Consciousness: Activity Theory and Human Computer Interaction, pp. 17–44. MIT Press, Cambridge (1995)
17. Bardram, J.: Designing for the dynamics of cooperative work activities. In: Proceedings of the 1998 ACM Conference on Computer Supported Cooperative Work, pp. 89–98 (1998)
18. Barthelmess, P., Anderson, K.M.: A View of Software Development Environments Based on Activity Theory. Computer Supported Cooperative Work 11(1-2), (2002)
19. Kuutti, K.: The Concept of activity as a basic unit of analysis for CSCW research. In: Proceedings of the European Conference on CSCW, pp. 249–264. Kluwer, Dordrecht (1991)
20. Foorthuis, R.M., Brinkkemper, S.: A Process Model for Project Members Conforming to Enterprise Architecture. Technical Report, Utrecht University (2008), http://www.cs.uu.nl/research/techreps/repo/CS-2008/2008-023.pdf
21. Rational: Rational Unified Process. Version 2003.06.00.65. Rational (2003)
22. Engeström, Y., Brown, K., Christopher, L.C., Gregory, J.: Coordination, cooperation, and communication in the courts: Expansive transitions in legal work. In: Cole, M., Engeström, Y., Vasquez, O. (eds.) Mind, culture, and activity. Cambridge University Press, Cambridge (1997)
23. Engeström, Y.: Developmental Work Research: Reconstructing Expertise Through Expansive Learning. In: Nurminen, M.I., Weir, G.R.S. (eds.) Human Jobs and Computer Interfaces. Elsevier Science Publishers B.V, Amsterdam (1991)
24. Kruchten, P.: The Rational Unified Process. An Introduction, 3rd edn. Addison-Wesley, Boston (2003)
25. Baskerville, R.L.: Investigating Information Systems With Action Research. Communications of the Association for Information Systems 2, Article 19 (1999)
26. Davison, R.M., Martinsons, M.G., Kock, N.: Principles of canonical action research. Information Systems Journal 14(1), 65–86 (2004)

Aligning Information System Design and Business Strategy – A Starting Internet Company

Vincent Pijpers, Jaap Gordijn, and Hans Akkermans

VU University Amsterdam, FEW/Business Informatics, De Boelelaan 1083a,
1081 HV Amsterdam, The Netherlands
{v.pijpers,gordijn,elly}@few.vu.nl

Abstract. In this paper we aim to align an organization's information system with its strategic environment. We propose an alignment framework which takes four perspectives into account: Strategy, Value, Processes, IT/IS. This alignment framework is 1) intended for the exploration phase of information system design, 2) considers the complex environment in which an organization - and its IS - operates, and 3) uses conceptual modeling techniques (IS architectures and $e^3forces$) and provides clear steps to analyzes and align the perspectives. We have tested our approach in a real life case setting, where we assisted in aligning an enterprise's IS and business strategy.

1 Introduction

Although *"business strategy"* and *"Information Systems"* (IS) seem to be quite distant topics, their relationship has been of interest for both the academic and business world. Among the first to develop and test frameworks to understand the relationship between business strategy and IT/IS were Henderson and Venkantraman [6] and Luftman et al. [8].

However, these frameworks are limited to only offering fairly abstract, informal facilities to reason about alignment and usually after the information system is already in production. No clear guidelines are provided to practitioners - especially IS practitioners - on how to align both concepts during the *design* of information systems [3]. A second limitation of these traditional frameworks is that they focus on alignment *within* an organization. How the organization, or more specifically the organization's information system, interacts with its complex environment is traditionally not considered. Yet, nowadays organizations increasingly operate in *value webs*, which are (complex) collaborations between enterprises to jointly satisfy a consumer need [12], making the interaction with the environment an import concern for business-IT alignment.

To deal with these issues, we propose an alignment framework (see section 2) which 1) can be used during the exploration phase of information system design, 2) provides steps and guidelines for the actual process of alignment and 3) considers the organization's interaction with its *complex environment* from four different perspectives - "Strategy", "Value", "Process" and "IT/IS"- , each considering a specific concern. Taking multiple perspectives into consideration

J. Stirna and A. Persson (Eds.): PoEM 2008, LNBIP 15, pp. 47–61, 2008.

comes however with a price, as it implies that the perspectives should be properly *aligned*, and not only *intra*-organizational (eg. strategy and IS within a *single* organization), but also *inter*-organizational (eg. interoperability of *cross-organizational* IS) [4].

Although the proposed alignment framework consider multiple perspectives relevant for business-IT alignment, not all are always interesting to stakeholders, as was the situation with our case study. Therefore we focus in this paper on one specific alignment issue, namely the alignment of an organization's *business strategy* and *IS* design. Both business strategy and IS are however rather broad concepts. For instance a business strategy can be expressed in terms of competences, positioning, finances, etc. [7], whereas IS can be expressed in terms of process models, data models, etc. [15]. To bring both concepts closer to each other, we operationalize both in terms of "interaction with the environment", which is a well known operationalization in both strategic literature (eg. [11]) and IS literature (eg. [15]). From a *strategic* perspective interaction with the environment considers external business forces influencing the actor under investigation on a strategic level (eg. competitors forcing down prices) [11]. From a *IS* perspective, interaction is concerned with the exchange of information with actors in the environment [15].

To understand and create alignment between a business strategy and IS we use a *conceptual modeling* approach. For modeling the IS perspective we use basic IS architectures, since they can show how an information system interacts with other actors in its environment (section 3.1). For modeling the strategic perspective we use the $e^3forces$ modeling technique [10], since this technique enables us to analyze the strategic environment of an organization in terms of *external business forces* influencing an organization on a strategic level (section 3.2).

To demonstrate our alignment framework and corresponding alignment approach we present a case study for a start-up Internet enterprise. For over a period of six months we assisted the enterprise with various alignment issues. In the case presented we aim to align the organization's business strategy with the organization's information system, which enables the offering of a valuable service (section 5).

This paper is constructed as follows: First the alignment framework is discussed. Next the modeling techniques used for alignment are presented. Hereafter steps for achieving alignment are discussed. Next the alignment approach is applied on the case study. We end with related work, conclusions and suggestions for further research.

2   Alignment Framework

Figure 1a presents the proposed alignment framework. Figure 1b presents the steps to create alignment (see section 4).

Exploration. Before actually implementing information systems it must be understood - on a high level - what the system will do (eg. interact with its environment) and how this will impact the organization. This is vital since mistakes

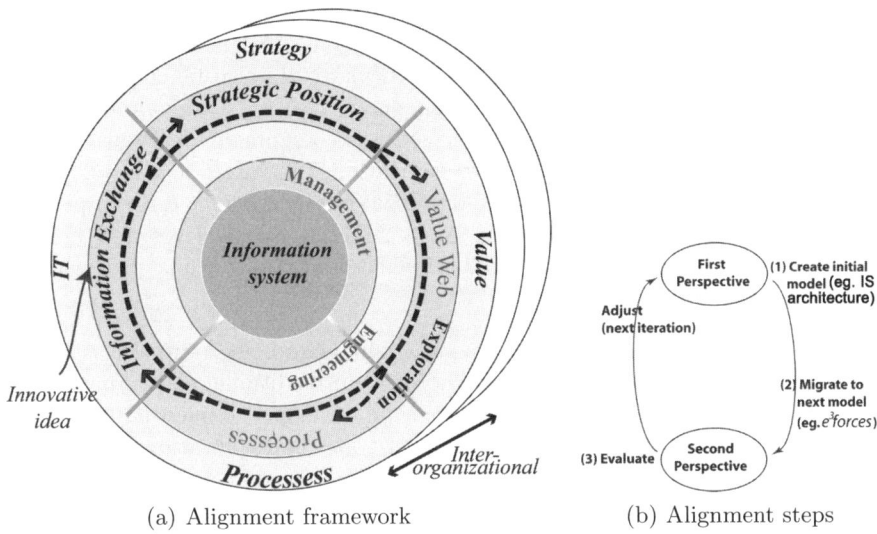

(a) Alignment framework   (b) Alignment steps

Fig. 1. Alignment

made in the early phases of information system design can have large (financial) consequences later on [5, 16]. So, the first step is to explore how the information system will interact with its environment from various perspectives (see outer circle alignment model (Fig. 1)). Only after the exploration phase is completed, further design (and alignment) should be considered; these additional steps are however outside the scope of this paper.

Multiple perspectives. To explore the *interaction* of a system/organization with its environment four different perspectives are taken into consideration (see also Fig. 1). Taking various perspectives on the system at hand to separate concerns is well known in traditional requirements engineering (eg. [9]). Although each perspective takes a different viewpoint, they all view the same phenomenon, which is in our case the interaction of a system with its environment. We consider the following perspectives to be relevant: 1) the *Business Strategy* perspective, which considers how other organizations influence the *strategic position* of an organization; 2) the *Value Creation* perspective, which considers how value is created by the *value web* in which the organization operates; 3) the *Processes* perspective, which considers the cross-organizational *coordination processes* to support the value creation; 4) the *IS* perspective, which considers information systems that interact with their surrounding to *exchange information*.

We must note that it depends on stakeholders which perspectives are actually explored. Stakeholders can find perspectives irrelevant, simply because they are at that point not (yet) interested in the specific concern explored by a perspective.

Alignment. A consequence of taking multiple perspectives on a system and its interactions with the world is that each perspective should be properly alignment with the others. However, alignment between the perspectives should not only be *intra*-organizational, which considers alignment decisions between perspectives within a *single* organization [4]; alignment should also be created *between* organizations. This results in two more alignment issues: 1) *inter*-organizational alignment *within* a perspective, which considers alignment decisions per *single* perspective but between *multiple* organizations (eg. interoperability between cross-organizational IS) and, 2) *inter*-organizational alignment *between* perspectives, which considers alignment decisions *between* perspectives and between *multiple* organizations (eg. alignment between cross-organizational processes and cross-organizational IS).

Iterative tuning. A naive way to reason about alignment, is to use a kind of top-down or "waterfall" approach as known from traditional software engineering methods. Each perspective would then be developed sequentially, and in a top-down way. We argue that this is, at least for the exploration phase, not a realistic approach. In case studies conducted, innovative ideas came from either the IS perspective (eg. new technologies), process perspective (eg. process optimalization) or value perspective (eg. business opportunities). Also, the world (including the competition) is continuous and fast moving in terms of enterprises, services, and technologies. So, we consider the alignment process a continuous and iterative "tuning" between the four perspectives within an organization *and* between organizations.

Where to start. If an opportunity for an innovative idea occurs, a basic question is which of the four mentioned perspectives to explore first. In case studies we have performed, we learned that an idea explained by stakeholders initially has a bias to one of the four mentioned perspectives (and actually often toward the IS perspective, as many business ideas stem from technological innovations). Often, this bias is grounded in the stakeholders themselves. We use this biased perspective as the starting point for the exploration of the development of the information system at hand, as stakeholders are familiar with this perspective, and therefore can provide the most information about it. For example, the stakeholders in our case have a technical academic background, so we started with exploring the IS perspective first.

Business Strategy - IS alignment. For the stakeholders in our case study two perspectives were of most interest: the business strategy perspective and the IS perspective. These perspectives were considered most relevant, since the stakeholders sought an IS design which "matched" their business strategy. Subsequently the focus of this paper is on aligning the organization's business strategy and IS by aligning the organization's interaction with its environment as seen from the business strategy perspective and the IS perspective. Understanding an organization's interaction with its environment is a well know construct for both understanding an organization's business strategy (see eg. [11]) and an organization's information systems (see eg. [14,15]). To this end we operationalize both the "business strategy" and "IS" in terms of interaction with the environment, resulting in interactions on a:

- *strategic* level, considering the strategic position of the organizations in its "strategic environment", where other organizations influence the organization at hand, thereby determining the success of the organization [11].
- *IS* level, considering the exchange of information/data between the organization's information system(s) and actors in its "information environment" [15].

Subsequently, in this paper we aim to design an information system operating in a complex environment, which from a IS perspective enables the offering of a valuable *service* and from a strategic perspective supports the execution of the organization's *business strategy*.

3   Alignment Modeling

Where traditional alignment frameworks offer no concrete methods to address alignment during the design of information systems [3], we take a *conceptual modeling*-based approach to create alignment within and between organizations. One of the major benefits of utilizing modeling techniques is creating shared understanding over various aspects among stakeholders of the system to be developed [2]. In addition, using modeling techniques provides a method to proper elicit the various perspectives on the system to be developed in a structured manner and allows for traceability of changes from one perspective into another [9]. Finally, the models we develop in this exploration phase provide a suitable starting point for the follow-up steps required for designing and implementing the information systems.

Since the focus on this paper is on aligning the strategic environment with the information environment for a system to be developed we take two modeling techniques into account: IS architectures (eg. [1]) and $e^3forces$ [10].

3.1   Information Environment Modeling

There is a substantial amount of literature on modeling an information system's interaction with its environment (see eg. [15]). Techniques commonly used are UML Use Case Diagrams [14], Data Flow Diagrams and IS architectures (eg. [1]). Since all techniques provide an apt description of an information system's interaction we aim at a notation which is easy and tractable. To this end we have chosen IS architectures. With these models we are interested in identifying two specific aspects: 1) what key technologies are needed for the system at hand, and 2) how the (sub) information systems interact with their environment. Furthermore, based on our field experience, if one of these aspects of the information system changes, chances are high that the business environment will also change.

So for the actor under investigation we model the (sub) information systems and data stores required with squares and rounded squares. Subsequently, we model, via simple arrows, which information is exchanged between the system(s) and actors in its environment (an example can be found in figure 2a). For these actors we also model which (sub)-information systems and data stores they require to interact with the actor under investigation. Technologies needed to enable the exchanges are also included (textual), since the selected components reflect important technology choices. For instance in our case study the choice for a GPS or GSM based positioning system had to be made. As we will see, such choices influence the strategic position of an organization.

3.2 Strategic Environment Modeling

We use $e^3 forces$ (see [10]) to model the strategic environment of an organization. As there is to the best of our knowledge no other model-based approach which analyzes the strategic environment of an organization in relation to information system design, the utilization of $e^3 forces$ to do so is an important contribution of this paper. The $e^3 forces$ technique provides modeling constructs for representing and analyzing strategic related concepts, such as "strategic position" and "business forces". It enables practitioners to analyze the strategic environment of an organization by analyzing the influence of environmental business forces on a product/service offered by the actor under investigation. The business forces analyzed are directly based on Porter's Five Forces framework [11]. In an $e^3 forces$ model, business forces and their strength are explicitly stated and are related to actors (see figure 2b for example). Furthermore, $e^3 forces$ enables practitioners to quantify a business force's strength such that it is possible to evaluate and compare various alternative strategic positions. Finally, $e^3 forces$ provides a clear and compact graphical overview of an organization's strategic position and related environmental business forces. The $e^3 forces$ technique uses the following constructs:

Actor. Actors, modeled as squares, are independent economic (and often also legal) entities [7], which interact with their environment by exchanging objects of value with external business forces [11]. Furthermore, an actor has a predetermined *business strategy*. The business strategy of an organization is the direction and scope of the organization's configuration and position in its environment such that it creates competitive advantage [7]. For an organization to successfully execute its business strategy a matching strategic environment is required [11].

Business Force. Business forces are those organizations that operate in the *environment* of the actor under study. From a modeling perspective, a business force is not an independent organization but a set of organizations, called *market*. These external organizations are grouped in markets because by considering sets of organizations we abstract away from the individual and limited influence of many single organizations [11]. This abstraction simplifies the $e^3 forces$ models to be made, and suffices for the business forces analysis we conduct. Therefore, we consider relationships between actors and specific markets in the actor's environment, rather than the many relationships between actors and each individual organization in the actor's environment. A business force, or market, has a certain *strength*. The strength of a force indicates to what extent that specific force can *influence* the price and/or configuration of a value object offered to or acquired from an actor. A business force or market is modeled as a layered square. The strength of a business force is expressed by a "strength" arrow. A strength arrow is graphically bundled with the exchange of a value object and points from the business force toward the actor.

Types of Business Forces: Buyer Markets are sets of organizations which are part of the environment of an actor and acquire value objects from the actor under study. Buyer markets influence value objects because they negotiate down prices, bargain for higher quality and, desire different specifications [11]. All this is at the expense of the profitability of actor under study [11]. Note that we, as described above, do not look at buyers independently, instead we analyze the buyer *market* of which the individual buyer is part. *Supplier Markets*, the second business force, are those organizations which provide value objects to actors in the constellation. Suppliers influence value objects provided to actors in a constellation by threatening to alter the configuration of value objects, to increase the price or to limit availability of value objects [11]. All this is at the expense of the profitability of the actor under study [11]. *Competitors*, the final business force, are actors that operate in the same industry as the constellation and try to satisfy the same needs of buyers by offering the same value objects to buyer markets as the constellation does [7]. Competitors are a threat for actors because they try to increase their own market share, influence prices and profits and influence customer needs; in short: they create competitive rivalry [11]. Due to space limitations we consider "substitutes" and "New Entries" as competitors, which is motivated by the fact that they also try to satisfy the same customer needs.

Determining business force's strength. To analyze the influence of a business force on a value object, n different aspects (Q_n) need to be analyzed depending on the business force. These aspects are directly derived from the Five Force Model (see [10, 11]). To be able to measure and compare the strength of the business force, each of the business aspects related to the business force is scored on a five points scale. The scoring of business aspects is performed with the aid of *domain experts*. The score "5" indicates that the extent to which the business force can influence the value object exchanged is high and "1" indicates that it is low. Because the relevance of the aspects can vary per value object exchanged, domain experts give each aspect a *weight factor* (β_j), as done in CBAM [1]. The domain expert have to divide 100 points over the n aspects $(\sum_j^n \beta_j = 100)$; more points indicate higher relevance. When the weighted expert scores are summed the "strength" of a business force is expressed and indicates to what extent the business force is able to influence the value objects exchanged with the actor.

$$Strength_{businessforce} = (\sum_j^n \beta_j * Q_n)/5$$

The total sum is divided by 5 to range buyer market's strength from a maximum "100" to a minimum of "20". For *visual* purposes a score in the range of "20-48" indicates low strength (light gray arrows), "48-76" indicates medium strength (medium gray arrows) and, "76-100" indicates high strength (dark gray arrows).

Value object. Markets and actors in a constellation exchange products and services which are, in generic terms, *value objects* (see also [5]). A value object has two attributes [11,7]: 1) the *configuration* consisting of the qualities the object offers and, 2) a *price* which is expressed in terms of another value object, wanted in return by the provider of the original value object (the price to be paid is usually money, although not obligatory).

4   Alignment Steps

To create alignment a number of steps have to be performed (see Fig. 1b):

Step 0: Preconditions. To align the business strategy of an organization and its IS, we need to know two things: what the business strategy is and what (high level) service the IS will offer (eg. why is the IS needed?). The business strategy will specify how the service offered by the information system is used to create competitive advantage [7]. We consider three generic strategies [7,11]: 1) *cost-leadership*, which is trying to offer value objects with similar quality as competitors but against a lower price; 2) *differentiation*, which is to offer value objects with qualities that are unique or differ from competitors; 3) *focus*, which is focusing on a specific (small) buyer market. What service the IS will offer, is needed to know to elicit what functionalities and technologies the IS will need.

Step 1: Explore First Perspective. As stated, we use the stakeholders' bias to one of the perspectives as a guideline to determine which perspective to explore first. We reason that the stakeholders are most familiar with this perspective, and therefore can provide the most information about it. For example, in the case study at hand the stakeholders were biased toward the IS perspective. Therefore we started with exploring the IS perspective. Subsequently the first step was to create an (initial) *IS architecture*. With this model we aim to elicit *key-technologies* used and with what actors (eg. organizations, persons, or even hardware) the system exchanges information, both inbound and outbound.

Step 2: Explore Second Perspective. In step 2 we construct an $e^3forces$ model based on the IS architecture from the previous step. The $e^3forces$ model will show the *strategic interactions* whereas the IS architecture shows the information interactions of the system to be designed. For creating the $e^3forces$ model we use the following guidelines:

- Actors in the IS architecture are translated into business forces in the $e^3forces$ model. Actors providing information become supplier markets. Actors acquiring information become buyer markets.

- In addition, information exchanges in the IS architecture are translated into value exchanges. We analyze what of value an information exchange represents and what of value is exchanged in return (see also [5]). The basic question answered is: What of value does the information represent for the receiving actor?
- Finally, we model *competitors*. Information on competitors is not found in the IS architecture, but is required to fully understand the strategic environment of an organization [11]. So to complete the e^3*forces* model, we add business forces which offer products/services similar as to offered by the organization under investigation.

Step 3: Evaluate. The next step is to *evaluate* the strategic interactions by evaluating the various business forces modeled by following the e^3*forces* 's guidelines on how to do so (see sec. 3.2). This evaluation provides us with information on which actors have a large influence on the organization at hand and how (eg. on the service's price or configuration). Subsequently, we can determine if the organization's strategic environment supports the execution of the chosen business strategy. For example, if various actors have a large influence on the price of a service, then a low-cost business strategy might not be the best choice. Note that the analysis performed here heavily relies on business strategy literature by Porter (eg. [11]).

Next Iteration. If it appears that the strategic environment does *not* properly support the execution of the organization's business strategy, then a better strategic environment needs to be found. This is however done by adjusting the information interactions and thus repeating step 1. We aim to re-position the information system (eg. different technologies) in its environment on an information level such that it still can offer a valuable service to its environment, but from a strategic perspective better supports the execution of the organization's business strategy (which will be evaluated in step 3). To modify the IS architecture in step 1, we present the following guidelines:

- *Alternative Resources.* If there is a strong supplier force in the strategic environment we try to find alternative sources for the value objects offered by these markets. Translated to the information perspective this means that we try to find different *information sources* or *technologies* needed by the information system.
- *Alternative Buyers.* If there is a strong buyer force we search for other buyer markets to which the service/product can be offered. In the information perspective this means that we try to find *new actors* which could use the information offered by the information system.

Final design. We basically repeat step 1-3 until we find an IS architecture for the information system which enables the execution of a valuable service and on a strategic level supports the execution of the business strategy chosen by the organization at hand.

5   Case Study: Mobzilli - Location Based Advertisement

Mobzilli, a starting Dutch "Internet" company (www.mobzilli.com), offers the e-service "location based advertisement", which offers organizations the possibility to bound advertisements to geographical locations. Potential customers can request the advertisements utilizing a small java application on their mobile phone. So if a customer would be in a shopping street s/he would be able to request the advertisements of the shops in her/his vicinity using her/his mobile phone. Obviously an information system is needed to provision such a service.

We have had intensive contact with Mobzilli for over a period of six months. During these contacts we were not only able to gather information about Mobzilli and its surroundings but we were able to assist in the design of Mobzilli's information system. We consulted Mobzilli during various meetings on aspects ranging from strategic issues to technical issues. In return, they provided us with feedback on our approach and the modeling technique $e^3forces$ (eg. what was clear and practicable and what was not).

Step 0: Preconditions. As stated, we need to know the business strategy chosen by Mobzilli to be able to analyze if their strategic environment is desirable. Selecting this strategy itself is not part of out approach, since a business strategy spans multiple years. So, we just ask for the selected strategy. Mobzilli has chosen the business strategy "differentiation", which states that competitive advantage is created by offering a product with a unique configuration but not at low-cost. For the strategic environment of Mobzilli this means that they prefer business forces which do not influence the configuration of their service but which are allowed to influence the price of the service [11].

5.1   First Iteration

Step 1: Exploring the Information Perspective. Since Mobzilli's founders had a bias for the IT perspective due to the technical innovation of their idea, we start with exploring the IS perspective. So as a first step, we create an IS architecture. We aim to elicit here not only what information is exchanged between the information system and its environment, but also to elicit a number of technologies used to facilitate these communications. Fig. 2a shows the IS architecture for Mobzilli's information system initial design.

The IS architecture shows Mobzilli as the central actor incorporating three sub-information systems: 1) a database system, which stores all the ads received from various organizations, 2) an ads generator, which retrieves the ads from the database depending on the location given and forwards the advertisement to the clients mobile, and 3) an analysis system, which serves to provide statistical information of advertisements requested. Furthermore the model shows that 1) a GPS module provides the coordinates of a customer, 2) a GSM with mobile Internet and Java, which is owned by the customer, receives ads, and 3) "Shops" provide ads for the database and retrieve statistical information. We assume a mobile Internet connection to exist and therefore do not include providers.

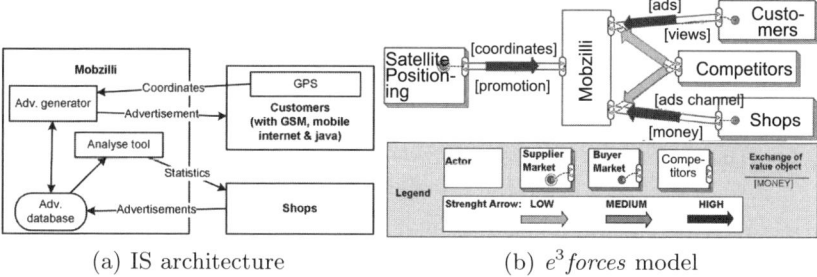

(a) IS architecture   (b) e^3 forces model

Fig. 2. First Iteration

Step 2: Exploring The Strategic Perspective. In consult with Mobzilli we developed an e^3 forces model for their initial design to provide insight into their strategic environment (see Fig. 2b).

The e^3 forces model itself is based on the IS architecture. The actors (organization or sub-system) in the IS architecture are translated into a market that influences Mobzilli. So "Consumers" become the buyer market "Customers", since they acquire a value object from Mobzilli. The actor "Shops" becomes the buyer market "Shops", since they acquire a value object from Mobzilli. Finally, the "GPS" sub-system becomes the supplier market "Satellite Positioning" since the GPS technology supplies valuable information to Mobzilli. In addition, alternative satellite positioning techniques exist (eg. the European Galileo) and the strength of this business force depends on alternative organizations offering the same service.

Based on the information exchanged between Mobzilli and the various business forces, we determined what of value is actually exchanged. For example, the provision of "ads" and acquisition of "Statistical information" by "Shops" is part of the value object "location based advertisement" offered by Mobzilli, which is their main service offered.

Step 3: Evaluate. Together with Mobzilli we applied the metrics described in sections 3.2, and after a few iterations we found the final scores. According to the supplier metric the score for the supplier market "Satellite Positioning" is 90, due to an imbalance in the market. The score indicates a strong influence on the value object "position coordinates" offered to Mobzilli. The value object is however free, therefore the strong influences is on the configuration (eg. accuracy) of the value object and not on the price. Furthermore, for Mobzilli to utilize GPS technology each user must have a GPS module. This however limits the amount of possible customers, resulting in a high score of 79 for "Customers". The strength of "Shops" for "Advertisement Channel" is also high (87) since the service is not important for "Shops" (eg. plenty alternatives for advertisement).

Based on these first results it can be concluded that their information system design results in a strategic environment which is not optimal for the execution of their chosen business strategy ("differentiation"). Not only is their a *strong* supplier force which influences the configuration, there are also two *strong* buyer forces which influence the configuration of Mobzilli's service. Since the service is new the influence of competitors is still low and therefore neglected.

This analysis provided rationale for Mobzilli's feeling that their initial information system design had a strategic environment which does *not* support the execution of their business strategy, even though the design allows for the service to be provisioned.

5.2   Second Iteration

Step 1: Exploring the Information Perspective. Mobzilli focused on specific technology used as a first step to create more alignment between their business strategy and IS. As the first e^3*forces* model shows, using GPS limits the client group size and results in a strong supplier. To this end, alternative methods for client positioning were considered. Mobzilli chose to replace satellite positioning with positioning via triangulation of a GSM's signal strength.

In relation to the original IS architecture, the modified architecture (Fig. 3a) shows that "GPS" is replaced by a GSM with Java app, which computes the customer's location based on triangulation of signal strengths.

Step 2: Exploring the Strategic Perspective. Based on the second IS architecture an e^3*forces* model was made (see Fig. 3b). The main modification is that the market "Satellite Positioning" is replaced by the market "Position Software". Since the technology to triangulate signal strength from GSM's has to be acquired, "java app" is translated into the market "Position Software".

Step 3: Evaluate. Together with Mobzilli we again determined the strength of the various business forces, and after a few iterations we found the final scores. The score for the supplier market "Position Software" is 80, although still high, it is lower than the score for "Satellite positioning". Again the strong influence is on the configuration (eg. interfaces) and not on the price of the value objects (eg. free licenses exist). Using the metric for buyer markets resulted in a score of 72 for "Customers" and 87 for "Shops". Note that the score for "Shops" has remained the same, but the score of "Customers" decreased. This is the result of more customers *without* GPS. Therefore, there is only one strong force on the buyer side remaining ("Shops") which can make demands in regard to the

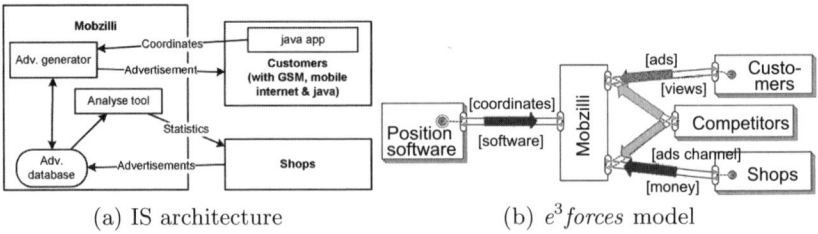

(a) IS architecture   (b) e^3*forces* model

Fig. 3. Second Iteration

configuration of Mobzilli's service. Since the service is still new the influence of competitors is still low and therefore not relevant.

The strategic environment is still not optimal for the execution of the chosen business strategy. The scores of the various forces are however better than in the initial design. This indicates that the revised information environment of Mobzilli's information system is better then in the first iteration. This notion was supported by Mobzilli. However, Mobzilli wondered if an even better strategic environment could be found, so again revisions were made.

5.3   Final Iteration

Step 1: Exploring the Information Perspective. Mobzilli chose to keep using GSM triangulation technology. However, Mobzilli did consider a new group of users for which their "location based advertisement" service is valuable: "Musea". The final IS architecture (Fig. 4a) again does not show many difference in regard to the previous IS architecture, yet an additional actor is modeled "Musea", which has the same interaction with the system as "Shops".

Step 2: Exploring the Strategic Perspective. The e^3*forces* model for the strategic environment is presented in figure 4b. The model is based on the final IS architecture and shows a new buyer market ("Musea"), which acquires the same value object from Mobzilli as "Shops" does.

Step 3: Evaluate. In cooperation with Mobzilli the various metrics were applied. The score for "Positioning Software" (80) remained the same. Using the metric for buyer markets resulted in a score of 69 for 'Customers", the score decreased since again an even larger population exists. The new score for "Shops" is 78. By adding a market, more trading areas for Mobzilli are available and thereby the strength of "Shops" decreased. For "Musea" the scores is 65. The strength of "Musea" is less than that of "Shops" because less alternatives are at hand for this buyer market. With this new design only one strong force remains. Since the service is still new, also for the new buyer market, the influence of competitors is still low and therefore not relevant.

Analysis Conclusion. It was concluded that the final design provides a strategic environment which is acceptably aligned with the system's final information

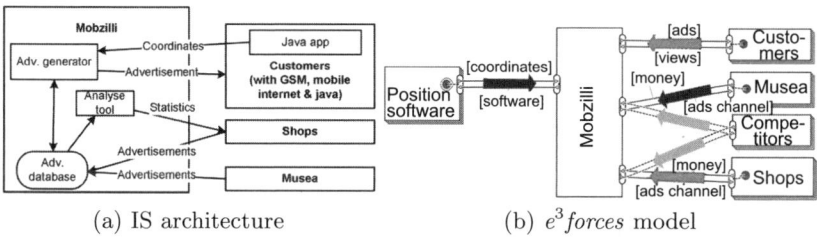

(a) IS architecture   (b) e^3*forces* model

Fig. 4. Final Iteration

environment. This notion was supported by Mobzilli. By carefully adjusting the IS architecture, based on findings from the strategic environment, an environment was found which has as minimal as possible influence on the configuration of Mobzilli's service and subsequently allows for the execution of the chosen business strategy. Although Mobzilli often had a feeling concerning various design choices (eg. which technology). They were however unable to properly related technical issues to their business strategy. With the aid of our alignment approach we were able to provide Mobzilli with theoretical rationale for their design choices.

6   Related Work

The most relevant related work it that of Thevenet and Salinesi [13]. Their method, INtenional STrategic Alignment (INSTAL), analyzes organizations at two levels: the strategic level and the operational level. Using documentation from both levels a third level is created where the synergy between both levels is documented, both the strategic and operational level are modeled within one single model [13]. However, in contrast to our approach, which has an external view of organizations, INSTAL has an internal view on organizations. Furthermore, modeling both strategic and operations aspects within one model might cause confusion since both viewpoints highlight quite different aspects of organizations.

7   Conclusion

The aim of this paper was to align an organization's business strategy and information system design within a complex environment. We accomplished this by analyzing - and subsequently aligning - the organization's interactions from a strategic perspective and information perspective. Furthermore, we provided clear steps on how to explore and align both perspectives. The application of our methodology in a real-life setting showed that we are able to align an organization's IS interactions on an informational level and the organization strategic interactions. This alignment resulted in a IS design which enables the provision of a valuable service and interacts with its environment such that the corresponding strategic interactions allow for the execution of the organization's business strategy. However, as our alignment framework indicates, various other alignment issues have to be considered during the exploration phase of information system design, leaving room for further research.

Acknowledgments. The authors wish to thank E. Dubois, J. A. Pastor Collado, J. Falcão e Cunha, M. Léonard, C. Salinesi, A. Persson, L. Patrcio, N. Castell, and P. Botella for discussions about the framework in Fig. 1 and W. Chowanski and R. Ladchartabi from Mobzilli for providing case material. This work has been partly sponsored by NWO project COOP 600.065.120.24N16.

References

1. Asundi, J., Kazman, R., Klein, M.: Using economic considerations to choose amongst architecture design alternatives. Technical report, Software Engineering Institute (2001)
2. Borst, W.N., Akkermans, J.M., Top, J.L.: Engineering ontologies. International Journal of Human-Computer Studies 46, 365–406 (1997)
3. Chan, Y., Horner Reich, B.: IT alignment: what have we learned? Journal of Information Technology 22, 297–315 (2007)
4. Derzsi, Z., Gordijn, J.: A framework for business/IT alignment in networked value constellations. In: Latour, T., Petit, M. (eds.) Proceedings of the workshops of the 18th International Conference on Advanced Information Systems Engineering (CAiSE 2006), Namur, B, pp. 219–226. Namur University Press (2006)
5. Gordijn, J., Akkermans, H.: Value based requirements engineering: Exploring innovative e-commerce idea. Requirements Engineering Journal 8(2), 114–134 (2003)
6. Henderson, J., Venkantraman, N.: Strategic alignment, leveraging information technology for transforming organizations. IBM systems journal (1) (1993)
7. Johnson, G., Scholes, K.: Exploring Corporate Strategy. Pearson Education Limited, Edinburgh (2002)
8. Luftman, J., Papp, R., Brier, T.: The strategic alignment model: Assessment and validation. In: Proceedings of the Information Technology Management Group of the Association of Management (AoM) 13th annual International Conference, Vancouver, pp. 57–66 (1995)
9. Nuseibeh, B., Kramer, J., Finkelstein, A.: A framework for expressing relationships between multiple views in requirements specification. IEEE Transactions on Software Engineering 20(10), 760–773 (1994)
10. Pijpers, V., Gordijn, J.: e3forces: Understanding strategies of networked e3value constellation by analyzing environmental forces. In: Proceedings of the 19th Conference on Advanced Information System Engineering 2007. LNCS, vol. 4495, pp. 188–203. Springer, Heidelberg (2007)
11. Porter, M.E.: Competitive advantage. Creating and sustaining superior performance. The Free Press, New York (1980)
12. Tapscott, D., Ticoll, D., Lowy, A.: Digital Capital - Harnessing the Power of Business Webs. Harvard Business School Press, Boston (2000)
13. Thevenet, L.H., Salinesi, C.: Aligning is to organization's strategy: The instal method. In: Krogstie, J., Opdahl, A.L., Sindre, G. (eds.) CAiSE 2007 and WES 2007. LNCS, vol. 4495, pp. 203–217. Springer, Heidelberg (2007)
14. UML. Uml 2.0, www.uml.org
15. Wieringa, R.J.: Design Methods for Reactive Systems. Morgan Kaufman Publishers, San Francisco (2003)
16. Yu, E.: Models for supporting the redesign of organizational work. In: COCS 1995: Proceedings of conference on Organizational computing systems, pp. 226–236. ACM Press, New York (1995)

Towards a Communicational Perspective for Enterprise Information Systems Modelling*

Arturo González[1], Sergio España[2], and Óscar Pastor[2]

[1] Departamento de Sistemas Informáticos y Computación
Universidad Politécnica de Valencia
`agdelrio@dsic.upv.es`
[2] Centro de Investigación en Métodos de Producción de Software
Universidad Politécnica de Valencia
`{sergio.espana,opastor}@pros.upv.es`

Abstract. This paper presents an overview of Communication Analysis, an approach to enterprise information systems (ISs) modelling that adopts a communicational perspective. It consists of a method and its underlying requirements structure. The proposed approach is conceived to be conceptually sound (it is founded on settled knowledge from various scientific fields), practically prescriptive (it offers guidance and criteria) and flexible (it offers specific strategies to deal with static and dynamic aspects of ISs). Both the method and the structure have been proved to be successful in complex projects.

Keywords: Enterprise Information Systems, Requirements Engineering.

1 Introduction

Enterprise modelling covers the set of activities, methods, and tools related to developing models for various aspects of an enterprise [1]. In this paper, the term enterprise refers to an organisational system that needs to manage its activity and its knowledge. An enterprise model is a consistent set of complementary models (a.k.a. viewpoints) describing the various facets of an enterprise to satisfy some purpose of some business users (a.k.a. stakeholders) [1]. Proposals for enterprise modelling may differ in their purpose, the content of the model, the quality of formalism, the level of abstraction, and the span of existence [2]. Concerning information systems (ISs), the purpose of an enterprise model can be to serve as a requirements specification for the information system (IS) computerisation [3]. This paper focuses on this purpose. We consider requirements elicitation to be a process that involves not only gathering requirements and constraints related to a software product (solution viewpoint), but also understanding and specifying organisational work practice (problem viewpoint).

* Research supported by the Spanish Ministry of Science and Innovation (MSI) project SESAMO (TIN2007-62894), the MSI FPU grant (AP2006-02323), and FEDER.

J. Stirna and A. Persson (Eds.): PoEM 2008, LNBIP 15, pp. 62–76, 2008.
© IFIP International Federation for Information Processing 2008

This paper proposes a requirements elicitation[1] method and a requirements structure that have been specifically conceived for the development of enterprise ISs. We refer as enterprise IS to a system of people, processes, data and material resources that supports the management and daily activity of an enterprise, by providing the strategic, tactical and operational levels with the information that they need for their performance. We share the view of Langefors that the IS is a support for organisational communication [4]. This paper proposes Communication Analysis as an approach to IS modelling. Communication Analysis adopts a communicational perspective by focusing on communicative interactions while eliciting requirements. Communication Analysis covers several enterprise model viewpoints (e.g. resources, activities, information, organisation). In case of necessity, it can be complemented with other viewpoints (e.g. economic, optimisation).

Special emphasis is placed on the structure of the requirements specification (RS). We consider that the lack of a proper structure is one of the factors that hinder the industrial adoption of Requirements Engineering (RE) proposals. In this paper, we argue about the concept of requirement and we enumerate issues related to their structure. E.g., a requirements structure should facilitate the elicitation process by supporting fact finding: we advocate binding together method and structure. The proposed requirements structure is founded on Systems Theory and Communication Theory, among other fields of science. The method borrows concepts and revises techniques from RE and Software Engineering, among other disciplines. Furthermore, specific modelling techniques are proposed to deal with communicational aspects of ISs (e.g. Communicative Events Diagram and Communication Structures). Communication Analysis (the method and the requirements structure) is the result of many years of applied research. The approach has been successfully put in practice in several enterprise ISs development projects.

The paper is outlined as follows. Section 2 motivates the work; several issues that hinder the industrial adoption of RE proposals are discussed. Section 3 introduces Communication Analysis; the underlying requirements structure and the main activities that compose the method are explained. Section 4 discusses the qualities of the proposal with respect to the motivating issues. Section 5 reviews related work. Section 6 presents the conclusions and future work.

2 Motivation: Recurrent Problems in Requirements Engineering

There is no agreement in ISs development project failure rates. The widely cited 1994 Chaos Report suggests that 84% of projects are unsuccessful [5]. The report uses an ambiguous concept of failure and, therefore, its validity has been questioned [6]. A 2006 Chaos Report highlights "a major up-tick" (sic) in success rates: the rate of unsuccessful projects drops to 65% [7]. In any case, it is recognised that information and communication technologies development is a risky activity. Various factors are considered to cause failure. E.g. project complexity increases risk significantly [8], and an inadequate requirements practice is also considered a major factor [9].

---

[1] We refer to the discovery and description of requirements as *elicitation*. We acknowledge that some of the terms that we use appear sometimes in the literature with a different meaning.

The sizeable scientific production in the area of RE indicates that we are dealing with an open problem. Many challenges issued by Bubenko in 1995 [10] are still valid today. As some studies show [11][12], new requirements elicitation techniques keep on being proposed but they do not live up to industry expectations. Many factors hinder RE industry adoption [13][14]; among these factors we will focus on those related to the inherent complexity of RE. We claim that there exist differences in criteria about the concept of requirement itself. We consider that the following issues are source of bad practice in requirements specification (RS).

1. **Requirements should offer an external view of the system under development.** Many authors agree on the fact that requirements should describe the user perception of the system [15][16]. Requirements are considered as functions and characteristics of a system that can be perceived externally [17]. Yet, something as basic as information needs is not the essential element of many RS proposals. Instead of determining what information the users need to carry out their tasks, many RS proposals emphasise the viewpoint of how the application is used. An IS is a socio-technological system [18], a medium that supports the communications of an organisation [4]. Therefore, we consider that input and output messages are the external concept par excellence. We believe that IS requirements elicitation should be organised around the communicative interactions between the system and its environment.

2. **Requirements should differentiate the problem space and the solution space.** Our stance is that input and output messages are the basis of an IS RS. They define user's needs (i.e. problem space), independently of the implementation technology. The way in which messages are built and conveyed, and the technological support that allows treating these messages efficiently determine how the problem is solved (i.e. solution space). E.g. an order (input message) requested by a client can be 'solved' by introducing data via a keyboard, scanning bar codes, reading magnetic cards, etc. Whatever the solution chosen, the input message is invariable.

3. **Requirements elicitation practices should facilitate user-developer communi-cation.** So as to establish shared knowledge. However, in many cases, stakeholders do not understand the RS language. The lack of shared knowledge between business experts and the development team hinders aligning the software with the needs of the enterprise.

4. **Requirements specifications should be well structured.** It is necessary to determine a structure for the set of requirements (i.e. for the RS document) and a structure for each individual requirement. In many cases, the structure of the set of requirements consists of a enumerated list of requirements and the structure for each individual requirement consists of a description template [19][20][21]. Templates facilitate a cognitive reasoning process that is *local* to a given requirement; that is, they allow to interact with the user in order to ask for details of the requirement that the analyst could miss without the template. The structure of the set of requirements should facilitate the cognitive reasoning of requirements that are *adjacent* to a given one; that is, when a stakeholder expresses a requirement, the structure of the set should promote the discovery of requirements that are related to the initial one (by helping the analyst ask the proper questions). However, enumerated lists are poor from the methodological and cognitive points of view. Solely enumerating facts hinders systematising fact finding. It is hard to

support an interactive and structured search process by means of enumeration, since the search space is not sequential. We consider that a proper structure for the set of requirements would improve requirements elicitation and management.

5. **Methods should be adaptable (and should provide flexible guidelines).** In a development project, there appear distinct types of problems that may need distinct problem-solving approaches. E.g. each kind of stakeholder recounts knowledge that can be related to derived-information needs (e.g. managerial staff tend to need listings and printouts), or to input-information needs (e.g. operational staff tend to need business forms). The way to elicit requirements is contingent upon the characteristics of the problem. When designing a requirements elicitation method it is advisable not to force a single orientation. The method should guide the analyst to tackle each problem with the proper reasoning tool. Note that flexibility does not mean indefiniteness: requirement elicitation guidelines should be prescriptive.

6. **The (inevitable) ambiguity of the concept of requirement should be overcome.** Some authors have given widely-accepted definitions of term requirement. But those definitions do not help much to deal with requirements. For instance, it is common to express that a RS should specify *what* the system does, instead of *how* the system does it. In fact, we did so above (see issue 2). However, the difference between the *what* and the *how* is not objective, as Davis shows in [17]. Standard definitions of requirement (e.g. a condition or capability needed by a user to solve a problem or achieve an objective [15]) neither specify the scope, granularity or structure of a requirement. To overcome this problem, the concept of requirement needs to be reinforced with instructive RS exemplifications, prescriptive elicitation guidelines and a requirements structure that facilitate the process. The need for requirements structure is argued in issue 3 and is a major contribution of this paper (see Section 3). Regarding exemplification, it is the instances (the examples) that complete the meaning of a concept [22]. Unfortunately, authors are not in the habit of illustrating their work with instructive examples that serve as reference. As stated in [12], examples found in RE literature are usually irrelevant.

7. **Requirements elicitation methods and structures should provide an integrated perspective of all the viewpoints of the analysed system.** In the current RE scene there exists a wide range of requirements elicitation techniques. Each technique is focused at a specific viewpoint of the system. Some techniques offer a similar viewpoint and can be considered mutually exclusive (e.g. BPMN and UML activity diagrams). Other techniques offer complementary viewpoints and can be used combinedly (e.g. UML class diagrams and state-transition diagrams). Methods should choose a set of combinable techniques and exploit their complementarity in order to integrate their viewpoints. This integration would foster the requirements structure navigability.

The above-mentioned issues are the subset of RE problems that motivates our work. We do not claim to have found a solution to each and every RE problem. Our main concern is providing a method that allows dealing with complexity and providing a requirements structure that is properly organised. Next section presents the proposed approach.

3   Requirements Structure Underlying Communication Analysis

There are, at least, three systems involved in ISs development [23]. The enterprise (a.k.a. organisational system) is a social system that needs the information that the IS provides in order to achieve its goals. The IS is a system composed of heterogeneous agents and it is intended to facilitate the enterprise work practice by means of supporting information tasks (e.g. acquiring, storing, retrieving, distributing information). The subject system[2] is the portion of the world that the enterprise wants to observe, control or influence [18]; the enterprise does so by means of performing communicative interactions and storing relevant facts about the subject system. RS should be organised around the set of interactions/messages that enterprise actors need in order to carry out their tasks. Communicative interactions constitute *what* the enterprise needs (the problem); therefore we consider them to be the main requirements to be discovered and described. The rest of requirements qualify communicative interactions by stating aspects, qualities, constraints, etc. of the communication. These solution requirements constitute *how* the system has to be implemented or has to perform. Communication and information requirements are related to *efficacy*; that is, the adequacy of the information supplied to achieve a task. Solution requirements relate to *efficiency*, to the minimisation of operation and usage costs. E.g. usability requirements and response-time constraints are intended to reduce costs. We further differentiate two kinds of solution requirements: usage requirements offer an external viewpoint and lead to interface design; operational requirements offer an internal viewpoint and lead to internal component design.

We propose a layered structure for requirements that covers both the problem and the solution spaces. This structure is the backbone that supports requirements elicitation (both the discovery and the description of requirements). The first level of the requirements structure corresponds to the systemic levels involved in enterprise ISs modelling. Each requirement is ascribed to one systemic level. We will also refer to the proposed systemic levels as requirements levels. The Communication Analysis method can be explained in terms of a composition of activities that are associated to the requirements levels. Figure 1 shows the requirements levels (to the left) and the Communication Analysis workflow (to the right). Today it is widely accepted that an iterative and incremental software lifecycle facilitates software development. However, the workflow is presented sequentially for the sake of understandability; it can be considered that this flow can be repeated on each development process iteration (in Figure 1, this fact is informally expressed by means of a spiral).

This structure offers two dimensions. One dimension is related to the static-dynamic duality (horizontal axis of Figure 1). The other dimension is related to refinement (vertical axis of Figure 1).

In organisations, a duality appears among dynamic and static aspects: business interactions are such things because they affect business objects and, in the opposite way, certain objects are considered business objects because organisational interactions deal with them. Communication Analysis eases to deal with this duality by offering techniques for interaction analysis (activities 2, 4 and 6) and for the analysis of business objects (activities 3, 5 and 7). This way, following a systemic

---

[2] In the literature, the *subject system* is sometimes refered to as *Universe of Discourse*.

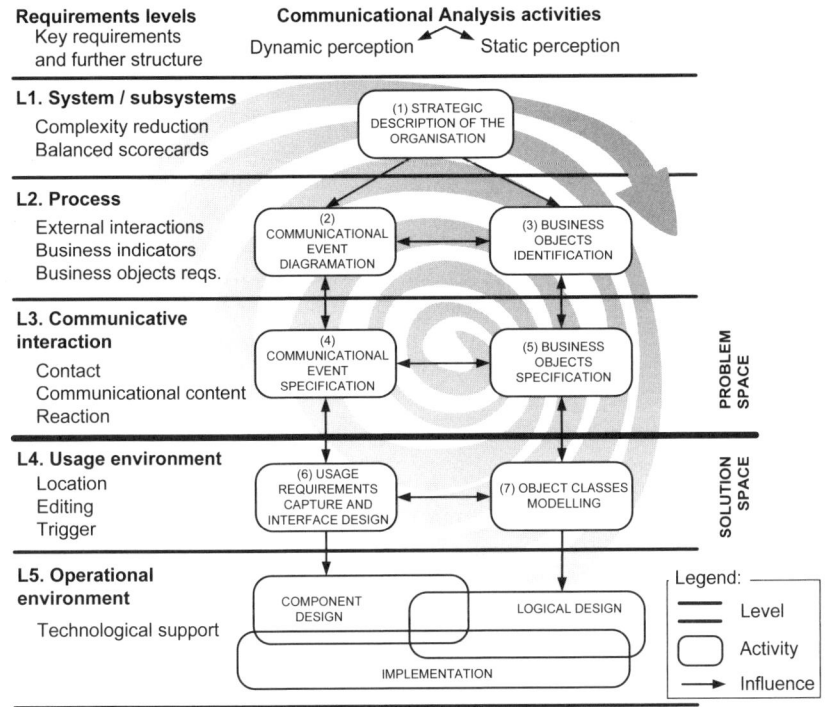

Fig. 1. The requirements structure and the Communication Analysis workflow

approach, Communication Analysis allows to use stepwise refinements techniques in a twofold perspective. From a dynamic perspective, analysing business processes and obtaining, from the process specification, the business objects structure. From a static perspective, discovering the business objects structure and, then, reasoning the communicative interactions that allow the users to deal with those business objects. This intertwining of both perspectives makes the method flexible and contingent.

We consider each elicited requirement to be of one of these kinds:

- A communicative interaction between the information system and its environment. E.g. a balanced scorecard, the reception of an order from a customer.
- A refinable aggregate of interactions. E.g. the accounting department (seen as a set of interactions), the set of communications related to sales management.
- Part of the specification of a communicative interaction. E.g. a message structure description, the description of a particular data field.
- A characteristic of a (set of) requirement(s) of any the previous kinds. E.g. statements such as "every amount shall be stored with 9 decimals", "every listing for the accounting department shall have a timestamp".

Each and every requirement is associated to a specific interaction or to a set of interactions. This way, the communicational perspective of the Communication Analysis forces every requirement to be subordinated to communicative interactions.

During the first stages[3] of requirements elicitation, the analyst seeks to obtain the repertoire of communicative interactions that the users need for their work practice. In later stages, the analyst (or designer) confronts the design of the interface that will support the editing of messages. Also, the memory of the system is designed to ensure the persistence to the communicative interactions. Lastly, the technological architecture is designed and the software application is implemented. In many ways, the techniques that we propose are an evolution and enhancement of existing techniques. For instance, the analysis of external interactions (done during activity 2) is a revision of business process modelling techniques. Next, the requirements structure and the method are explained in more detail. For the sake of brevity, only the techniques with a clear communicational nature are exemplified; namely the Communicative Events Diagram and Communication Structures.

L1. System/Subsystems Level

The first requirements level proposed is related to the point of view of business strategy; i.e. the information needed to manage the enterprise. The two main kinds of requirements ascribed to this level are: (a) communicative interactions (mainly outputs) that enable strategic management and decision making; (b) refinable aggregates of communicative interactions in the shape of subsystems.

Activity 1 consists of creating a strategic description of the organisation. Strategic requirements allow the definition of balanced scorecards [24]. In addition, when big enterprises are confronted, it is convenient to decompose the problem into subsystems or organisational areas. This way the analyst obtains aggregates of interactions that are more manageable, and problem complexity is reduced.

L2. Process Level

Communication is the essence of business process analysis in Communication Analysis. The analyst seeks to discover the set of communicative interactions of the enterprise. The method offers unity criteria to help determine the granularity of communicative interactions. Then, these interactions are ordered in space-time.

Activity 2 consists of determining the set of external interactions of the IS with its environment. By external we mean that we seek to describe system behaviour and not system composition. Communication Analysis offers a set of unity criteria that allow to objectify the appropriate granularity of communicative interactions. The term *communicative event* is used to refer to a complete communicative interaction (an interaction that satisfies the unity criteria)[4]. The elicited communicative events are interrelated by means of temporal precedence relations, creating a *Communicative Events Diagram*[5]. This diagram specifies the set of interactions of a business process, highlighting the information needs of the involved stakeholders.

---

[3] We refer as *stage* to the set of those activities that are related to the same requirements level.

[4] Unity criteria for the communicative event are not explained herein for reasons of space.

[5] Note that the Communicative Events Diagram actually specifies *classes of* communicative events; we omit this qualifier to keep the name shorter (just as the Activity Diagram does).

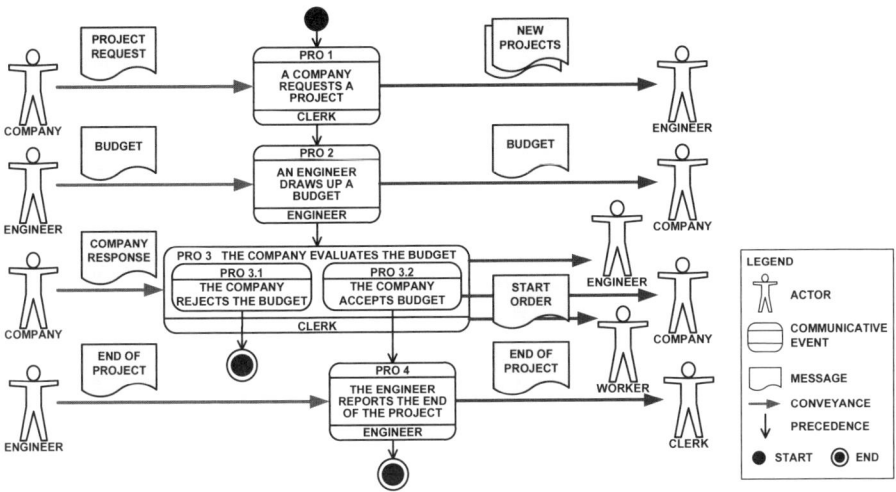

Fig. 2. Communicative Events Diagram of a projects office

Consider the case of a projects office that carries out industrial electrical installations[6]. A company (customer) contacts the projects office clerk, who opens a project record where data about the requested project and the customer company is registered. Every morning, the electrical engineer checks new projects, s/he visits the company and, depending on the customer needs, s/he draws up a budget and attaches it to the project record. A copy of this budget is sent to the company. The company either accepts or rejects the budget. If the budget is accepted, the clerk issues an order to start the project. Once the project is completed, the engineer reports this fact so the clerk can manage the payment. Figure 2 shows the Communicative Events Diagram that specifies the projects office IS, from a communicational perspective.

Activity 3 consists of identifying business objects[7]. Interviews with stakeholders (mainly representative users) are conducted and an ontological approach is followed. The aim is to identify the static perceptions that the users have of their business elements. During activity 3, business objects are identified and outlined; their detailed description is done during activity 5. Business process indicators are also specified. These indicators allow an organisation to monitor their running and performance (e.g. the state of an order, number of outstanding orders waiting to be served, mean response time to an order). Some business indicators appear during activity 3, others appear during activity 5.

The bidirectional arrow between activities 2 and 3 represents that the identification of business objects may involve the identification of new communicative events and vice versa. Communication Analysis is flexible and adaptable in this sense.

---

[6] This exemplification is neither big nor detailed, but it is relevant to enterprise information systems; bigger examples are to be offered in future publications.

[7] Herein, we use the term *object* where other authors would use the expression *class of objects*.

L3. Communicative Interaction Level

If the business process analysis done in the level above was intended to discover communicative events, now it is the turn for describing them.

Activity 4 consists of the specification of communicative events. Requirements related to communicative events are further structured in three wide classes: contact, communication and reaction requirements. *Contact requirements* are related to the triggering of the event by an actor who wishes to communicate something to the IS. *Communication requirements* specify the contents of the message being communicated to or from the IS. Practice has shown us that *Communication Structures*, a form of structured text, is convenient to describe messages. Figure 3 shows the Communication Structure associated to the communicative event PRO1. The structure of message fields lies vertically (at the right). Many other details of the fields can be arranged horizontally; e.g. the information acquisition operation, the data domain, the link with the business object, an example value provided by users. *Reaction requirements* are related to the IS reaction to the conveyed message; that is, it has to do with processing the information, updating the system memory and distributing the reaction result to other actors so that they can act accordingly.

Activity 5 consists on the specification of business objects. Business objects are complex aggregates of properties. At this stage, business objects are not specified from a (typical) object-oriented perspective. Object orientation splits business knowledge into homogeneously identifiable aggregates of properties. For instance, users consider an order to be a single business object, but object orientation splits an order into several object classes (e.g. order head and order lines). During activity 5, the structure of properties of each business object is specified. Then, each property (either elementary or complex) is linked with communicative interactions; i.e., the corresponding Communication Structure column is filled (B.OBJECT in Figure 3).

The bidirectional arrow between activities 4 and 5 represents that new business-object requirements may arise from the specification of communicational content, and vice versa.

PRO1 A company requests a project				
FIELD	OPERATION	DOMAIN	B.OBJECT	EXAMPLE VALUE
NEW PROJECT=			PROJECT	
< project code+	g projcode()	char[7]	< code+	P0034/08
request date+	i	date_time	req_date+	24-04-2008
COMPANY=				
< VAT number+	s Company<vat>	char[16]	vat+	19.345.631-Q
company name+	d Company	char[124]		Delicioso Olive Oil, SA
address+	d Company	char[256]		Polígono Sur, prc.64, nº 7
contact person+	i	char[64]	contact+	Sergio Pastor González
contact phone#+	<d Company + i>	char[16]	phone+	963870000 ext 83534
>+				
project description+	i	char[124]	description	Install air conditioning
>			>	unit in a 1000m2
				warehouse
LEGEND a=<b+c > aggregation g generation i input s selection d derivation				

Fig. 3. Communication Structure associated to the Communicative Event PRO1

L4. Usage Environment Level

In the usage environment, the essential interactions are related to the *editing* of the messages that are associated to communicative events. In order to do so, the user needs to navigate through the interface and to *locate* the corresponding editorial environment, to *trigger* a start signal to begin the editing process, and to trigger an end signal that initiates the expected reaction of the system. Editing, location and trigger are the types of interactions that guide usage requirements elicitation. Also, requirements related to ergonomics are addressed (e.g. layout, look and feel).

Activity 6 consists of capturing usage environment requirements in order to design the interface. Communicative events are restructured in editorial environments since a system interface usually supports several external interactions combinedly (both for interface usability reasons and for component reuse). Each editorial environment is then modelled in terms of abstract interface patterns (e.g. a grid) that are arranged in containers (e.g. a window form). Communication Analysis considers the interface to be a message editor and displayer, and it offers techniques that allow to reason the interface from the Communication Structures. Furthermore, a strong traceability is achieved among the interface patterns and the Communication Structures.

Activity 7 consists of modelling classes of objects. The business objects specified during activity 5 need to be fragmented in order to computerise them. The IS memory is specified in terms of object classes (as object-oriented and relational models do).

The bidirectional arrow between activities 6 and 7 represents that interface design often originates new classes of objects, and that decisions taken during object class modelling influence interface design.

L5. Operational Environment Level

This level is very conditioned to the chosen implementation technology. We only draft the activities associated to this level for the sake of brevity, and because these activities are clearly out of the scope of this paper[8]. This level concerns the design of software components that support the interface, the reaction, and the system persistence. The software architecture is chosen depending on several factors; e.g. technological and budgetary constraints. Lastly, the software is implemented.

At this point in the article, the Communication Analysis workflow (i.e. the activities) and the first level of the underlying requirement structure (i.e. the requirements levels) have been presented. Also, further levels of the requirements structure have been mentioned (e.g. L3: contact, communicational content, and reaction), although not explained in detail due to space restrictions. It is worth insisting that Communication Analysis induces an external viewpoint of the system; the proposed RE techniques elicit (aggregates of) messages/interactions. Next section argues how our proposal contributes to deal with the issues enumerated in Section 2.

4   Qualities of the Proposal

Structure levels L1 and L2 are related to communicational requirements (e.g. balanced scorecards, communicative events). At these levels, the analyst refines sets

---

[8] To focus the paper on requirements elicitation techniques, other development process activities -such as project management, testing and deployment- are neither addressed.

of communicative interactions (i.e. groups of messages). Level L3 sets the limit for communicative interaction refinement, by offering unity criteria that allow to determine the granularity of communicative events with as much objectivity as possible. At level L3, messages are described. Levels L4 and forth involve taking design decisions; system composition is specified. For instance, communicative interactions are reorganised around editorial environments, which in turn are composed of interface components. In short, each level allows the refinement of upper level requirements and the addition of requirements of that specific level. In the following, it is argued how the issues enumerated in the motivation (see Section 2) can be ameliorated or even solved by following the approach proposed in this paper.

Communication Analysis offers an external point of view; that is, the initial (and main) focus is put on discovering and describing the messages communicated between the IS and its environment (motivating issue 1).

The separation of the requirements associated to the problem space from those of the solution space (issue 2) allows an enterprise to concentrate on specifying the organisational knowledge (the problem), and then to outsource the technological solution. Software development providers can propose interface prototypes taking as input the problem specification and (if there exist) organisational standards regarding interface style guides, usability guidelines, etc. Furthermore, the specification of communicational and informational needs (problem) tends to be stable whereas technological designs and constraints (solution) are usually more volatile. The separation of problem and solution spaces facilitates requirements management, allowing this activity to focus on those requirements that change frequently over time.

Regarding the facilitation of user-developer communication (issue 3), Communication Analysis promotes two communication-enhancing techniques. Firstly, the definition of a glossary of business objects (during activity 3). Secondly, the specification of each communicative event using as input business forms used (or even designed) by users (during activity 4). This way, the user informational model is faithfully represented. See, however, some comments regarding this issue in conclusions and further work (Section 6).

Moreover, the requirements structure and the unity criteria diminish the ambiguity of the concept of requirement and allow an effective methodological guidance for requirements elicitation (issue 6). Our experience with the use of this method has demonstrated that it facilitates the ascription of each discovered requirement to the place in the structure where it belongs, as well as the determination of a proper granularity for the specified communicative interactions.

The concept of communicative interaction and its granularity are maintained at every requirements level. This conceptual homogeneity allows every requirement to be strictly linked to an interaction or to a set of interactions. This prescriptive interrelation in the requirements structure facilitates organising, searching for and tracing requirements (issue 4). The proposed requirements levels allow to search for requirements of a certain systemic level (searching or classifying requirements using a different requirement attribute may need tool support). In current traceability[9]

---

[9] In this paper, we refer to the aspect of requirements traceability that concerns understanding how high-level requirements are transformed into low-level requirements. It is therefore primarily concerned with the relationships between layers of information [26].

proposals, the interrelation is set a posteriori by means of linking requirement identifiers with structures meant for aggregation [25]. Explicit mappings among problem-space and solution-space requirements come standard in our approach.

Communication Analysis allows forward and reverse elicitation strategies (issues 5 and 7). A *forward* strategy consists of first eliciting input communicative interactions (those that report new information to the IS) and then inferring output communication needs. A *reverse* strategy consists of considering output interactions (e.g. listings and printouts) as complex objects; then the analyst defines derivation formulas until s/he finds the input interactions that provide the information included in the object (or in a part of it). These strategies deserve to be explained in detail in future work.

The method and requirements structure proposed in this paper have been put in practice in several complex and broad scope projects. Communication Analysis has been adopted (a) by the Valencia Port Authority, (b) by the Infrastructure and Transport Ministry of the Valencian Regional Government, (c) and by Anecoop S. Coop.[10]. Anecoop is a second degree cooperative and the major commercialisation agent in the Spanish fruit and vegetables sector. Anecoop intermediates between its associated cooperatives (>100) and its worldwide clients. Therefore, its IS is highly complex, since it has to deal with disparate information needs (e.g. invoices conforming to different tax laws). Communication Analysis has changed the way Anecoop tackles ISs development. Anecoop has attained a successful software development process. A 2-6 people team elicits requirements. All the implementation effort is outsourced. They have implemented a software framework to support their internal business processes and they have also deployed a web service-based B2B solution to work with their associates. At the moment, Anecoop leads a big project aimed to unify the internal processes of their associates. Obviously, this success can not be attributed only to the requirements practice; other practices as project management and risk management have also been undertaken.

5 Related Works

We claim that requirements elicitation and systems analysis methods have to be founded on the knowledge structures that they intend to discover and describe. It is not sufficient to offer a requirements structure without offering a sound method to provide the content, and vice versa. We consider that there exist comprehensive surveys of requirements elicitation techniques [14][27][28][29], so we focus the study of the state of the art on proposals that offer structure and taxonomy for requirements.

Some proposals consider systemic aspects that are characteristic of IS development [30][31][32][33][34][35]. For instance, the following levels of the Requirements Abstraction Model (RAM) [35] are similar to the levels proposed in this paper: Product level and L1; Function level and L3; Component level and L5. The difference between the RAM and our approach is that the RAM has been conceived for market-driven product development and it lacks a proper structure for supporting business process-related requirements. Some proposals offer structure for requirements of an specific level [19][20][35][36]. For example, Volere [20] offers an atomic requirement specification template. Now then, this template is the same independently of the type

---

[10] (a) Autoridad Portuaria de Valencia; (b) Consellería de Infraestructuras y Transporte.

of requirement. In this paper we propose the use of specific structures and notations for specific types of requirements (e.g. Communication Structures for message-related requirements). Some proposals support refinement [19][20][35].

Information systems must support enterprise communication. However, aspects related to communication are barely present in the above proposals. Some frameworks deal with communication [33], but Communication Analysis confers more pre-eminence to these aspects. In any case, the communicational strategy for IS analysis and design is not an unexplored idea. There exist proposals based on speech act theory [37] and the language action perspective [38] [39]. For example, Cronholm and Goldkuhl propose Communication Analysis as a perspective and method for requirements elicitation [39]. Their proposal coincides with ours in the communicational perspective. With regards to the method, we coincide in highlighting the importance of studying enterprise documents. However, discovery guidelines and the requirements structure are different. Cronholm and Goldkuhl focus their method on enterprise documents and use them as a guide for discovering requirements. The communicative situations in which a document is used are subordinated to the document. Therefore, the requirements structure that they propose (graphically materialised in the Document Activity Diagram) can be said to be document-centred. The method and structure proposed in this paper focuses on the communicative situations (that we refer to as communicative events) and messages are specified by means of Communication Structures. As a result, our requirements structure (graphically materialised in the Communicative Events Diagram) is communicative interaction-centred. Communicative Events Diagram is a revision of business process modelling techniques. The Communication Structures technique is influenced by DeMarco's proposal for data structures in Structured Analysis [40].

6 Conclusions and Future Work

This work is motivated by the inherent complexity of enterprise information systems (ISs) requirements elicitation, and by the lack of requirement elicitation techniques widely-adopted by the industry. We consider that this paper offers interesting insights into ISs requirements. The contribution of this paper is double. Firstly, it presents Communication Analysis, an approach to ISs development that is based on the communications between the IS and its environment. Secondly, it provides a structure for requirements. The requirements structure is founded on systemic concepts; that is, it takes into consideration the diverse systemic levels that are involved in computerised ISs development. Each and every requirement is ascribed to a specific level. Whenever a requirement needs to be refined, this is done in subsequent levels. This way, the structure allows to organise requirements in order to support and facilitate both requirements discovery and description. Also, the requirements structure has a clear communicational perspective. It fits perfectly Communication Analysis. This paper describes the Communication Analysis workflow. The activities are related to their corresponding systemic level. The method is flexible and contingent in the sense that it provides specific techniques to deal both with dynamic aspects (e.g. business processes are viewed as flows of communicative interactions) and with static aspects (e.g. business objects) of the IS. Two modelling techniques for communicative interactions are proposed: Communicative Events Diagram and

Communication Structures. These techniques have been drafted for reasons of available space; they will be tackled in more detail in future publications.

The way in which our proposal satisfies the motivating issues is argued. In any case, we plan to demonstrate the advantages of Communication Analysis empirically. We consider that sharing our industrial experience using the method will be of interest (qualitative research). Also, we are currently carrying out lab experiments to assess specific characteristics of the method, such as the unity criteria (includes quantitative research). Practice has shown us that the communicational perspective facilitates user-developer communication and mutual understanding, but we acknowledge that other influential factors deserve deeper research. E.g. in projects where stakeholders have markedly differing opinions, the analyst must play the role of facilitator.

Currently, several tools that will support Communication Analysis are under development. Also, we are researching the integration with model-based software production methods (e.g. the OO-Method [41]), in order to take advantage of automatic software generation.

References

1. Vernadat, F.: Enterprise Modeling and Integration: Principles and Applications. Springer, Heidelberg (1996)
2. Szegheo, O.: Introduction to Enterprise Modeling. In: Enterprise Modeling: Improving global Industrial Competitiveness, pp. 21–32. Kluwer, Dordrecht (2000)
3. Bubenko, J.A., Kirikova, M.: Enterprise Modelling: Improving the Quality of Requirements Specifications. In: Information Research Seminar IRIS 17, Olou, Finland (1994)
4. Langefors, B.: Theoretical Analysis of Information Systems, Studentlitteratur, Lund (1977)
5. The Standish Group International, Inc.: CHAOS Report 1994 (1994)
6. Glass, R.L.: The Standish Report: Does it Really Describe a Software Crisis? Commun. ACM 49(8), 15–16 (2006)
7. The Standish Group International, Inc.: CHAOS Summary 2008 (2008)
8. Daniels, C.B., LaMarsh, W.J.: Complexity as a Cause of Failure in Information Technology Project Management. In: IEEE Intl. Conf. on System of Systems Engineering (SoSE 2007) (2007)
9. IT Cortex Project Failure Statistics, http://www.it-cortex.com/Stat_Failure_Cause.htm
10. Bubenko, J.A.: Challenges in Requirements Engineering. In: 2nd IEEE International Symposium on Requirements Engineering. IEEE Computer Society, Los Alamitos (1995)
11. Juristo, N., Moreno, A., et al.: Is the European Industry Moving Toward Solving Requirements Engineering Problems? IEEE Software 19(6), 70–77 (2002)
12. Kaindl, H., Brinkkemper, S., et al.: Requirements Engineering and Technology Transfer: Obstacles, Incentives and Improvement Agenda. Requir. Eng. 7(3), 113–123 (2002)
13. Morris, P., Masera, M., et al.: Requirements Engineering and Industrial Uptake. In: 3rd International Conference on Requirements Engineering: Putting Requirements Engineering to Practice, Colorado Springs, Colorado, USA. IEEE Computer Society, Los Alamitos (1998)
14. Zowghi, D., Coulin, C.: Requirements Elicitation: A Survey of Techniques, Approaches and Tools. In: Aurum, A., Wohlin, C. (eds.) Engineering and Managing Software Requirements, pp. 19–46. Springer, New York (2005)
15. IEEE: Standard glossary of software engineering terminology IEEE Std 610.12-1990 (1990)
16. Zave, P., Jackson, M.: Four Dark Corners of Requirements Engineering. ACM T Softw. Eng. Meth. 6(1), 1–30 (1997)

17. Davis, A.M.: Software Requirements: Analysis and Specification. Prentice Hall, Englewood Cliffs (1990)
18. Lockemann, P.C., Mayr, H.C.: Information System Design: Techniques and Software Support. In: Kugler, H.-J. (ed.) IFIP 1986. North-Holland, Amsterdam (1986)
19. IEEE-STD-830-1998 Recommended Practice for Software Requirements Specifications (1998)
20. Volere: Requirements Specification Template & Atomic Requirements Template, Atlantic Systems Guild (2006), http://www.volere.co.uk
21. Davis, A.M.: Just Enough Requirements Management, Dorset House (2005)
22. Sager, J.C.: A Practical Course in Terminology Processing, 23 p. John Benjamins Publishing, Amsterdam/Philadelphia (1990)
23. Pastor, O., González, A., España, S.: Conceptual Alignment of Software Production Methods. In: Krogstie, J., Opdahl, A.L., Brinkkemper, S. (eds.) Conceptual Modelling in Information Systems Engineering. Springer, Berlin (2007)
24. Kaplan, R.S., Norton, D.P.: The Balanced Scorecard: Translating Strategy into Action. Harvard Business School Press (1996)
25. Ramesh, B., Jarke, M.: Toward Reference Models for Requirements Traceability. IEEE T Software Eng. 27(1), 58–93 (2001)
26. Hull, E., Jackson, K., Dick, J.: Requirements Engineering. Springer, Heidelberg (2004)
27. Goguen, J.A., Linde, C.: Techniques for Requirements Elicitation. In: IEEE International Symposium on Requirements Engineering, San Diego, CA, USA, pp. 152–164 (1993)
28. Sommerville, I., Kotonya, G.: Requirements Engineering: Processes and Techniques. Wiley, Chichester (1998)
29. Wieringa, R.: A Survey of Structured and Object-Oriented Software Specification Methods and Techniques. ACM Comput. Surv. 30(4), 459–527 (1998)
30. UN/CEFACT's Modeling Methodology - UMM Meta Model - public draft 2.0 (2008)
31. Wieringa, R.: Requirements Engineering: Frameworks for Understanding. Wiley, Chichester (1996)
32. ISO/IEC: 10746-1:1998 Information Technology - ODP Reference Model Overview (1998)
33. Wieringa, R.: Design Methods for Reactive Systems: Yourdon, Statemate and the UML. Morgan Kaufmann, San Francisco (2002)
34. Myers, D., Hathaway, T.: On Business Requirements and Technical Specifications: A Requirements Taxonomy. Requirements Solutions Group LLC (2005)
35. Gorschek, T., Wohlin, C.: Requirements Abstraction Model. Requir. Eng. 11(1), 79–101 (2005)
36. White, S., Edwards, M.: A Requirements Taxonomy for Specifying Complex Systems. In: 1st Intl Conf on Eng of Complex Computer Systems. IEEE Computer Society, Los Alamitos (1995)
37. Falb, J., Popp, R., et al.: Fully-automatic generation of user interfaces for multiple devices from a high-level model based on communicative acts. In: 40th Annual Hawaii International Conference on System Sciences. IEEE Computer Society, Los Alamitos (2007)
38. Dietz, J.L.G.: Enterprise Ontology: Theory and Methodology. Springer, Heidelberg (2006)
39. Cronholm, S., Goldkunhl, G.: Communication Analysis as Perspective and Method for Requirements Engineering. In: Mate, J.L., Silva, A. (eds.) Requirements Engineering for Socio-Technical Systems. Idea Group Inc. (2004)
40. Demarco, T.: Structured Analysis and System Specification. Yourdon Press (1979)
41. Pastor, O., Molina, J.C.: Model-Driven Architecture in Practice: A Software Production Environment Based on Conceptual Modeling. Springer, New York (2007)

Integrating System Dynamics with Object-Role Modeling

P. (Fiona) Tulinayo[1], S.J.B.A. (Stijn) Hoppenbrouwers[1],
and H.A. (Erik) Proper[1,2]

[1] Institute of Computing and Information Sciences, Radboud University Nijmegen
Toernooiveld 1, 6525 ED Nijmegen, The Netherlands, EU
`F.Tulinayo@science.ru.nl, stijnh@cs.ru.nl`
[2] Capgemini, Papendorpseweg 100, 3500 GN Utrecht, The Netherlands, EU
`e.proper@acm.org`

Abstract. We put Object-Role Modeling (ORM) to work in the context of the creation of System Dynamics (SD) models. SD focuses on the structure and behavior of systems composed of interacting feedback loops. The art of SD modeling lies in discovering and representing the feedback processes and other elements that determine the dynamics of the system (typically, a process in an organization). However, SD shows a lack of instruments for discovering and expressing precise, language-based concepts in domains. At the same time, the field of conceptual modeling has long since focused on deriving models from natural expressions. We therefore turn to ORM as a prime example of this school of thought to integrate its strong natural language based modeling approach into the creation of SD models. A two-step schema based approach for transforming an ORM domain model into a SD stock and flow diagram is presented. We discuss how typical ORM conceptualization can be linked to SD conceptualization and how such a transformation can be performed. Examples are provided.

Keywords: System dynamics and Object-Role modeling.

1 Introduction

Integration of methodological concepts can be viewed as an improvement of process development. This is because concepts from different approaches supplement each other; hence the weaknesses of one approach are overcome by the strength of the other. The current effort was inspired by an observed lack of concept-level modeling power in SD. We set out mainly to augment SD modeling by first laying down a sound foundation of domain concepts by means of fact-based ORM modeling. This enables us eventually to link the ORM model to an SD stock-flow diagram SD as a method has been in existence since 1961, developed by Jay Forrester to handle socio-economic problems with a focus on the structure and behavior of systems composed of interacting feedback loops. A review and history is given in [4]. The art of SD modeling lies in discovering

J. Stirna and A. Persson (Eds.): PoEM 2008, LNBIP 15, pp. 77–85, 2008.

and presenting the feedback processes and other elements of complexities that determine the dynamics of a system [10]. SD provides a high level view of the system emphasizing the interactions between its constituent parts, as well as the impact of time on its dynamic behavior [6]. In the context of enterprise modeling SD is typically used in process analysis design and optimization. SD models are usually supported by software that allows for process simulation. A main advantage of improving SD's conceptual foundation through ORM is that SD models can be more soundly and readily linked to databases.

In this paper we first explore the conceptual links between SD and ORM, and then present a three step schema based approach for transforming an ORM domain model into an SD stock and flow diagram. Thus this paper presents an exercise in usefully linking two existing and rather different methods in enterprise modeling.

2   System Dynamics Structure

In SD, two diagrams are most commonly used: causal loop diagrams (CLD) and stock-flow diagrams. CLDs show the main feedback loops in a process. They are composed of two concepts (*influences* and *elements*). The influences have a direction indicated by an arrow, and another indicator as to whether the influenced element is changed in the same direction (+) or in the opposite direction (-). The stock and flow diagrams include four different concepts (*Stocks, Flows-Rates, Connectors* and *Converters*). Stocks can be considered reservoirs containing quantities describing the state of the system. Flows (inflows to and outflows from the various levels) can be imagined as pipelines with a valve that controls the rate of accumulation to and from the stocks. The converters contain information in the form of equations or values that can be applied to stocks, flows, and other converters in the model [7].

Connectors and converters measure the quantities in levels and, through various calculations, control the rates. They appear as lines with arrows (connectors) and as circles (converters). In the conventions for the stock and flow diagram:

- Connectors can feed information into or out of flows and converters but only extract information out of the stock.
- Stocks are influenced by flows (in and out) and can influence flows or converters but cannot be influenced by other stocks and Converters.
- The flows can be influenced by stocks and converters but cannot influence converters or other flows, and converters can influence flows or other converters.

The Stock and Flow Diagram in fig. 5 provides an example.

3   Using ORM as a Foundation for SD Models and Modeling Processes

The first step in our approach consists of three sub-steps in which an ORM diagram is augmented and replaced by process concepts that lean towards SD-like conceptualization. The second step consists of two sub-steps that concern the construction of actual CLD and Stock and Flow diagrams. ORM is a fact-oriented approach for modeling information at a conceptual level [5]. Its use is comparable to that of ER [3]. In this paper we use as an example the procedures a paper might go through en route from writing to publication. The procedures are stated as:

1. A person (author) writes intent of submission. This can be in the form of an abstract.
2. Then the content (text of the paper) is submitted, whereby the paper becomes a submitted paper.
3. Each submitted paper receives a classification.
4. Each submitted paper is reviewed
5. Some submitted papers are accepted and some are rejected
6. For each submitted paper new content is submitted, which makes the paper a published paper that is added to the publications.

These statements can be represented on an ORM diagram as indicated below

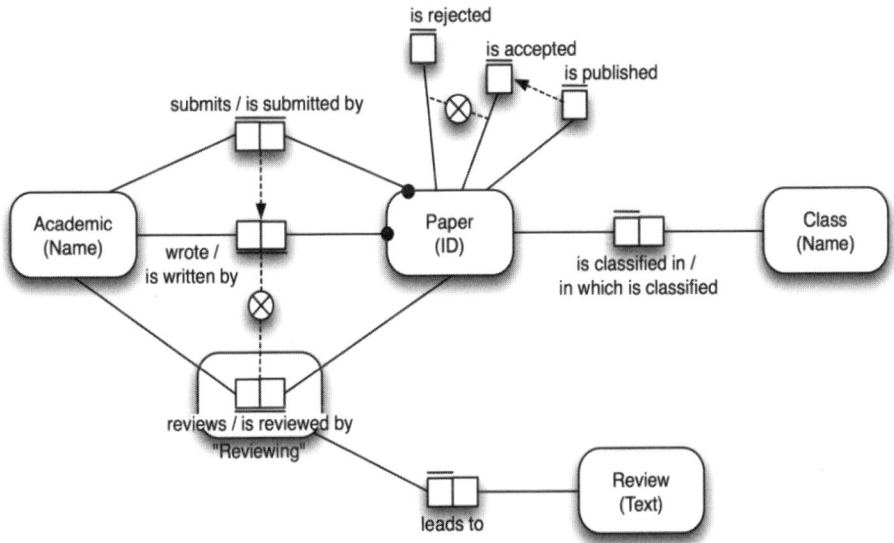

Fig. 1. Paper flow concepts in ORM

Step 1.(a) We started with fig.1 which is an ORM diagram of events (reported as elementary facts) that may be observed in a domain (in this case, the reviewing domain). This approach is in line with the PSM^2 [2] approach. Note the constraints requiring that the submitting academic is indeed one of the authors of a paper, and that a reviewer of a paper cannot be author of that paper.

Step 1.(b) We add temporal dependencies between the roles associated to the paper. This leads to the flow depicted in fig. 2. The left hand side depicts the

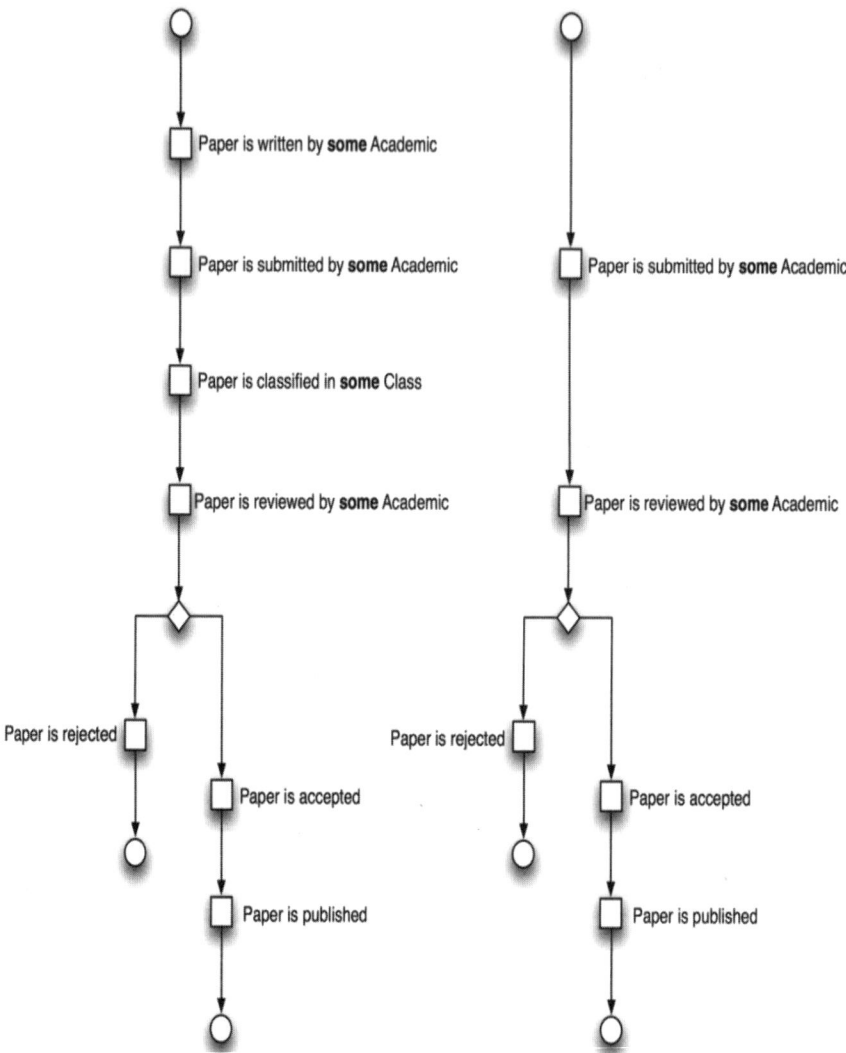

Fig. 2. Paper Flow

full diagram based on the facts types (event types) in the original ORM diagram. The diamond shape is the BPM [11] symbol for a XOR split. Our interest is in the flow statics of submissions, reviews, acceptance, rejection and publication. This leads to the abstracted view depicted on the right hand side.

3.1 ORM Integrated with SD

Step 1.(c)we now make explicit the relations between, in particular, the ORM model and stock-flow model.

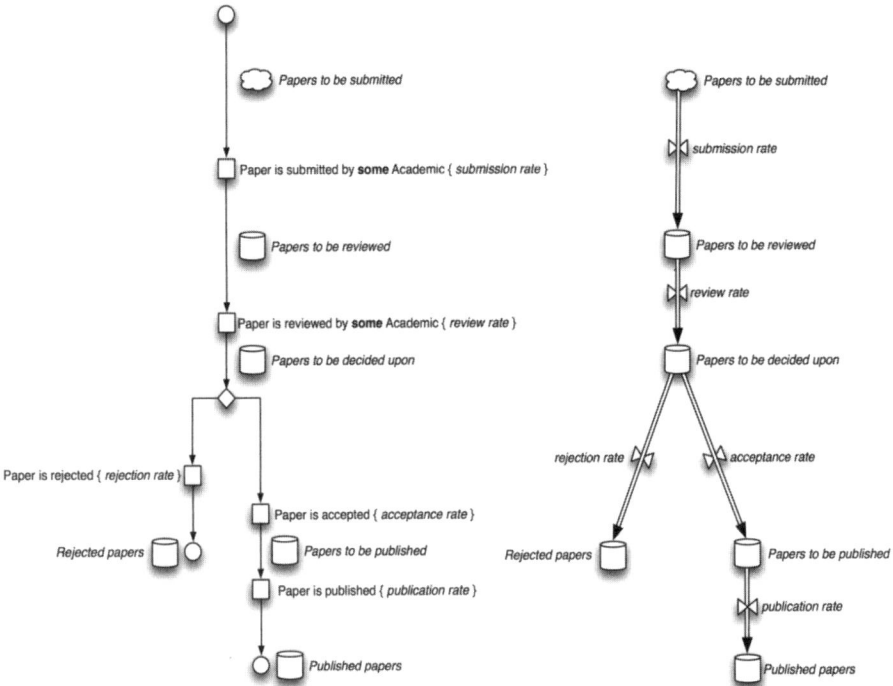

Fig. 3. An integration of ORM with SD

In fig. 3 the left hand side shows fig. 2 (right) with some extra information. The extra information pertains to the flow based interpretation. We now see stores of papers that are ready to flow from one state to another. Each time a paper "flows", this is an event (the original events related to ORM diagram, fig. 1). So:

- A paper is **reviewed**
- A paper is **decided upon**
- Etc.

Associated to the event-types, we can now also add a rate. Leading to:

- Review rate
- Acceptance rate
- Etc.

The right hand side then depicts the SD diagram. This is the prelude to the complete SD Stock and Flow diagram as depicted in fig.5

Step 2.(a) We now embark on identifying the key variables for the SD model: first we create a CLD (in our case, using Vensim simulation software). This helps us identify the influences ('+', '-') variables have on each other.

In SD the system behavior is described as a number of interacting feedback loops, balancing or reinforcing and delay structure. The arrows come together to

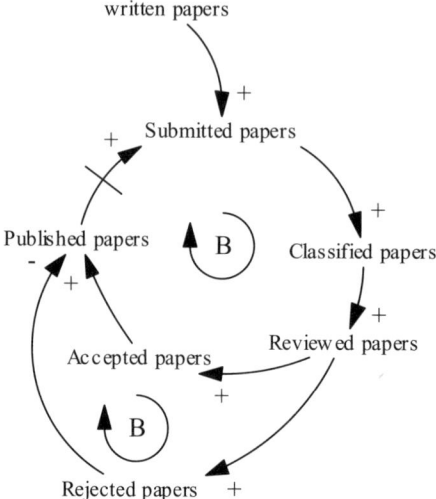

Fig. 4. A causal Loop Diagram for paper flow

form loops, and each loop is labeled with an (R) or a (B). "R" means reinforcing; i.e., the causal relationships within the loop create exponential growth or collapse and "B" means balancing; i.e., the causal influences in the loop keep things in equilibrium. In this case we only have balancing loops. Causal links from one variable to another can be marked as positive or negative based on how their variables change. If number of links with negative sign on the loop is even, then the loop is self-reinforcing (R) and if the number of links with negative on the loop is odd, then the loop is a balancing loop (B).

In Fig.4 a number of variables are used inline with the prior diagrams, each with a direction (arrow) and an indicator (+/-). There is a delay mark between variable published papers and submitted papers indicated with a single slash on the arrow. The delay mark implies that there is a time lapse before the variable at the arrow tip is affected. In this case the submitted papers move in the same direction as classified papers; if one increases the other also increases; the reverse is also true. This holds for all cases where there is a '+' influence (polarity). Once the papers are submitted they are reviewed and the results are released. Based on this, papers are either accepted or rejected. The rejected papers affect the published papers in the opposite direction; an increase in the rejected papers causes a decrease in the published papers and *vice-versa*. Yet the accepted papers affect the papers to be published in the same way where an increase in the accepted papers causes an increase in the published papers.

3.2   Stock and Flow Diagram

After developing the CLD and identifying the different polarities required, we convert the model into a Stock and Flow diagram to show how the system components interact. The Stock and Flow diagram is more complex and detailed than the CLD because it includes nodes for each of the model parameters. It is also used to develop a set of equations, which are used in a numerical simulator to generate (simulate) the behavior of the system.

Step2.(b) The stock and flow diagram is constructed using the Powersim application which takes its name from "Powerful Simulation." It is a simulation tool based on the system dynamics methodology. The Stock and Flow diagram is used to show flow dependencies and how quantities are distributed within the system. Stocks hold quantities that are subject to accumulation through inflows, or are subject to reduction through outflows.

We have the stocks as submitted papers, papers to be decided upon, rejected papers, Accepted papers, and published papers. These stocks have inflows and out flows that are regulated by means of valves. The valves determine the rate at which an inflow or outflow of material applies to the stock (box). In this model there are different factors that affect the flows, and these are either positive or negative as reflected in the CLD. These effects can be indicated as constants linked to the flows or stocks with a connector. During the development of the stock and flow model a number of experimental simulations is normally run to show the different behaviors of the system studied. In our case, such simulations were also carried out, on selected simulation parameters. While doing so, the

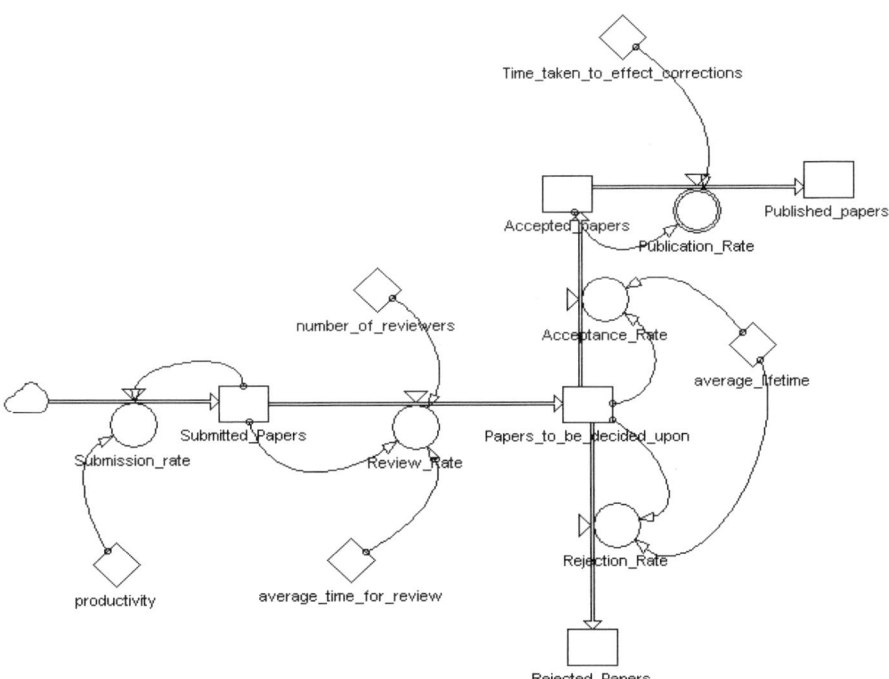

Fig. 5. A stock and flow diagram for the paper life cycle

model can be paused, and each of the stocks continues to hold their quantity for observation. If the value of a particular stock is not important to the problem at hand, then the stock is shown as a cloud, to indicate that it is outside the boundary of the model. This procedure is also known as sensitive analysis [8].

From fig.5 each rate is clearly defined as follows;

Let X and Y be the input and output of some flow $X \Rightarrow Y$:
Then the rate for this flow at time t is defined as

$$\mathsf{Rate}(X \Rightarrow Y) \triangleq \frac{\mathsf{TotalPop}_t(Y)}{\mathsf{TotalPop}_t(X)}$$

Where Totalpop $_t(X)$ is the set of all instances ever of stock.
For cases where we have more outflow rates from the same stock and more inflow rates from different stocks we would have for each stock X:

$$\mathsf{TotalPop}_t(X) \triangleq \mathsf{Pop}_t(X) \cup \bigcup_{Y:X \Rightarrow Y} \mathsf{AddedFlow}_t(X,Y)$$

$$\mathsf{AddedFlow}_t(X,Y) \triangleq \mathsf{TotalPop}_t(Y) - \bigcup_{X':X' \Rightarrow Y \wedge X' \neq X} \mathsf{TotalPop}_t(X')$$

$$\mathsf{TotalPop}_t(X) \triangleq \mathsf{Pop}_t(X) \cup$$

$$\bigcup_{Y:X \Rightarrow Y} \left(\mathsf{TotalPop}_t(Y) - \bigcup_{X':X' \Rightarrow Y \wedge X' \neq X} \mathsf{TotalPop}_t(X') \right)$$

Note that in general this will lead to a recursive system of equation. As all instances have assigned unique location at each moment, this recursive system of equations will have a unique location.

4   Conclusion

In this paper we have identified the extent to which features of ORM static models can be transformed (with added information) into SD models. The two methods are rather different but when used together for a common goal we believe the results are not only better grounded but also more decisive and reliable. The ORM methodology equips the modeler with strong conceptualization of the domain. This is key to developing any model. By combining SD concepts with ORM style modeling we manage to better capture the static part of the model, and to link it satisfactorily with the dynamic aspect. This can enable stakeholders to make better decisions in BPM and process optimization.

5   Further Research

In the near future we will apply the approach presented in context of various case domains. We will further develop and refine the method and its diagrams and also devote more attention to formalizing its syntax and semantics. In addition we intend to use the techniques suggested in this paper in collaborative settings such as group model building which is a sub discipline with in the field of SD [9]. Finally, we intend to explore further links between SD and process modeling, in particular with the YAWL method [1].

References

1. Aalst, W.M.P.v.d., Hofstede, A.H.M.t.: YAWL: Yet Another Workflow Language. Information Systems 30(4), 245–275 (2005)
2. van Bommel, P., Frederiks, P.J.M., van de Weide, T.P.: Object–Oriented Modeling based on Logbooks. The Computer Journal 39(9), 793–799 (1997)
3. Chen, P.P.: The entity-Relationship model-Towards a unified view data. ACM Transactions of database systems 1(1), 9–36 (1976)
4. Forrester, J.W.: Industrial Dynamics. The MIT Press, Cambridge (1961)
5. Halpin, T., Wagner, G.: Modeling Reactive Behavior in ORM. In: Song, I.-Y., et al. (eds.) ER 2003, vol. 2813, pp. 567–569. Springer, Heidelberg (2003)
6. Hustache, J.-C., Gibellini, M., Matos, P.L.: A System Dynamics Tool for Economic Performance Assessment in Air Traffic Management 4th USA/Europe Air Traffic Management R and D Seminar Santa, December 3-7 (2001)
7. Leaver, J.D., Unsworth, C.P.: System dynamics modeling of spring behavior in the Orakeikorako geothermal field. Elsevier Ltd., Amsterdam (2006)
8. Mutschler, B., Reichert, M.: On Modeling and Analyzing Cost Factors in Information Systems Engineering. In: Bellahs'ene, Z., Leonard, M. (eds.) CAiSE 2008. LNCS, vol. 5074, pp. 510–524. Springer, Heidelberg (2008)
9. Rouwette, E., Hoppenbrouwers, S.J.B.A.: Collaborative systems modeling and group model building: a useful combination? In: 26th International Conference of the System Dynamics Society (2008)
10. Sharma, D., Sahay, B.S., Sachan, A.: Modeling Distributor Performance Index Using System Dynamics Approach., vol. 16(3) (2004)
11. White S.A.: Business Process Modeling Notation (BPMN) Version 1.0. BPMI. org (May 3, 2004), http://www.bpmn.org

Enhancing the Usability of BPM-Solutions by Combining Process and User-Interface Modelling

Hallvard Trætteberg and John Krogstie

Norwegian University of Science and Technology (NTNU), Trondheim Norway
{hal,krogstie}@idi.ntnu.no

Abstract. BPMN has over the last years appeared as a major approach for modelling process-oriented solutions. The approach is meant to work well both towards human understanding and execution. Executability is normally based on a mapping of BPMN-models to BPEL and defining a form for each flow where the user is the source or target. As we argue in this paper, this often gives sub-optimal and inflexible user interfaces. This paper describes our experiences with using BPMN for process and task modelling and Diamodl for model-based user interface dialog design. Although the added expressiveness and flexibility comes at the cost of introducing a model-oriented approach for dialog design, the necessary modelling steps follows the same kind of logic that is needed when going from a conceptual BPMN-model to an implementation-oriented model for a naïve generation of BPEL and forms UI, thus is interpreted as not extending the conceptual load of the approach significantly.

Keywords: Process modelling, user interface modelling.

1 Introduction

Models of business and work processes have for a long time been utilized to learn about, guide and support practice in a number of areas. In software process improvement [3], enterprise modelling [5], active knowledge modelling [12], and quality management, process models describe methods and standard working procedures. Simulation and quantitative analyses are also performed to improve process efficiency [11]. In process centric software engineering environments [1] and workflow systems [23] model execution is automated. Thus process modelling is not done for one specific objective only, which partly explains the great diversity of approaches found in literature and practice. Five main categories of usages of process modelling can be distinguished [10]:

1. Human sense-making and communication to make sense of aspects of an enterprise and to support communication among different stakeholders. Sense-making models are used within an activity in order to make sense of something in an ad-hoc manner, and will usually not be maintained afterwards.
2. Computer-assisted analysis to gain knowledge about the enterprise through simulation or deduction based on the contents of the model.

J. Stirna and A. Persson (Eds.): PoEM 2008, LNBIP 15, pp. 86–97, 2008.

3. Quality Management, following up the adherence of the work process to standards and regulations and to support process improvement. Here the model is meant to act as part of a corporate memory meant to exist as a reference point over time.
4. Model deployment and activation to integrate the model in an information system. Deployment can be manual, automatic (in automated workflow systems), or interactive [9].
5. Using the model as a context for a system development project, without being directly implemented (as it is in category 4).

Business Process Management (BPM) is a structured, coherent and consistent way of understanding, documenting, modelling, analyzing, simulating, executing and continuously changing end-to-end business process and all involved resources in light of their contribution to business performance. Thus we see that the potential usage of modelling in BPM is covering all the areas of use for process modelling as outlined above. In BPM and workflow there has traditionally been a wide variety of approaches and notations used. BPMN has over the last years been pushed forward and suggested as a standard and is met with the same kind of diverse needs; i.e. to be understandable for both humans and machines. The main approach for execution of BPMN is a translation to BPEL. The focus of BPEL engines is on process execution and not on the user interface of the application, which in practice can result in internally good process support systems that is hampered by an inappropriate, inflexible user interface, thus meeting unnecessary implementation problems when being introduced in an organization. Along the same line is the issue of the limited possibilities of tailoring such generated systems.

In this article, we will present the state of the art of combining process modelling notations such as BPMN and user interface modelling, to make it possible to guide the design of the process solution and take into account both process execution and user interface at a sufficiently early stage to have impact on the working solution. In addition to having a potential large impact in traditional development, as argued by e.g. Sousa et al [18], there is a need to better support the combined *evolution* of the business process and the interfaces of the systems. A combined model-based approach may improve on the current situation where process and UI must be considered individually, and it is hard to spot the places where user interface changes have impact on the process supported and vice versa.

In the next section we present BPMN in a sufficient detail to follow the argument. Then we present the field of MBUID (model-based user interface design), indicated how BPMN can be used for task modelling and present the Diamodl approach for the dialog part of user interface modelling. The following chapter will present the practical integration of these approaches, before summarizing the work.

2 Business Process Modelling Using BPMN

In this section we briefly introduce BPMN in order to give the reader sufficient background for understanding our subsequent arguments. The presentation is based on [17].

BPMN has over the last years been propelled as the most prominent candidate for an industry standard in process modelling, similar to the position of UML in object-oriented design. BPMN was originally developed by the Business Process Management Initiative (BPMI.org). Its specification 1.0 was released in May 2004 and adopted by OMG for standardization purposes in February 2006 [2]. The development of BPMN was based on the revision of other notations, including UML, IDEF, ebXML, RosettaNet, LOVeM and EPCs, and stemmed from the demand for a graphical language that complements the BPEL standard for executable business processes. Although this gives BPMN a technical focus, it has been the intention of the BPMN designers to develop a modelling language that can be applied for typical business modelling activities as well. The complete BPMN specification defines thirty-eight distinct language constructs plus attributes, grouped into four basic categories of elements, *viz.*, Flow Objects, Connecting Objects, Swimlanes and Artefacts. *Flow Objects*, such as events, activities and gateways, are the most basic elements used to create Business Process Diagrams (BPDs). *Connecting Objects* are used to inter-connect Flow Objects through different types of arrows. *Swimlanes* are used to group activities into separate categories for different functional capabilities or responsibilities (*e.g.*, different roles or organizational departments). Finally, *Artefacts* may be added to a diagram where deemed appropriate in order to display further related information such as processed data or other comments. Fig.1 gives an example of a BPMN model that shows a simple review process. The Customer sends in an application that is received by our User role. The User performs a shallow review and may decide to either let the Expert role perform a deep review or do it himself. The review is then sent back to the Customer.

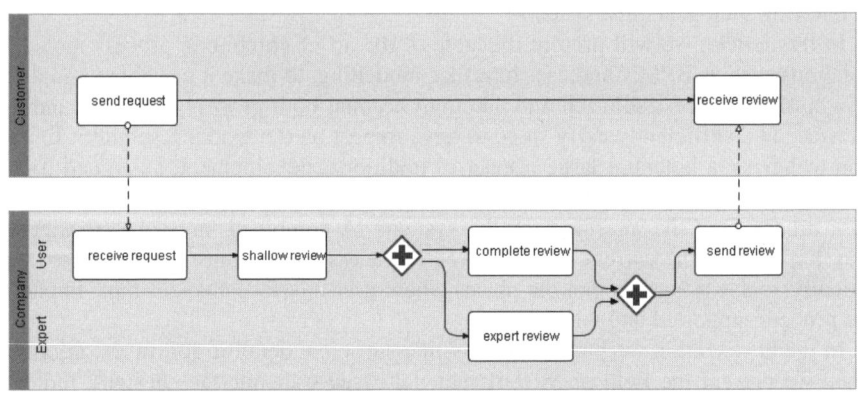

Fig. 1. BPMN model of a simple review process

3 Model-Based User Interface Design

The field of model-based user interface design (MBUID) has a long tradition [15], but it has been noted that diagrammatical UI modelling is not very common [13]. One of the reasons is that the methods, models and activities of MBUID are not aligned with the traditional system development practice including business process modelling. Generally a closer integration of MBUID and standard analysis and design modelling is called for. The attempts to link user interface modelling to design notations such as by creating particular UML-profiles (e.g. [7,14]) has had limited impact in this regard since it is necessary to think on the user interface on an earlier level than detailed design.

Research in model-based UI design has resulted in many specific modelling languages methods. Although there is no UML of UI design, there seems to be a general agreement on three classes of models [22].

1. Task and domain models focus on the user's and designer's knowledge of the user, their goals and the tasks they need to perform.
2. Dialog models focus on input and output of information, Abstract Interaction Object (AIO) structure and dynamic behaviour. Dialog models abstract away details of interaction style and client platform.
3. Models of concrete design describe the structure and details of Concrete Interaction Objects (CIOs) and is specific to interaction style and client platform.

In the model-based approach, design progresses from task models, through dialog models to concrete interaction design, in a top-down process. Parts may be generated, based on logical dependencies, using formal systems like predicate logic, process algebra, Petri nets, state machines, etc [15].

In [16] several task and process modelling languages are compared, to see how they may support model-based design of eServices in eGovernment applications. We have previously discussed the relation between process modelling and task modelling in [7]. Our focus on this paper is on a lean method based on BPMN for process and task modelling and the Diamodl language for dialog modelling and deployment using standard, open-source tools and modern service-oriented architecture. [19] also take a business process model (BPM) as a starting point, but uses a less formal UI model with a weaker coupling to the BPM.

3.1   Using BPMN for Task Modelling

According to www.bpmn.org "... Business Process Modelling Notation (BPMN) will provide businesses with the capability of understanding their internal business procedures in a graphical notation...". Such a business procedure is a set of coordinated tasks performed by a set of roles and structured in hierarchy.

Tasks in different processes communicate and implicitly coordinate by means of message connections. Tasks in the same process use flow connections for controlling sequencing and variables for storing XML data as process state. A task may repeat and be conditional. Web services are used for communicating with external systems, including business objects and UI clients. A task modelling language typically structures tasks in a hierarchy. Operators are used for controlling the enablement and sequencing of tasks, e.g. tasks may be performed in sequence, in parallel, one of several tasks may be conditionally selected, a task (structure) may repeat, etc. Events from the environment, including objects representing the domain, may trigger or enable tasks, and operations may be performed on the environment.

The main difference between BPMN and a task modelling language is more a matter of perspective than expressive power and both essentially model a task hierarchy. Similarly, the control flow connections of BPMN and operators in task modelling languages are visually different, but have essentially the same expressive power.

Finally, messages may take the role of events, to model tasks that are triggered by changes in the environment.

The weakest point of BPMN is domain and data modelling. Due to its focus on process message exchange and integration of web services, XML schemas and XML data has been chosen as the data model. Fortunately, many tools for object-oriented modelling, e.g. EMF [4], can generate XML schemas, serialize models as XML and in general interoperate with XML, so this is more a practical obstacle than a conceptual problem. E.g. although a variable cannot be declared to reference an object of a particular class, it can be declared to refer to an XML fragment that represents an object of a particular class.

What is still missing is a way of declaring pre-conditions and post-conditions in terms of objects and their life-cycle (creation and destruction) and state. E.g. a precondition for performing a review of an application is the application, and the postcondition is that the review has been created. Hence, we augment the BMPN "task" model with annotations on each task that makes these conditions explicit, not very different from how UML Use Case diagrams are elaborated by means of structured text.

3.2 Diamodl

The Diamodl notation [20,21] is a visual language for modelling abstract dialog, covering both information handling and activation logic, which is particularly suited for business applications. The interactor and gate concepts specify the input and output function of an AIO. The variable, computation and connection concepts are used for specifying how data is stored, transformed transported among interactors.

Fig. 2 shows a simple model where these five concepts are used. The upper left box is a variable and is used to store data. This particular one is limited to holding a

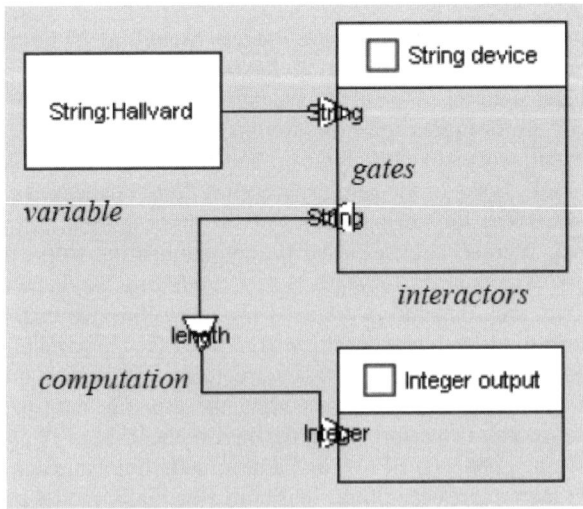

Fig. 2. The variable, interactor, gate, computation and connection concepts

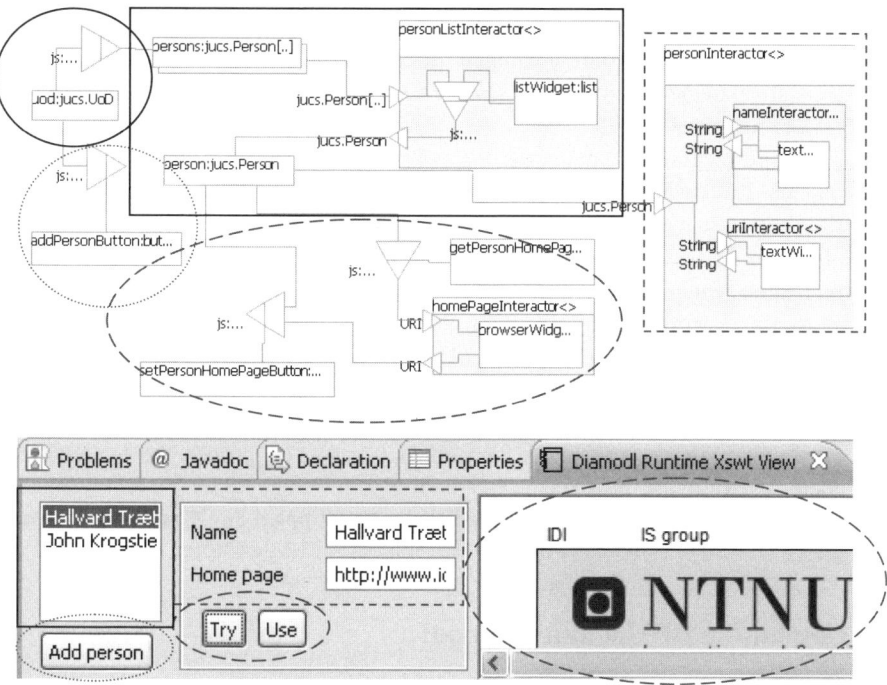

Fig. 3. Diamodl example

String and currently contains "Hallvard". The two boxes with title bars to the right are interactors and the attached triangles are gates. As indicated by the gates, the upper interactor may output and input a String, while the lower one may output an Integer. The variable is connected to the output gate of the former interactor, while the input gate is connected to a computation, the output of which is further connected to the output gate of the latter interactor. The name and the input/output types suggest that the computation computes the length of the input String. Hence, this particular model specifies a UI through which the user may edit a String and see its length.

In addition to these five concepts, states (an interactor is also a state) and transitions are used for specifying the activation and deactivation of interactors, while UML class and object diagrams are used for data modelling.

In Fig. 3, a more comprehensive Diamodl example is shown, also indicating how the different parts of the model relate to the concrete user interface. As above, interactors are shown as rectangles with gate triangles on their left side, either pointing into for user output or out for user input. Variables are labelled with class names and multiplicity.

Computations are shown as free-floating triangles, and are labelled by attribute, association or operation names from the UML class diagram (not shown). Connections are shown as edges and may optionally be labelled with attribute or association names, to indicate an embedded computation. The links to the interface can be seen through:

- The solid circle contains a variable named uod holding the root UoD object, in which all other objects are contained (directly or indirectly). All the Person objects are extracted by following UoD's allPersons association and sent to the persons variable.
- The solid rectangle contains the list widget that is used for viewing the Person objects. It includes Javascript for extracting the Person instances' names. The person variable holds the selected Person.
- The person variable is connected to personInteractor inside the dashed rectangle, which models the fields used for viewing and editing the name and homePage properties.
- The browser widget and "Try" and "Use" buttons are modelled inside the dashed oval. The "Try" button triggers a computation which sends the selected Person's homePage property to the browser, while the "Use" button triggers a computation that sets the same Person's homePage property to the URI currently shown by the browser.
- The "Add person" button is modeled inside the stippled circle and creates a new Person instance and adds it to the UoD object's allPersons association.

4   Combining BPMN and Diamodl

In the prototypical MB-UID process, a task model is the starting point for developing a dialog model and subsequent concrete user interface design. The task model may be seen as capturing human behaviour, the dialog model describes software behaviour. The deployment of the UI will be a combination of concrete user interface elements and the software and models necessary for implementing the dialog behaviour, like state machines, data binding, etc. and the concrete interface describes what is actually deployed. This is actually fairly similar to the standard approach of business process modelling using BPMN and execution and deployment using the Business Process Execution Language (BPEL) [6]. First, the behaviour of the process, or rather the roles and systems taking part in the process, is described as communicating processes, activities and tasks in a BPMN diagram. This model is transformed to a (automation of) coordination (also called choreography or orchestration) of the process and relies on web services for linking all the participants (people, processes and external services). The BPEL model is then deployed, together with other supporting software like business objects, web services, data bases etc.

As can be seen, the overall approach and role of the models is similar, although they have the (group) system perspective instead of the (individual) UI perspective. This suggests that the models can be related across the domains of business process management and user interface design, as illustrated in the architectural figure of Fig. 4. According to this figure, process models (in BPMN) may be related to task models since they both capture the behaviour of people, BPEL models may be related (architecturally, not methodologically) to dialog models, since they both model software for supporting people and BPEL and a deployed BPEL model executed by a server-side engine may interact with the client-side UI runtime. We are currently investigating how this may be more than an analogy, i.e. we propose a method whereby BPMN is

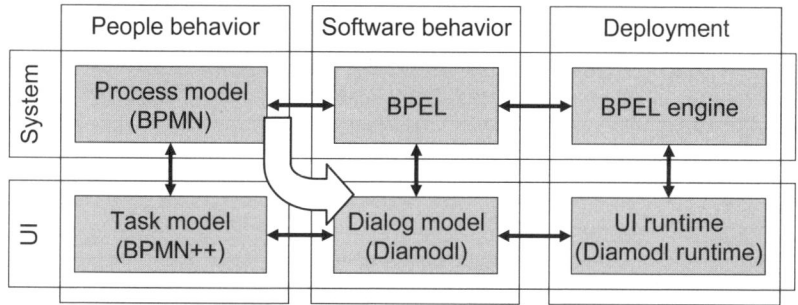

Fig. 4. Relationship between system and user interface domains

used for both business process and task modelling and BPEL and Diamodl are used for modelling software support and deployment on a SOA-based platform. The analysis and design tasks travels from the traditional BPMN model to the task model to the dialog model as indicated with the bold white arrow in Fig.4.

4.1 Step-by-step Modelling Method

Fig. 4 shows the relationship between system and UI perspectives on the process of going from a process/task model to a deployed system which combines a BPEL engine and the Diamodl runtime. In this section we detail the practical process. The process is illustrated by a simple example, that of reviewing a request (for something) and returning the answer as first illustrated in Fig 1. Creating this BPMN model is the first step in our method, combined with domain modelling, where concepts in the domain are formalized in a class diagram.

In practice, the domain model may already exist, either from previous projects or as a reference model for a well-established domain, e.g. order management. Since BPMN is XML-centred we need to be able to convert the domain model to an XML Schema, before annotating the connections between processes (and possibly internal variables) with XML types. We use Ecore, the Eclipse Modeling Framework's modelling language for domain modelling, and export the XML Schema from the Ecore editor. The Intalio Designer Eclipse application, which we use for BPMN modelling, allows us to open the XML Schema in the Process navigator and drag XML types into the connections in the diagram.

This model is system centric, in that it does not focus on any particular user or distinguish between the user and the system. The next step in the method is disentangling the users' task from the system. The general idea is to model the User role in a process of its own and make the connection (interface) to other roles and processes explicit. The design oriented process model is shown in Fig. 5. As can be seen, this process interacts with both the Executable process, i.e. the system, and the Expert role.

This design oriented process model is similar to a task model, in that it makes explicit what each uses does (task structure) and how it interacts with its environment (events and data). It may require further decomposition to be detailed enough, and in addition we annotate it with pre- and post-conditions that make explicit how domain data is operated on. E.g. the pre-condition for the User task "shallow review" is that

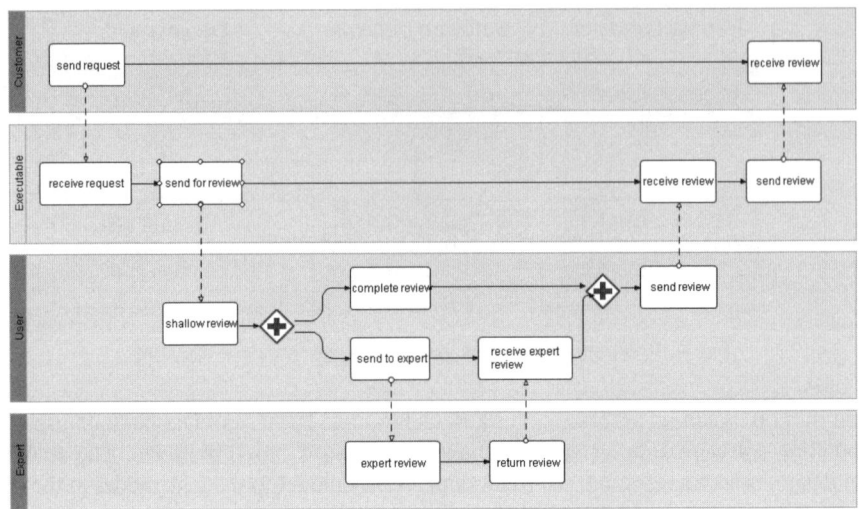

Fig. 5. Design-oriented process model

there exist an unhandled request and the post-condition is that a review has been created and is in progress. This step may result in a refined domain model, to better capture the objects' possible states.

The connections flowing into and out of the User process, defines the necessary input and output of the user interface, and hence the dialog model, which is the next step. Our dialog modelling language Diamodl fits well with the dataflow nature of process models and web services. The connections are modeled as computations in Diamodl, the in-flowing connections become computations without input (sources of data), while out-flowing connections become computations with one input and no output (sinks of data).

Although the BPMN diagram is a model of how the user works, it is not a model of how the user works with the to-be-designed UI. In our experience, one of the main decisions to be made is how the user manages multiple and possibly parallel instances of the process. This possibility is implicit in the process model and if not considered in the design process, we may end up with a user interface that forces the user to work with each process instance independently. E.g. in this case, we should consider if the user should be able to see the finished review of one request while performing the shallow review of another, and perhaps support copying the former review.

Part of the dialog model and corresponding GUI prototype is shown in Fig. 6. The two large, shaded triangles are computations that represent connections from the process model, receiving a request and sending a review to the expert, respectively. This model lets the user see the list of unhandled requests, select and view one and choose to review the selected one. There is also a list of reviews in progress, from which the user may select one and send to the expert. The GUI prototype has mostly been generated from the model, with only the layout and labels added by hand. The sample data that populates the GUI has been created with standard EMF tools, based on and validated against the domain model.

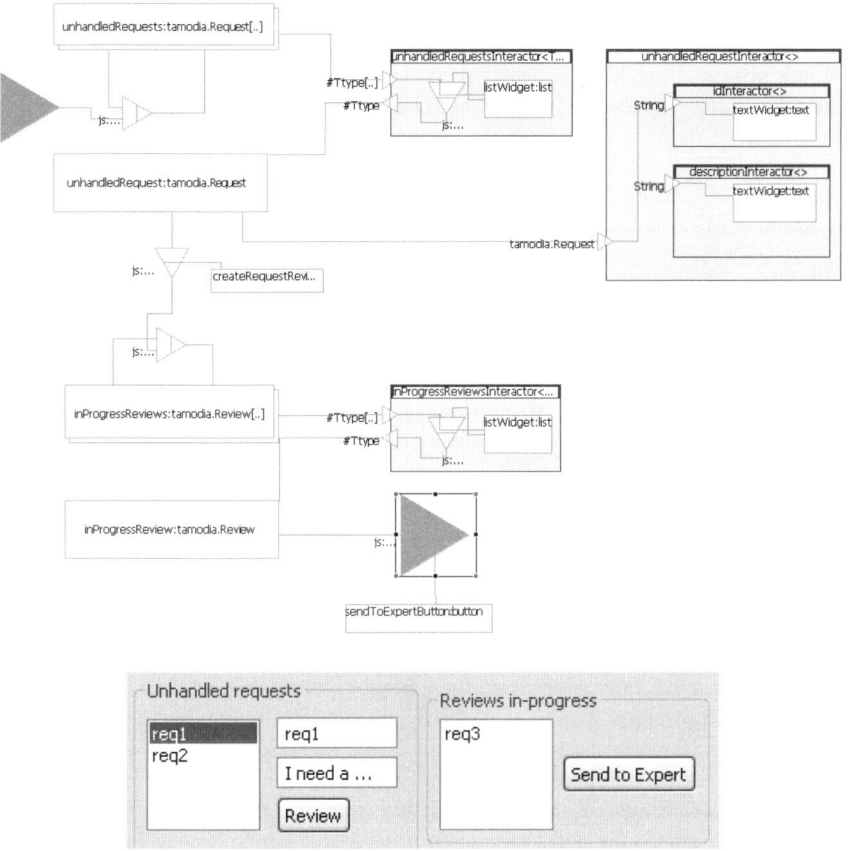

Fig. 6. Dialog model fragment and GUI prototype

The last step is deployment, which in general will include the part of the BPMN process marked as executable, the GUI and dialog and supporting services like task and data management. A valid (and executable) BPMN process fragment may be translated to BPEL code and deploying it on one of several open source BPEL engines, and Intalio Designer is able to generate and deploy to a standards-compliant server in a few clicks.

The GUI and dialog model is executable, but the Diamodl runtime currently lacks general support for web services, so the final link between GUI and the BPEL engine is missing. We have, however, validated that we can initiate tasks from the Diamodl runtime and receive data from the BPEL engine, using the existing support for JavaScript and XML. Similarly, although EMF-based data hasn't been integrated into the BPEL engine, EMF supports serializing and de-serializing Ecore instances as XML, so in principle any BPEL engine can store and communicate EMF-based data to and from the Diamodl runtime and web services. In addition to doing this ourselves, we had last year 20 students using the approach as part of their regular master BPM-course. After the normal introduction to the different parts of the approach, and the environment, the students were able to develop simple applications using the approach.

5 Conclusions and Further Work

Business process modelling and management is getting increasing attention and use, as are other process-oriented approaches. The focus on process, originating from more radical ideas of BPR, has traditionally emphasized the improvement of organizational solutions. Although useful to avoid sub-optimalization within the different functions, we have seen e.g. in ERP-systems that this often create non-optimal solutions for the *individual* worker. Systems developed or generated to directly support the inter-organizational or organizational process often focus on a different aggregation of tasks than solutions geared towards supporting the individual worker.

This is only one area where traditional process solutions need improvement. The limited success of traditional workflow management systems (WMS) has partially been attributed to the lack of *flexibility*. Thus over the last years flexible workflow has been investigated. Most work within this area looks at how conventional systems can be extended and enhanced in other words how static workflow systems can be made *adaptive and tailorable*.

Traditional ERP systems for instance tend to be quite inflexible, hardly adaptable, and primarily support the organizationally agreed processes in a uniform manner independent on personal needs of the users. Existing workflow management systems have typically been focused on dealing with exceptions and have thus offered some support for adaptive processes. These types of systems, however, have typically overlooked emergent processes, which seem to encompass an increasing part of organized activity.

On the other hand, only supporting the emergent work style and individual needs of the individual knowledge worker is probably at times inefficient, because routine parts of the work can be prescribed and automated, and because sharing of explicit process models facilitates co-ordination, collaboration and communication between multiple parties. Thus there is a need for a balance between prescription and emergent tailorable representations. This is parallel to the main issue in this paper, how to balance the need of the organizational process with the need of user interfaces appropriate for the individual worker. How the integrated process and user-interface modelling approach discussed in this paper can be extended to address also this problem area is material for further work. As a first step, we plan a more thorough validation of the approach described in this paper.

References

1. Ambriola, V., Conradi, R., Fuggetta, A.: Assessing Process-Centered Software Engineering Environments. ACM Transactions on Software Engineering and Methodology 6(3) (1997)
2. BPMI. org and OMG (2006): Business Process Modeling Notation Specification. Final Adopted Specification, Object Management Group, http://www.bpmn.org (February 20, 2006)
3. Derniame, J.-C., Kaba, B.A., Wastell, D. (eds.): Promoter-2 1998. LNCS, vol. 1500. Springer, Heidelberg (1999)
4. The Eclipse Modeling Framework home page, http://www.eclipse.org/modeling/emf/
5. Fox, M.S., Gruninger, M.: Enterprise modeling. AI Magazine (2000)
6. Havey, M.: Essential Business Process modeling. O'Reilly, Sebastopol (2005)

7. Kovacevic, S.: UML and User Interface Design. In: Bézivin, J., Muller, P.-A. (eds.) UML 1998, LNCS, vol. 1618, pp. 253–266. Springer, Heidelberg (1999)
8. Kristiansen, R., Trætteberg, H.: Model-based user interface design in the context of work-flow models. In: Winckler, M., Johnson, H., Palanque, P. (eds.) TAMODIA 2007. LNCS, vol. 4849, pp. 227–239. Springer, Heidelberg (2007)
9. Krogstie, J., Jørgensen, H.: Interactive models for supporting networked organizations. In: Persson, A., Stirna, J. (eds.) CAiSE 2004. LNCS, vol. 3084, pp. 550–563. Springer, Heidelberg (2004)
10. Krogstie, J., Dalberg, V., Jensen, S.M.: Process modeling value framework, Enterprise Information Systems. In: Manolopoulos, Y., Filipe, J., Constantopoulos, P., Cordeiro, J. (eds.) Selected papers from 8th International Conference, ICEIS 2006, Paphos, Cyprus, May 23-27, 2006. Lecture Notes in Business Information Processing, vol. 3. Springer, Heidelberg (2008)
11. Kuntz, J.C., Christiansen, T.R., Cohen, G.P., Jin, Y., Levitt, R.E.: The virtual design team: A computational simulation model of project organizations. Communications of the ACM 41(11) (1998)
12. Lillehagen, F., Krogstie, J.: Active Knowledge Modeling of Enterprises. Springer, Heidelberg (2008)
13. Myers, B., Hudson, S.E., Pausch, R.: Past, Present and Future of User Interface Software Tools. ACM Transactions on Computer-Human Interaction 7(1) (March 2000); Applied Computing. Springer, London
14. Nunes, N.J., Cunha, J.F.: Towards a UML Profile for Interaction Design: The Wisdom Approach. In: Evans, A., Kent, S., Selic, B. (eds.) UML 2000, LNCS, vol. 1939, pp. 101–116. Springer, Heidelberg (2000)
15. Paternò, F.: Model-based Design and Evaluation of Interactive Applications. Series of Applied Computing. Springer, London (2000)
16. Pontico, F., Farenc, C., Winckler, M.: Model-based support for specifying eService eGovernment Applications. In: Coninx, K., Luyten, K., Schneider, K.A. (eds.) TAMODIA 2006. LNCS, vol. 4385, pp. 54–67. Springer, Heidelberg (2007)
17. Recker, J., Indulska, M.: An Ontology-Based Evaluation of Process Modeling with Petri Nets. Journal of Interoperability in Business Information Systems 1(2), 45–64 (2007)
18. Sousa, K., Mendonca, H., Vanderdonckt, J.: User Interface Development Lifecycle for Business-Driven Enterprise Applications. In: Proceedings of Seventh International Conference on Computer-Aided Design of User Interfaces CADUI 2008, Albacete, Spain (June 2008)
19. Sukaviriya, N., Sinha, V., Ramachandra, T., Mani, S., Stolze, M.: User-Centered Design and Business Process Modeling: Cross Road in Rapid Prototyping Tools. In: Baranauskas, C., Palanque, P., Abascal, J., Barbosa, S.D.J. (eds.) INTERACT 2007. LNCS, vol. 4662, pp. 165–178. Springer, Heidelberg (2007)
20. Trætteberg, H.: Dialog modelling with interactors and UML Statecharts - A hybrid approach. In: Markopoulos, P., Johnson, P. (eds.) Proceedings of DSV-IS 1998. Springer, Heidelberg (1998)
21. Trætteberg, H.: Dialog modelling with interactors and UML Statecharts - a hybrid approach. In: Jorge, J.A., Jardim Nunes, N., Falcão e Cunha, J. (eds.) DSV-IS 2003, vol. 2844, pp. 346–361. Springer, Heidelberg (2003)
22. van der Veer, G.C., van Welie, M.: Task Based Groupware Design: putting theory into practice, van der Veer, G. In: van der Veer, G.C., van Welie, M. (eds.) Proceedings of DIS 2000, New York, United States, August 17-19 (2000)
23. Workflow management coalition (WfMC), Terminology & Glossary (1999), http://www.wfmc.org/standards/docs.htm

Fractal Modeling Approach for Supporting Business Process Flexibility

Julija Stecjuka, Marite Kirikova, and Erika Asnina

Institute of Applied Computer Systems,
Riga Technical University,
1 Kalku, Riga, LV-1658 Latvia
{julija.stecjuka,marite.kirikova,erika.asnina}@cs.rtu.lv

Abstract. Ability to support various business models has been recognized as one of the essential competitive advantages of companies operating in global networked business environment. The use of several business models simultaneously, requires availability of flexible business process models. Flexibility of business process models, in turn, depends on appropriate information systems support. One of the ways how to support business process flexibility is to use a fractal paradigm in information systems development. The fractal paradigm can be applied at two levels of abstraction: the level of business process system and the level of software system. Applications of the fractal paradigm at two abstraction levels correspond to two different opportunities of supporting flexible business processes.

Keywords: business process, flexibility, information system.

1 Introduction

Ability to support various business models has been recognized as one of the essential competitive advantages of companies operating in global networked business environment [1]. The use of several business models simultaneously requires flexible business process models. Flexibility of business process models, in turn, depends on appropriate information systems support inside and outside the business organization. One of the important problems to be resolved in information system development for supporting business process flexibility, is the possibility to adapt an information system's functional model to business processes needs on a high level of detail, so that both domains (business domain and computer system domain) become a whole in the context of business process implementation.

The goal of this paper is to discuss applicability of a fractal approach in business process modeling and information systems design. The approach is based on the idea of a fractal enterprise that has been presented in [2] as well as on the research of business process flexibility on different levels of abstraction [3]. Fractality of an enterprise implies goal adaptability and similarity at different levels of scale (or granularity) of the enterprise. Flexibility of a business process implies that two different constituents of the business process are recognized: (1) the core of the process that

J. Stirna and A. Persson (Eds.): PoEM 2008, LNBIP 15, pp. 98–110, 2008.

changes relatively slowly and (2) the "rural" parts of the process that may be changed relatively frequently. In this paper we conceptually distinguish between (1) a fractal business process system and (2) a fractal software system. The first concept is used for supporting business process flexibility at the abstraction level of enterprise business processes; the second concept is used for achieving flexibility of software design that supports the business processes of the enterprise. The concepts are supported by corresponding fractal information systems development approaches, which are briefly presented in the paper.

The paper is structured as follows. Basic concepts and related work are discussed in Section 2. Information systems design approach for fractal process systems is presented in Section 3. Object-oriented approach for designing fractal information systems is presented in Section 4. Discussion of applicability of the approaches and conclusions are given in Section 5.

2 Basic Concepts and Related Work

The use of fractal approach in systems development has been applied in a number of different contexts [4]. Theoretically, fractal systems are self-organizing, cooperative, self-similar at different levels of scale systems that can adapt to changing systems goals and environment [5, 6 and 7]. Vitality and dynamics of such systems seem to be attractive features of enterprises operating in turbulent global environment.

One of the central notions in fractal systems is the *scale* of the system. In a fractal enterprise the scale is identical to the structure of enterprise decomposition [2], where the largest scale refers to the whole enterprise and the smallest to the smallest organizational unit exposing fractal properties. From the point of view of processes, self-similarity can be considered in at least three different dimensions, namely: agent (enterprise organizational units), process (functionality), and information architecture (Fig. 1). While each organizational unit (including an individual employee) performs particular processes and uses particular information structures, there is no simultaneous scaling commonality between organizational, process and information architectures, i.e., a small scale organizational unit can perform processes of different scales

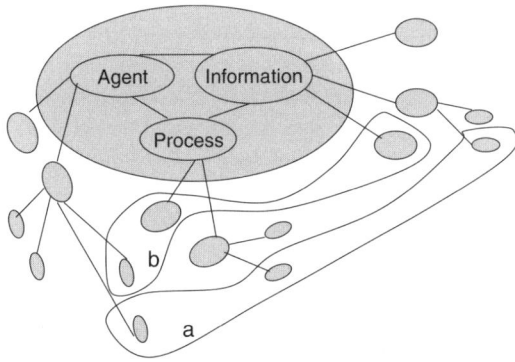

Fig. 1. Fractal architecture of organizational units, processes and information

and use information structures of different scales (see a and b in Fig. 1). Each process at different levels of scale may be performed by different agents and use different information architectures. In general, fractality of the process can be considered from several viewpoints or according to several dimensions simultaneously, i.e., it could be reflected by a multi-fractal model. Models and approaches described in Sections 3 and 4 deal with multi-fractality, however, this aspect of the models is not emphasized in the paper in order not to overcomplicate the discussion about the possibilities of supporting business process flexibility.

Usually the processes in fractal systems are addressed via functions of agents. The following basic process taxonomies may be found in fractal systems development approaches:

- sensing, observing, analyzing, resolving, organizing, reporting, actuating [8]
- sensing, requirements definition and planning, execution, delivery, responding [7]
- monitoring, analyzing, reporting, planning, executing [9]
- goal dissociation, partner selection, business coordination, task execution, schedule-progress monitoring [10].

Above-mentioned taxonomies are applicable in many cases, however, their generality is not always helpful for identifying information systems requirements for business process support (see more details in Section 5).

As regards the agent perspective the following information flows are to be taken into consideration [8, 11]:

- information flows inside a fractal entity
- information flows between the same scale level fractals
- information flows between different scale level fractals
- information flows between external environment and fractal entities.

Information flows between external environment and fractal entities are used for the assessment of the change against specific levels of work environment such as cultural, strategic, socio-informal, financial, informational and technological [11, 12].

In fractal systems, information architecture has at least two orthogonal dimensions. The existence of those dimensions depends on (1) different modes of information processing (human brain, software) and (2) the particular fractal hierarchy under consideration. Fractal hierarchy relates to the living systems theory [13] where hierarchical levels emerge to achieve a higher communication efficiency. With respect to computer systems supported information transfer and processing, in a fractal level software system, part of information is to be processed by software of a higher fractal entity and, at the same time, each fractal entity may have independent information processing functionalities.

There are different definitions of business process flexibility; however, most of them focus on the ability to respond to external changes in the appropriate period of time using a reasonable amount of resources [14, 15 and 16]. Flexibility, however, possesses some degree of stability because whenever a part of the system is made flexible, some other part is made inflexible [17]. From the information systems viewpoint different approaches could be used to support relatively rigid and relatively flexible (or more rapidly changing) business process constituents.

Fractal approach may seem to be somewhat similar to aspect-oriented methods of software development [18]. However, aspect-oriented approaches, in general, do not consider multiple scales of processes and goal adaptability, which are essential features of fractal systems.

3   Business Process Fractality Oriented Software Requirements for Flexibility Support: A Process-Oriented Approach

The approach discussed in this section focuses on fractal properties of the business process system. The notion of the fractal business process system is discussed in Subsection 3.1. The approach of identification of software services for fractal process system support is briefly presented in Subsection 3.2. The approach takes into consideration commonalities and differences of requirements at different levels of process fractals and tries to identify those functionalities that are least dependent on possible changes affecting the fractal system.

3.1   The Notion of the Fractal Process System

We define the fractal process system by modifying definitions given in [8] and [9]: the fractal is a functioning systems component (enterprise business process and/or software service), whose goals and performance can be precisely described, which has unique objectives, achieves concrete results and acts autonomously in a self-optimizing way whilst interacting with other system's fractals. The fractal processes system may be described as follows [19]:

- It consists of fractals (enterprise business processes and/or software services), where each of the fractals has unique objectives, which correspond to system's common objectives.
- Each fractal has its own structure in the fractal processes system, i.e., a unique set of interconnected activities.
- Each single fractal acts separately to meet the system's common objective and interacts with other fractals in the case of the lack of resources (e.g., information stored by other fractal component).
- The fractal processes system is organized as a multilevel structure, where the level is the scale at which the fractal is examined. In a sense, a large-scale fractal includes self-similar small-scale fractals. So the system's common objective could be achieved by implementing an appropriate fractal for each scale.
- Information flows exist between fractals in the fractal processes system.

The main fractals properties in the fractal processes system are implemented in the following way [19]:

- Self-similarity manifests when processes of different scale have a common objective and similar inputs and outputs.

- Self-organization in the fractal processes system could be expressed as follows:
  - Appropriate alternative selection during certain fractal task processing.
  - Modification and optimization of interacting fractal relationships.
  - Creation of a new fractal or a new alternative for accomplishing tasks of a fractal process.
  - Development of a new software service.
  - Adapting to changes in external requirements.
- Systems common objectives are achieved iteratively, by developing each single fractal's individual objective taking into account feedbacks.
- Dynamics and vitality means that coordination and cooperation between self-organizing fractals are characterized by individual dynamics and the ability to adapt to dynamical environment. The information system plays a vital role in achieving this property of the fractal business process system.

3.2 The Main Steps for the Identification of Requirements for Fractal Business Processes

The main idea of the suggested method is to create a relatively simple approach for describing the process system from the point of view of information processing. The process-oriented method for fractal information system development is based on the assumption that software services can be defined as soon as the fractal sub-system of enterprise business processes is discovered.

The process-oriented method includes the following main stages [19]:

- Stage 1 – Fractal processes system development. This stage includes the following three activities:
  - Perform analysis of existing enterprise business processes with the aim of identifying a business sub-process with common or similar goals, similar inputs and outputs.
  - Identify the dimensions of the scale of selected business sub-processes.
  - Define appropriate fractal hierarchy according to previously defined scales.
- Stage 2 – Software model development taking into account the fractal hierarchy. To develop software model, the following activities are needed:
  - Define software functional and non-functional requirements for each "fractal" in fractals' structure.
  - Identify common and specific requirements for all identified "fractals" in the fractal hierarchy.
  - Identify appropriate software services for "fractals" taking into account common and specific requirements identified in the previous step.
  - Define interactions between identified software services.
  - Define relationships between software services and process "fractals". Relationships have a very important role in "fractals" self-organization, thanks to which "fractal" system is able to restructure and tolerates replacement of some of its parts. Relationships help to track changes in fractals organization and introduce necessary changes in software services.

- Stage 3 – Detailed business processes model development for obtaining common vision of the situation in fractal information system. At this stage correspondence between business process decomposition and software services is defined by gradual business process decomposition up to the granularity where it is possible to identify, which software service directly corresponds to which business sub-process.

The approach is discussed in greater detail in [19].

Figure 2 illustrates to some extent the approach presented in this subsection by a simplified fragment of travel agency processes.

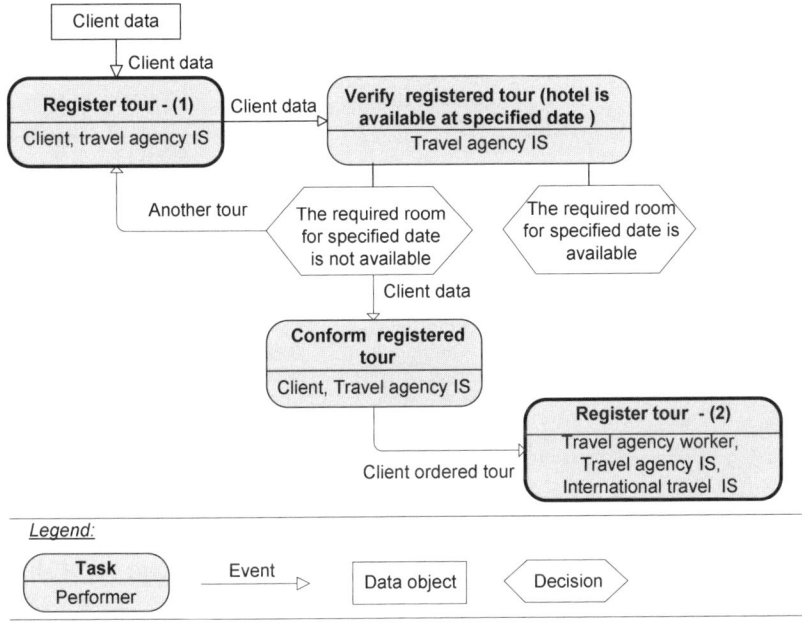

Fig. 2. A simplified fragment of a travel agency business process model

The main goal of the agency is to receive and process client orders, which contain the required tour code, hotel name and tour date [20] Analyzing the travel agency's business processes, a fractal business process "Register tour" was identified. It has common or similar goals, similar inputs and outputs on two scales: inter-organizational scale (Register tour 1) and travel agency scale (Register tour 2). According to similarities and differences in functional and non-functional requirements [20], software service "Register tour" corresponds to fractals identified in business process model Figure 3. The service supports business process flexibility in the sense that, if there are changes in the registration process, both business processes are supported by corresponding changes in one particular software unit.

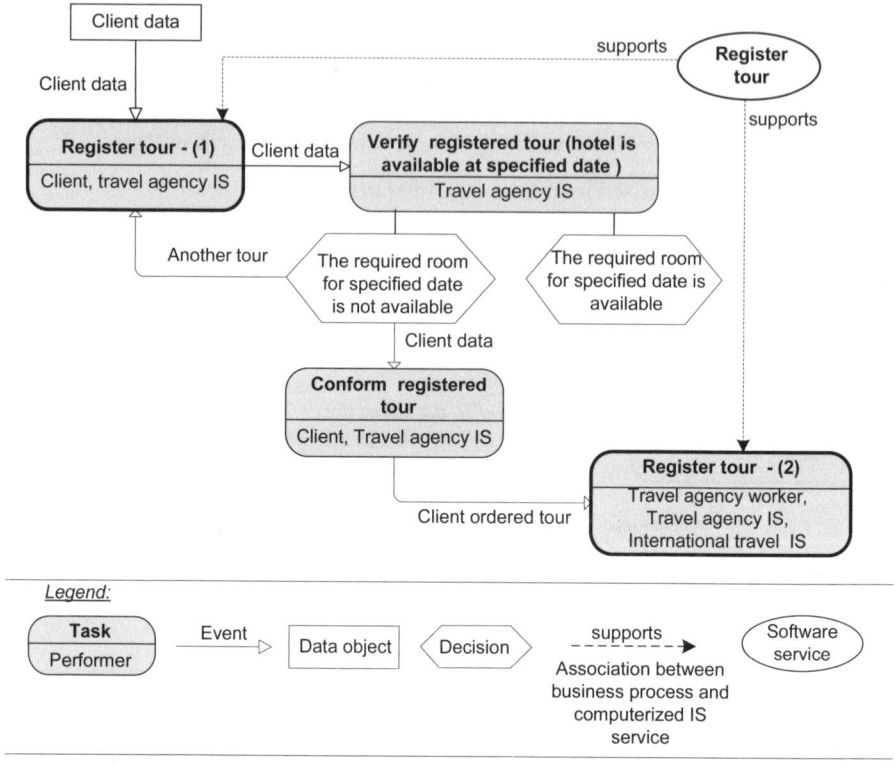

Fig. 3. Correspondence between business processes and software services

4 Fractal Software for Supporting Process Flexibility: An Object-Oriented Approach

The main idea of an object-oriented method is to create architecture of the system as polymorphic as possible. The suggested method includes the following three stages [21, 22]:

- Stage 1 – analysis of the system organization and behavior. The following are the main activities of Stage 1:
  - Define organizational structure of the system. Analysis of organizational structure facilitates the identification of actors and use cases. This relates to that in object-oriented analysis and design, system analysis starts with the identification of system's actors and use cases.
  - Define actors and their goals, use cases that are necessary for the achievement of those goals, and operation contracts, i.e., define the behavior of the information system under consideration. Use cases characterize the behavior of the software system that produces a measurable result of value to an actor. Use cases are goal-oriented. Additionally, one or several use cases can be used for the same

goal. Actors are humans or roles of other computer systems in an organization. Besides that, actors activate the execution of use cases. Thus, after the identification of *actors*, their *functional goals* are determined. In accordance with the identified functional goals, *use cases* needed for the goal achievement are identified. Use cases are specified by their scenarios that are main flow and alternate flow (in case of errors or exceptions) description of each use case. Here it is important to identify the so-called *operation contracts* for each actor's request. Each contract describes one operation with the specified name, parameter list, *references to other use case that use the same operation, pre and post conditions.* The result of this activity is a use case model and use case descriptions for each organizational level "fractal".

- Define a conceptual model. In addition the third activity is identification of concepts in the system's description. Concepts are ideas, things, or objects. Concepts and their relationships should be defined in the initial model of concepts.

- Stage 2 – definition of fractal scale invariants and organization. Scale invariants are properties of the system that do not change with the change of scale. The following are the main activities of Stage 2:
  - Define behavioral scale invariants. Initially the interactions in each identified use case should be analyzed and may be specified using UML interaction diagrams – sequence or collaboration diagrams. During the analysis of interactions, it is important to define messages that are sent and received by objects on different scales while acting towards the achievement of the same goal.
  - Define structural scale invariants. To define structural scale invariants, it is necessary to analyze the data of the structure. In fractal systems, structural data that are related to the fractal structure can be candidates to structural scale invariants. Those candidates that must be presented on all scales of the fractal system are separated as attributes of a fractal class (classes).
  - Define fractals' architecture. To support fractal's property "self-organization", a designer should define architecture (organization) of fractals by mapping it to the organizational structure of the system in the real world.

- Stage 3 – design of fractal classes and interfaces. Since the object-oriented approach supports inheritance and platform-independent modeling supports implementation of a defined behavior and structure at different platforms, it is useful to define all shared fractal related aspects as a distinct class – a fractal class. A *fractal class* is a class that specifies similar structure and functionality of fractals of the same kind. A *fractal interface* is an interface that should be implemented by a class that specifies a fractal. The interface specifies those scale invariants that are mandatory for specific kinds of fractals.

- Stage 4 – design of fractal classes' behavior on distinct scales. During Step 4 classes (and their behavior), which correspond to organizational scales and inherit fractal classes, must be defined. Here the important point is to make sure that all differences in operation implementations are taken into account.

A simplified use case model detected in Stage 1 is represented in Figure 4.

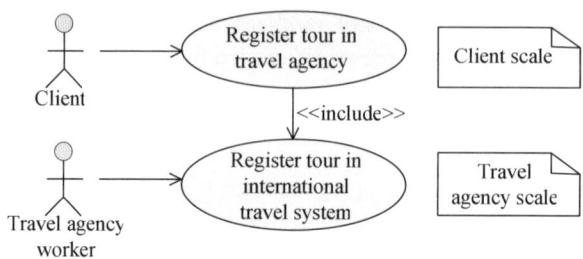

Fig. 4. Use case model for process "Order tour"

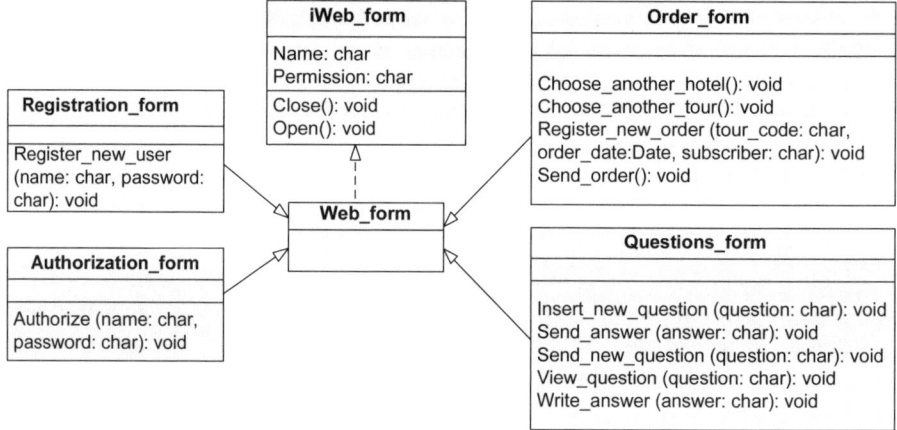

Fig. 5. Fractal interface iWeb_form

One of the fractal classes interfaces defined after analyzing use cases in Stage 3 is represented in Figure 5.

Figure 5 illustrates the fractal interface class *iWeb_form*. The fractal class *Web_Form* implements this interface. The interface *iWeb_form* specifies that a class, which realizes it, must contain information about its name and access permission and must perform its opening and closing if necessary. Hence, classes *Authorization_form*, *Registration_form*, *Order_form* and *Questions_form* inherit this responsibility and may realize this responsibility in their specific way. Interfaces of fractals support rapid propagation of changes in the behavior of agents from the business level to information system's functionality.

5   Discussion and Conclusions

Section 3 and 4 of this paper illustrate that, using fractal approach, several ways of business process flexibility support can be identified. The solutions depend on the

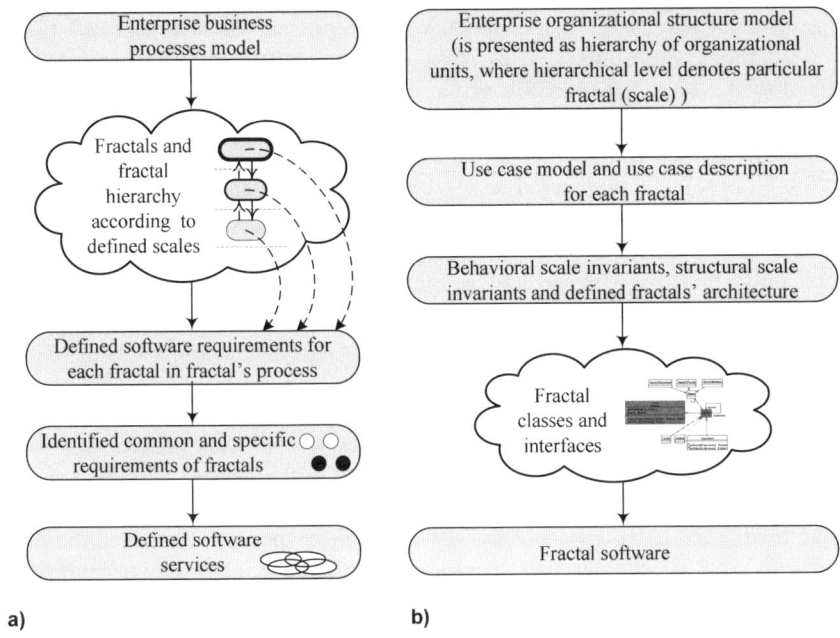

Fig. 6. Differences between process-oriented (a) and object-oriented (b) fractal approaches for information systems design

level of abstraction or decomposition where fractality of the system is identified or defined. Both approaches are compared in Figure 6. The process-oriented approach (discussed in Section 3) seeks to, first, identify fractal properties at the business process level and then structures software requirements according to identified fractal processes. In software systems design this allows to distinguish between more frequently and less frequently changing parts of the business process. The object-oriented approach (discussed in Section 4) analyzes goals of actors and seeks to identify fractals at the computerized information processing level thus introducing the fractal software architecture for business system support. Both object-oriented paradigm and fractal paradigm support flexibility. The contribution of a fractal paradigm in the object-oriented approach is in the utilization of self-similarity, i.e. fractals can organize themselves in order to perform some task due to their self-similarity. Flexibility in the object-oriented paradigm is effect of the realization of the "polymorphism" principle where the units that implement this principle may not be self-similar. It means that the object-oriented paradigm provides a technique to implement a certain property of fractals, namely, their self-similarity.

Process-oriented and object-oriented approaches were applied to 15 different medium complexity business systems by 15 information systems designers [23]. While theoretically it would be possible that both approaches suggest similar software for business process support, it was not so in any of 15 cases. Almost in all cases seeking fractals at the business process level led to service-oriented software architectures for business system support, while seeking fractals at the level of software processes led to object-oriented software architectures. With the process-oriented approach two different situations were observed: in some cases identified software services corresponded to the basic functionality of the business process, but in most cases these were "satellite" services such as saving data in the data base, data transfer from one location to another, etc. In addition, the depth of the analysis of processes was greater than the process taxonomies used in several sources devoted to fractal approaches in systems design (see Section 2). In the object-oriented approach, fractality of data in information flows was taken into consideration while in the process-oriented approach only intuitively perceivable similarity of information flows was analyzed. Thus the object-oriented approach utilized two and the process-oriented approach utilized one fractal hierarchy of three essential business systems dimensions represented in Figure 1.

The usefulness of the fractal process- and object-oriented approaches of system design was perceived differently by different designers. Two basic criteria they used in the evaluation of approaches were 1) compatibility of the method with their previous knowledge and 2) simplicity of defining fractal subsystems in the particular application domain. Thus practitioners of the object-oriented approach perceived the object-oriented method to be easier than the process-oriented one, and vice versa: designers used to process analyses preferred the process-oriented approach. In almost all cases it was possible to identify multi-scale "fractals" of software hierarchy. However, not all business processes exhibited this property. For instance, fractals were not found in VCOR framework [24], which initially seemed to be a very appropriate reference base for the use of process-oriented approach.

One of the expectations of the use of a fractal paradigm for supporting business processes was cutting of the time for user and software requirements definition. However, none of the designers reported shorter time for requirements acquisition when using a fractal paradigm in the systems development. Almost all pointed to the fact that the use of a fractal paradigm forces the requirements engineer to gather more detailed requirements and pay more attention to a variety of requirements with respect to different levels of scale in identified "fractals".

On the whole, the use of a fractal paradigm for support of business process flexibility has the following benefits:

- The process-oriented approach makes it possible to define software services that support fractal business processes and thus utilize flexibility support opportunities provided by service-oriented architectures.
- The object-oriented approach makes it possible to define flexible object-oriented software designs to support the user requirements of business process participants.
- Both approaches foster acquisition of detailed requirements with respect to individual differences at different scales of "fractals" in the business process or software respectively.

The application of a fractal paradigm is limited only to those business process and software subsystems in the enterprise, which exhibit fractal properties in at least one modeling dimension (agent, process or information architecture). The agent perspective was not analyzed in depth in the paper while it could to some extent contribute to both process- and object-oriented approaches. Actually, consideration of agents' fractality imposes analysis of agents' goals on a higher level of abstraction, i.e., not only with respect to software use as it was in Section 4. That suggests slightly different process- and object-oriented approaches to information systems design for support of enterprise flexibility and agility. Another direction of further research is the investigation of possibilities to integrate process- and object-oriented approaches in order to support business process flexibility simultaneously from both business and software perspectives.

References

1. Chapman, M., Berman, S., Blitz, A.: Foreword by Tushman M.: Rethinking innovation. Fast Thinking (2008)
2. Warneke, H.J.: The Fractal Company. Springer, Heidelberg (1993)
3. Kirikova, M., Strazdina, R., Grundspenkis, J., Osis, J.: Analysis of business process flexibility at different levels of abstraction. In: The 9th International Conference on Enterprise Information Systems: Software Agents and Internet Computing, Funchal, Madeira, INSTICC, Portugal, pp. 389–396 (2007) ISBN 978-972-8865-91-7
4. Kirikova, M.: Toward multi-fractal approach in IS development. In: 16th International Conference on Information Systems Development Challenges in Practice, Theory and Education (ISD 2007), Galway, Ireland (in print, 2008)
5. Bruneton, E., Coupaye, T., Stefani, J.B.: The Fractal Component Model. Specification, The ObjectWeb Consortium (2004)
6. Fryer, P., Ruis, J.: What are fractal systems: A brief description of complex adaptive and emerging systems (2006) (accessed April 14, 2007), http://www.fractal.org
7. Ramanathan, Y.: Fractal architecture for the adaptive complex enterprise. Communications of ACM 48(5), 51–67 (2005)
8. Ryu, K., Jung, M.: Fractal approach to managing intelligent enterprises: Creating Knowledge Based Organizations. In: Gupta, J.N.D., Sharma, S.K. (eds.), pp. 312–348. Idea Group Publishers (2003)
9. Canavesio, M.M., Martinez, E.: Enterprise modeling of a project-oriented fractal company for SMEs networking. Computers in Industry (2007), http://www.sciencedirect.com, doi:10.1016/j.compind.2007.02.-05
10. Hongzhao, D., Dongxu, L., Yanwei, Z., Chen, Y.: A novel approach of networked manufacturing collaboration: fractal web based enterprise. Int. Journal on Advanced Manufacturing Technology 26, 1436–1442 (2005)
11. Tharumarajah, A., Wells, A.J., Nemes, L.: Comparison of emerging manufacturing concepts. Systems, Man and Cybernetics 1, 325–331 (1998)
12. Sihn, W.: Re-engineering through fractal structures. In: IFIPWG5.7 working conference Reengineering the Enterprise, Ireland, pp. 21–30 (1995)
13. Cottam, R., Ranson, W., Vounckx, R.: Life and simple systems. Systems Research and Behavioral Science 22(5), 413–430 (2005)
14. Regev, G., Soffer, P., Schmidt, R.: Taxonomy of Flexibility in Business Processes (2006), http://lamswww.epfl.ch/conference/bpmds06/taxbpflex
15. Daoudi, F., Nurcan, S.: A Benchmarking Framework for Methods to Design Flexible Business Processes. In: Software Process Improvement and Practice, pp. 51–63 (2007)
16. Snowdon, R.A.: On the Architecture and Form of Flexible Process Support. In: Software Process Improvement and Practice. John Wiley & Sons, Chichester (2006)

17. Regev, G., Wegmann, A.: Business Process Flexibility: Weick's Organizational Theory to the Rescue (2006), http://lamswww.epfl.ch/conference/bpmds06/program/Regev_13.pdf
18. Chitchyan, R., Rashid, A., Sawyer, P.: Survey of Analysis and Design Approaches, OSD-Europe EU Network of Excellence (2005), http://www.comp.lancs.ac.uk/computing/aop/papers/d11.pdf
19. Stecjuka, J., Kirikova, M.: The process-oriented fractal information system development method. In: 14th International Conference on Information and Software Technologies (IT 2008), pp. 171–181. Kaunas University of Technology (2008)
20. Astahova, T.: Course work in Requirements Engineering. Riga Technical University, Riga (2007) (in Latvian)
21. Asnina, E., Osis, J., Kirikova, M.: Design of fractal-based systems within MDA: platform independent modeling. In: 3rd EuroSIGSAND Symposium 2008, Marburg/Lahn. GI-LNI P-129, pp. 39–53. Koellen-Verlag (2008)
22. Asnina, E., Osis, J.: Analyzing of multifractal system properties in object-oriented software development. In: 48th International Riga Technical University Conference, Scientific Proceedings of RTU, Series — Computer Science (5), Applied Computer Systems. RTU, Riga (2007)
23. Deliverables of project Nr. R7199 Development of fractal information systems design methodologies, Riga, RTU (2007) (in Latvian)
24. VCOR framework (2007), http://www.value-chain.org/

Supporting Collaboration in an Extended Enterprise with the Connector View on Enterprise Models

Anders Carstensen[1], Lennart Holmberg [2], and Kurt Sandkuhl[1]

[1] School of Engineering at Jönköping University,
P.O. Box 1026, 55111 Jönköping, Sweden
{anders.carstensen,kurt.sandkuhl}@jth.hj.se
[2] Kongsberg Automotive
P.O. Box 504, SE-565 28 Mullsjö, Sweden
lennart.holmberg@ka-group.com

Abstract. The work presented in this paper aims at contributing to enterprise interoperability. The focus is on collaboration in extended enterprises as general application field and active knowledge models as underlying technology. The starting point for the paper is an application case from automotive industry, where active knowledge models were developed for essential product development tasks. The paper concerns the development of a connector between these active knowledge models in order to support collaboration between two partners. The focus is on the operationalising phase of the connector development and on experiences. One result from this work is to propose three levels for the modeling, depending on the maturity level of the collaboration - searching for a partner, modeling existing collaboration and enhancing collaboration through detailed modeling.

Keywords: Enterprise model, extended enterprise, collaborative work, connector view, enterprise interoperability.

1 Introduction and Background

Enterprise interoperability has been a research subject since more than 20 years and still offers numerous challenges for the scientific community. Researchers have been examining the interoperability challenges on various levels (e.g. from the business models to technical details [17]) and from different perspectives (like those described by ODP [10]). The spectrum of solutions proposed spans form general reference models or frameworks (see [18] for an overview) to service description languages and protocols for heterogeneous environments.

The work presented in this paper aims at contributing to enterprise interoperability and focuses on (1) collaboration in extended enterprises as general application field, (2) enterprise knowledge modeling as underlying technology, and (3) networked manufacturing in the specific use case considered. An extended enterprise is a dynamic networked organization, which is created ad-hoc to reach a defined objective using the resources of the participating enterprises. The focus on collaboration in extended

J. Stirna and A. Persson (Eds.): PoEM 2008, LNBIP 15, pp. 111–126, 2008.
© IFIP International Federation for Information Processing 2008

enterprises indicates that not easily automatable routine activities are in the center of our interest, but complex processes involving several actors in different companies and their coordination. We take advantage of progress in the field of active knowledge modeling and propose to use such models for analyzing collaboration requirements, designing solutions in a participative manner involving relevant stakeholders, and operationalising these solutions. One important characteristic of collaboration in networked manufacturing is the weight of product knowledge in the enterprise knowledge models, i.e. knowledge about product structure, design concepts, configuration possibilities is essential for the collaboration.

The article is structured as follows: the remaining part of this section introduces the application context of this work and the subject active knowledge modeling. Section 2 summarizes previous work on the approach of connector views. Section 3 introduces first steps to operationalising of the connector view approach including material from the industrial case. Section 4 contains a discussion and related work. Future work and conclusions are presented in section 5.

1.1 MAPPER - Project

This paper is based on work in the EU-FP6 project MAPPER[1] (Model-adapted Process and Product Engineering). MAPPER had a runtime from autumn 2005 until spring 2008 and aimed at enabling fast and flexible manufacturing in networked enterprises by providing methodology, infrastructure and reusable services for collaborative engineering. One of the MAPPER use cases focused on distributed product development involving different subsidiaries of an automotive supplier. The collaboration of this automotive supplier with a sub-supplier forms the context for the work presented in this paper.

Product development in this context includes elicitation of system requirements based on customer requirements, development of functional, design of logical and technical architecture, co-design of material, electrical and mechanical components, integration testing and production planning. The process is geographically distributed, as it involves the sub-supplier and engineers and specialists at several locations of the automotive supplier. The purpose of the enterprise knowledge modeling in this use case was to capture the relevant product knowledge and process knowledge required for collaborative engineering. In particular, the knowledge model has to enable flexible collaboration processes between supplier and sub-supplier, i.e. an integration of both partners on work process, product model and collaboration service level is crucial.

1.2 Active Knowledge Modeling (AKM)

Enterprise knowledge modeling aims at capturing reusable knowledge of processes and products in knowledge architectures supporting work execution [2]. These architectures form the basis for model-based solutions, which often are represented as active knowledge models (AKM) [3]. An essential characteristic of active models vs. passive models is that "the model must be dynamic, users must be supported in

---

[1] See [1] for more information about MAPPER.

changing the model to fit their local reality, enabling tailoring of the system's behavior" [4]. Furthermore, the model must "first and foremost be available for the user in the operational information system at execution time. Second, the model must automatically influence the behavior of the computerized work support system or workplace. Third, the model must be dynamically extended and adapted; users must be supported in changing the model to fit their local needs, enabling tailoring of the work environment's behavior" [6, p. 5].

In MAPPER, the active knowledge models included the POPS* perspectives, which are mutually reflective [5]:

- process perspective (P): work processes and tasks,
- organization perspective (O): roles involved in the processes
- product perspective (P): components, configuration possibilities and dependencies of the product family,
- systems perspective (S): IT systems supporting processes and product development,
- further perspectives (*) depend on the purpose of the modeling project.

The overall modelling process was inspired by the C3S3P methodology. C3S3P is based on work in several EU projects, like EXTERNAL [7] and ATHENA[2]. C3S3P distinguishes between seven stages called concept study, scaffolding, scoping, solution modeling, platform integration, piloting in real projects and performance monitoring and management. More information about C3S3P is provided in [8] and [6].

In order to support the application of active knowledge models in everyday industrial practice an IT-platform was developed consisting of the enterprise modeling tool METIS[3], an execution environment, modeling templates and model-generated work places. In the remaining part of this paper, this platform will be called AKM-platform[4]. The most important part in the AKM-platform for the end user are model-generated and role-specific work places, which allow for capturing and modifying product knowledge during product development in collaboration with partners.

2 Previous Work

The work presented in this paper builds to a large extent on previous work presented in [9], which will be summarized in this section.

The starting point for our work is the use case briefly introduced in section 1.1. In this context, two companies (partner A and partner B) are setting up a new collaboration. Partner A is active as a supplier towards the automotive manufacturing industry, while Partner B is a supplier of wire products for Partner A. In the use case Partner A and B want to improve their collaboration concerning wire solutions for seat-heating. In this case the wire is a material for producing the seat heating product at partner A, while the wire at the same time is a product offered by Partner B. For the planned improvement at partner A, several negotiable solutions exist. These include different materials with different properties and price-levels. Hence the collaboration situation is not trivial and includes different departments and roles at each partner.

---

[2] http://www.athena-ip.org/
[3] http://www.troux.com. METIS was recently renamed to Troux Architect.
[4] http://www.akmodeling.com

The purpose of the work described in [9] was to model the collaboration between the two partners. Starting point were existing active knowledge models, which capture organizational knowledge in collaborative engineering using the POPS* perspectives, for example for tasks like "establish material specification" or "develop new test method". The main result of the previous modeling activity was an additional active knowledge model with the connector view, common for all collaborating partners, and a supporting view for each partner. The *connector viewpoint* defines the content of the connector view and a methodology to design the connector view.[5] Table 1 shows a definition of the connector viewpoint and the associated methodology. By using the connector view several advantages can be gained:

- "Existing models for the involved companies need not be changed, in the initial stages;
- Stakeholders have a natural place to relate collaborative elements;
- It is not necessary to align existing enterprise models according to one specific partner." ([9]).

The Reference Model for Open Distributed Processing (RM-ODP) is an ISO standard which among other things defines five different viewpoints for developing interoperability in distributed systems. These viewpoints are: the enterprise viewpoint, the information viewpoint, the computational viewpoint, the engineering viewpoint and the technological viewpoint [11]. In our use case we defined supporting views that consists either of elements that already are existing in the partners enterprise model or of triggering events that need to be added. Thus the supporting views can be seen as part of the enterprise views of the partners, while the connector viewpoint extends the set of viewpoints given in RM-ODP.

As described above we have developed a connector view common for both partner A and partner B, with a supporting view for each partner. In the connector view we have defined several different collaboration elements (23 to be exact). Each such collaboration element relates to one or several elements in each partner's supporting view and also to one or several *Information objects* in an *Information view*, common for both partners[6]. The collaboration elements define activities that emanate from the collaboration and thus cannot be said to belong to any partner's enterprise models and is not owned by a specific partner. Likewise, the information objects shared between the collaborating partners do not belong to just one of the partners, even though maintenance (such as storage etc.) of the information is a concern for the respective partner. By this approach we want to address the mutual need to explore what information and product knowledge is essential in the collaboration.

The first parts of the methodology in the connector viewpoint defines how to build (or establish) the connector view (see stage 1 to stage 3 in table 1) while the last part defines *Operationalising* the connector view (see stage 4 in table 1). In the previous work [9] *Operationalising* the connector view was not performed, and is a subject of this paper.

---

[5] More about viewpoint can be found in [10].

[6] The information viewpoint is one of the viewpoints of RM-ODP and should give a logical object-based representation of the distributed data and the constraints and possible manipulation of the data [11].

Due to the complexity of the operationalisation stage, the following sections will not cover this completely, but rather position the landmarks for this stage. The methodology for defining the connector view is a work in progress and requires additional use cases.

Table 1. Definition of the connector viewpoint

The connector viewpoint is an integrative viewpoint on different enterprise models exposing the intersection of these models including: <ul><li>Objectives of the collaboration between the enterprises in question;</li><li>Overlapping processes or tasks;</li><li>Information shared or exchanged in these processes;</li><li>Resources involved in the overlapping processes or supporting the collaboration, like IT-systems or machinery;</li><li>Roles involved in the overlapping processes or tasks and – if required their competences.</li></ul> A view based on the connector viewpoint may include *collaboration elements*, which identify subjects of organizational or technical change (transient nature) when the collaboration is implemented. These elements are not owned by any of the collaborating partners, and may correspond towards supporting objects.		
Stage	Step	Methodology description
1	a	Model goals and problems. It is important to find out from each partner what goals they want to meet with the system integration and what the problems are in meeting these goals.
1	b	Identify existing partner models reflecting the information usage. These can be the existing enterprise models that are relevant for the case to be modelled at the specific partner.
1	c	Identify collaboration elements in the connector view. E.g. how to connect tasks belonging to different collaborating partners, decisions to be taken, exchange of certain information etc.
2		Identify information necessary for collaboration elements in the connector view. Identified information objects are related to the collaboration elements in the connector view, (see 4b).
3	a	Identify supporting objects that relate to the collaboration elements. These are extensions of existing partner models that are relevant tasks or other objects in the enterprise for supporting the communication through the collaboration elements in the connector view.
3	b	Identify resources connected to supporting objects. Such as: roles, documents and systems as sources for information.
4	a	Relate collaboration elements through the supporting objects to the partner models. Collaboration elements are related to supporting objects and supporting objects to objects in the partner models.
4	b	Operationalise the connector view. Describe information usage in connector view. This includes defining the rules for how the information should be interoperable. It may include such things as: How terminology matches between systems, triggering mechanisms for connecting and exchanging information etc. In this step a re-evaluation of the initially stated goals and problems should be done in order to really focus on what is important when setting up the functionality of the connector view.

3 Towards Operationalising the Connector View

3.1 Describing the Collaboration (Elements)

The first step in operationalising the connector view is to define in a collaboration-description the correspondences between elements in the connector view and elements in the respective companies' supporting views. A question of interest is how the information objects related to the collaboration element is used in these correspondences? Due to the limited time given in the project for this analysis, only five collaboration elements have so far been included in the description. One such collaboration element included is "Meet to communicate requirements and decide on test methods", shown in figure 1. In the figure the relationships between the elements in the supporting views and the collaboration element and also between the information objects in the information view and the collaboration element are shown. The related elements are listed in tables 2 to 4. For this particular collaboration element the following collaboration description was written:

"At [*partner A*] requirements are specified and to get input for the requirement [*partner B*] is asked for technical support, this is an iterative procedure. When the requirements have been developed they are sent to [*partner B*]. [*partner B*] checks the possibilities of existing products in their portfolio, which meets the requirements on the wire. If no available solution exists an investigation of new development will be started. Requirement on the product (the wire) is important for determining which test method to use, but it is also necessary to discuss requirements on the test method as such. In order to meet the requirements from [*partner A*], [*partner B*] has to search for available test methods and this may trigger an investigation of new development of test method."

The written collaboration-description is an initial part of stage 4 b (see table 1) in the methodology for developing the connector view. The purpose is to analyze how the partners want to develop their collaboration and thus elaborate the specifics of the collaboration elements. There are several supporting elements at both partners which trigger the collaboration element and the specification of the collaboration element (in the collaboration-description) gives some directions of how these supporting elements act together.

The collaboration element is on a high level of conceptualization and we can state that there is no strict procedural order between the activities that trigger the collaboration element. This is illustrated by partner A, where we have (in accordance with stage 4a in the methodology described in table 1) associated the supporting elements with tasks in the active knowledge models forming the starting point for our work (see section 2). There are several elements in these models which in one way or the other may use the supporting object and thereby contribute to triggering the collaboration element. E.g. for the supporting object "Ask for technical support, suggestions of material" the model of "Establish material specification" has 4 associated tasks, "Internal testing" has 2 tasks and "Develop new test method" has 12 associated tasks. This indicates that there is no strict procedural order in which the supporting elements trigger the collaboration element. This seems also to be case for the other four described collaboration elements. Although there can be some activities that need to be performed before others there is often alternative or iterative paths where the order can not be strictly predicted in advance.

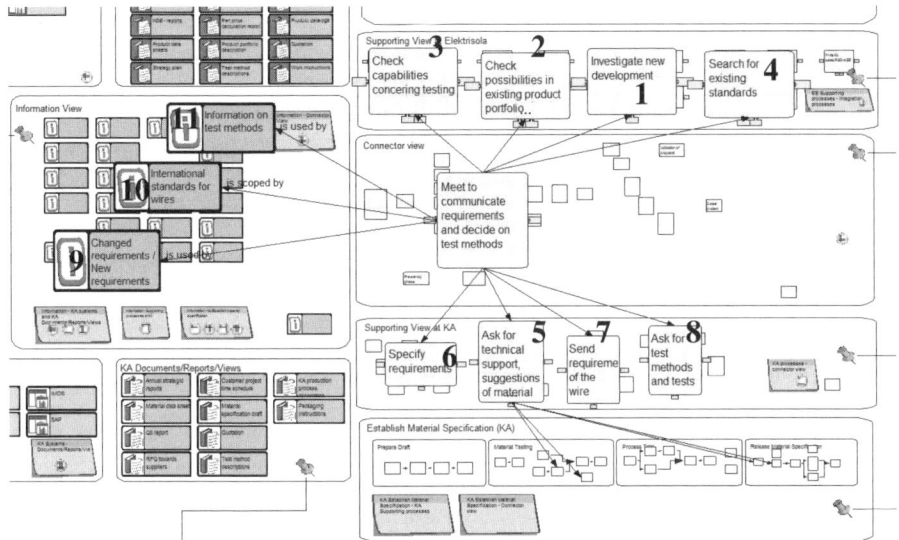

Fig. 1. On the right side, the connector view is shown in the middle with the supporting view for partner B above and the supporting view for partner A beneath. On the left side the information view. Some of the elements in the supporting views and information view are related to the collaboration element "Meet to communicate requirements and decide on test methods". These elements have been enlarged to make them more readable in the figure. The numbers reference the corresponding rows in tables 2 to 4 for the modeled supporting- and information elements.

Table 2. Elements in the supporting view for partner B, related to the collaboration element "Meet to communicate requirements and decide on test methods"

	Name	Description
1	Investigate new development	To think about new solution together with the team at [*partner B*]
2	Check possibilities in existing product portfolio	Compare requirements with properties of existing products
3	Check capabilities concerning testing	Test methods, test equipment, human resources and competences and experiences. Includes a meeting with QA/central lab, production and plant manager.
4	Search for existing standards	International wire standards (focused on the product and test methods), material safety data sheets, IMDS information, general data sheet of components, data sheet of specific solution.

Table 3. Elements in the supporting view for partner A, related to the collaboration element "Meet to communicate requirements and decide on test methods"

	Name	Description
5	Ask for technical support, suggestions of material	Initial communication concerning requirements and possible technical solutions
6	Specify requirements	Conclude on important properties and their requested values
7	Send requirements of the wire	The material specification is send usually by e-mail
8	Ask for test methods and tests	Ask the supplier for recommended test methods for the important properties

Table 4. Information object in information view related to the collaboration element "Meet to communicate requirements and decide on test methods"

	Name	Description
9	Changed requirements / New requirements	Can be find in the up-dated material specification
10	International standards for wires	Can be both standards concerning the product or test methods for the product
11	Information on test methods	Can be both inline test methods and offline test methods (tests made in the lab like tensile strength and bending tests). This can be further divided in existing test methods and new test methods developed either at [partner A] or at [partner B].

3.2 Further Analysis of the Connector View

In order to further refine and detail the collaboration elements in the connector view we decided to analyze the collaboration description by applying the IRTV-methodology from [6]. We have made this analysis on the specific collaboration element "Meet to communicate requirements and decide on test methods". Accordingly we modeled the four different dimensions: Information, Role, Task and View (IRTV), using the tool Metis and the AKM-platform. This is an iterative work, starting with modeling the Information and the Role dimensions, as seen in figures 2 and 3.

The application case is still under development and we will briefly present only some of the details from our work. It has to be mentioned that the AKM-platform is still under development and our work has been done using a prototype installation which does not have the full capacity that the platform is supposed to have when it is completed.

Stakeholders representing the different roles have been involved in the modeling at specific occasions. Between these meetings the modeling facilitator has prepared a solution, based on previous discussions, to be evaluated and further discussed. Information structures that should be possible to capture in the workplace are modeled in the information dimension. Such an information structure is "Component Specification",

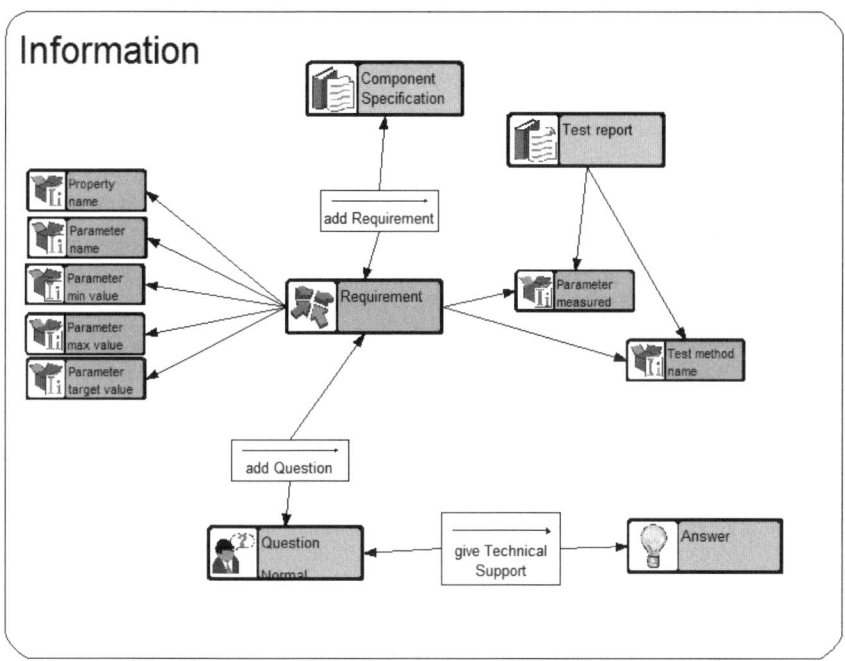

Fig. 2. The initially modeled Information dimension

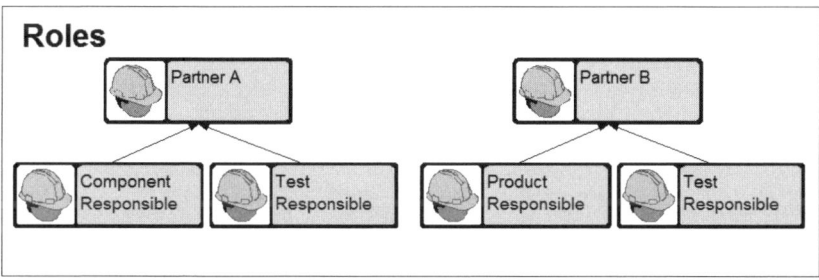

Fig. 3. The initially modeled Role dimension

which contains different "Requirement"-objects. A specific requirement-object contains some "Property"-objects such as "Property name", "Parameter name", "Parameter min value", etc. The information objects captured in the Information dimension relate to roles captured in the Role dimension through tasks modeled in the Task dimension. A specific task is implemented by a view in the View-dimension and defines how the involved information objects should be used by the task. The task and view dimensions from our use case are shown in figs. 4 and 5. The modeled tasks are those that concern the specific collaboration element and the involved roles.

Modeling the four different dimensions give other perspectives on how to operationalise the collaboration elements. In order to model the workplace for specific stakeholders at partner A and partner B, we are forced to think about questions like:

What are the main objectives with their work? Which information objects are they interested in modeling? What tasks are they interested in using? How can they use a modeling tool for performing their work? Etc. This will automatically involve the product that the stakeholder is working with, since this is a primary concern for the stakeholders.

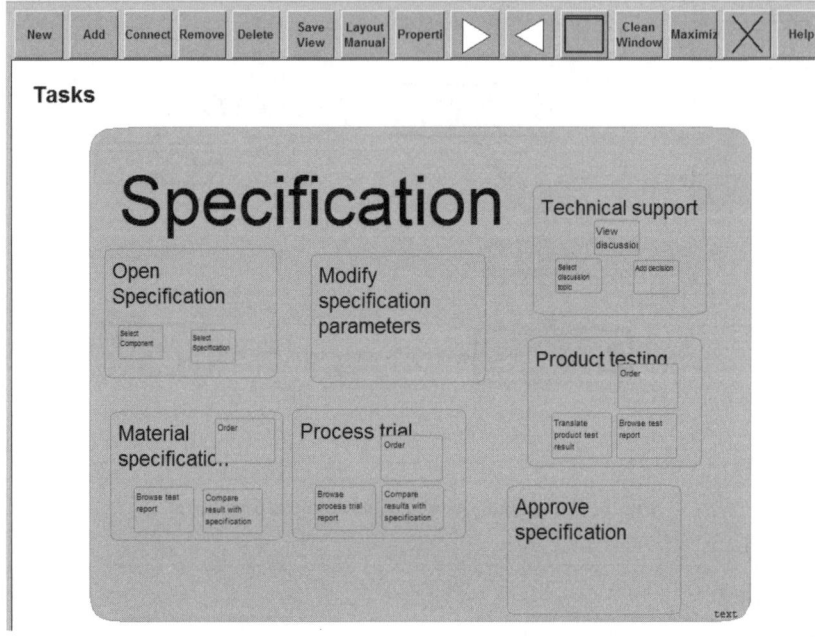

Fig. 4. Showing the modeled Task dimension

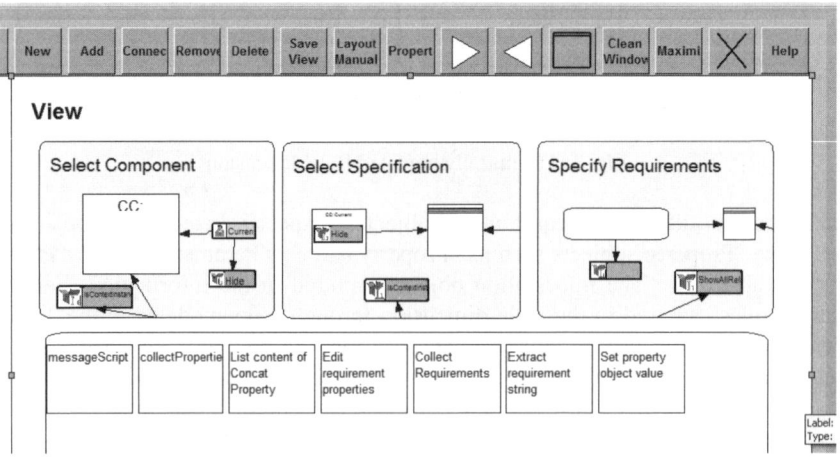

Fig. 5. Showing the modeled View dimension. The seven boxes in the lower part of the figure contains the added scripts.

The *component responsible* at partner A manages the component specification, a document which consists of several material specification documents. Document should not be taken in a literal sense since some documents, in the use case, will exist as models. It is actually a discussion point as such what information should exist as documents (in a literal sense) and which information should exist only as models. We will not take that discussion further here, albeit it is an important interoperability issue how to make document bound information available in the IT-systems. A specific material specification document contains several requirements which can be added by both the *component responsible* and the *test responsible* at partner A as well as by the *product responsible* and the *test responsible* at partner B. This requires that the modeled workplace can be used from both partner A and partner B. An interesting issue is the ownership of the information. Some requirements will be partly added by both partners. It is also a matter of the degree of maturity the documents have reached. In order to add requirements it is necessary for the *test responsible* at both partner A and partner B to perform tests on materials. These tests will add measured values and will require a specific test-method. The test method can be an in-house test-method created at partner A or partner B or it can be required from available sources. Sometimes questions arise when partner A performs tests and it is then necessary to pose these questions to partner B, who is responsible for delivering the material that is tested. These questions can have to do with the material as such or with the test-method used.

Several points of collaboration have been indicated: Entering of requirements from both partners; Investigation of available test-methods required from the other partner; The need to ask technical questions that arises during the testing. Specific tasks were modeled in order to implement these interactions as a workplace to be used by both partners. Such a task is e.g. to open and select a component and a specific requirement. The modeled tasks that are shown in fig. 4 become selectable choices in a menu in the workplace (see fig. 6). In the use case we have model-generated views (see fig. 5) that correspond to the tasks. For the task "Select component" it will be possible to select the component from a list of available components and for the task "Select specification" it is possible to select the specific requirement from the list of requirements belonging to the selected component. The task "Modify specification parameters" opens a view with possibility to add or modify components and requirements for the selected requirement.

By using the workplace information that belongs to the requirements for a specific product will be modeled. The models generated this way will be *active* in the sense we described earlier, they are available for the user and is actively updated and used.

Unfortunately, due to limits in the AKM-platform regarding work place generation, not all generation tasks could be done solely by modeling of views. It became necessary to add scripts to perform some specific operations. This requires that the programmer become acquainted with the metis-programming API. The modeled workplace is a prototype which in its present state is incomplete and need to be further developed in order to be put into operation.

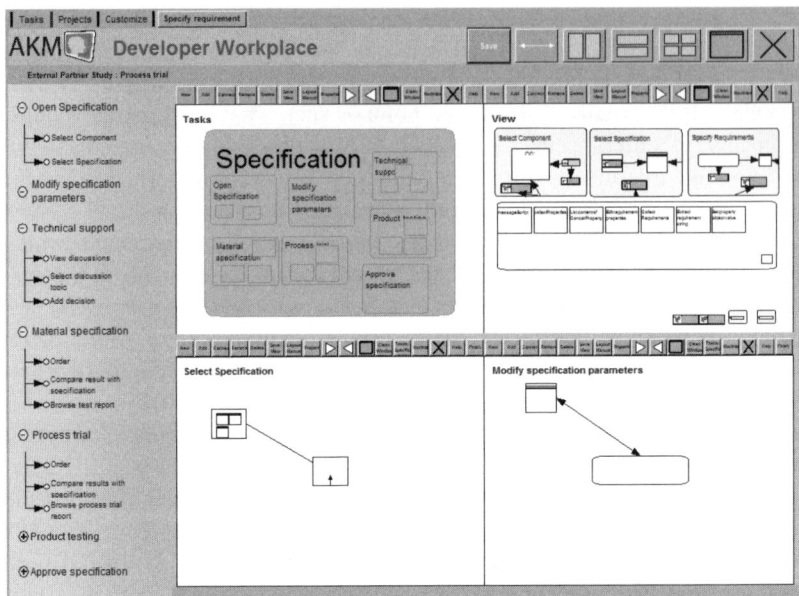

Fig. 6. The user workplace as it looks when you run it inside the workplace for generating workplaces. On the left side you can see the menu from which the user can select the tasks to perform. This menu is generated from the tasks modeled within the main task "Specification". When the user selects a task a window with the specific view is opened, much like the view shown in figs. 4 and 5. By using the small buttons "New", "Add" etc. (barely visible in this figure, but visible in figs. 4 and 5) the user can modify the model.

4   Discussion and Related Work

Different approaches that are relevant for the use case can be mentioned, such as Service Oriented Architectures (SOA), Model Driven Architecture (MDA) and Semantic Web. The following citation summarizes these approaches in a nutshell: "Though many of these approaches show promising results, they do not represent a holistic approach for capturing and nurturing enterprise knowledge" [6, p. 164]. It might however be seen as a paradox that collaboration between different approaches is necessary for solving interoperability problems. Process modeling is used for specifying how things should be performed, i.e. a procedural expression of actions. This can be put into contrast to business models that express what should be done. In process modeling as such it is many times difficult to see the logical reasons behind a specific design [12]. P. Johannesson proposes in the paper [12] that a combination of business and process modeling is fruitful since this places the process models on a declarative ground. Likewise in enterprise modeling it is important to perform goal modeling and to combine this with other types of models like process models.

Web services poses interesting aspects such as ways to combine different web services in order to create electronic business processes. Business Process Execution Language WS-BPEL (or BPEL4WS) and Web Service Choreography Definition

Language (WS-CDL) are evolving standards for designing web services. WS-BPEL can be used for defining business processes that can integrate user- as well as application activities. It does so by invoking already defined web services and by placing a process layer that defines how these web services are invoked. In WS-BPEL processes can be of two types: Executable processes with the purpose to "model the actual behavior of a participant in business interaction"; abstract processes with the purpose to define protocols for message exchange. The abstract processes, which are not executable, serve the function of defining a visible behavior while hiding the actual implementation. The reason for this is to make it possible for participants to not reveal sensitive business processes [13], however collaboration will always require some degree of openness in order to establish and maintain the collaboration.

The Object Management Group (OMG) is specifying a standard Business Process Definition Metamodel (BPDM), with the purpose to achieve integration between different ways of performing business process modeling. They are proposing two different views to be used: *Orchestration* and *Choreography*. Orchestration is about how to internally realize the activities in a web service and choreography is about how to combine collaborating services to achieve a business process [14]. Dijkman and Dumas have proposed four different views: the *choreography, orchestration, Interface behavior* and *Provider behavior* views. The *Interface behavior* and *Provider behavior* views cover what is necessary to model in order to receive and send messages between the collaborating web services [15]. Much of the described methodologies for modeling business processes are however perceived by the users as too technical and difficult to use in the initial modeling stages. The link to the goals for achieving collaboration does not become obvious. Alternative modeling strategies have been proposed, such as modeling views for capturing milestones and scenarios, which later are converted to executable models [16].

WS-BPEL and Choreography modeling has many interesting capabilities that can be combined with our approach of the connector view. Our purpose is however not only to create a model for delivering messages between the different stakeholders of the collaboration partners. It is to create active models which are dynamically changeable by the user. Active Knowledge Modeling can serve two purposes in our use case. First of all it can deliver a workplace for the collaboration between several partners. Secondly it can deliver a way of modeling an active connector view, which can be changed according to the collaboration needs. The described use case has concentrated only on the first of these challenges.

In our use case we have investigated the collaboration between two companies that already have some business relationship that they want to improve. It is reasonable that the companies, before they reach this level of maturity, have established contacts with collaborating partners. Although it can not be seen as a process which is done once and for all because the collaborating partners may change. Once the collaborating partner(s) have been found it is necessary to build the ways of how to collaborate. In this level it becomes necessary to meet and discuss matters for collaboration. This is as far as collaboration reaches in many situations today. It could also be possible to reach a higher level of maturity by integrating available information sources, which today are used in manual way even though IT is used on both sides.

5 Conclusions and Future Work

In this paper we have described work in progress for performing the last part, named *Operationalising*, in our methodology for developing the connector view. This work has given us some insights about the modeling work which the methodology requires.

In our work, we experienced it as useful to think in different levels for the use of the connector viewpoint:

Level 1: The companies try to describe how they want to start their collaboration. This includes finding a suitable collaboration partner and the initial steps to take.

Level 2: The companies want to develop and improve an already existing business relationship.

Level 3: The companies want to model their collaboration and implement it as executable models that are able to integrate information and software systems.

Most of the work we have presented in this paper can be considered to be on level 2. There is a distinction between how to proceed with the modeling and what becomes important to model on the different levels. On level 1 the companies need to establish their interface which declares and defines their need of collaboration. There is no need to reveal any detailed information about business interaction or products. On level 2 it becomes necessary to model the collaboration and information objects more thoroughly and describe the scenarios for how to perform the collaboration. On level 3 it is a necessity that the connector view models, in detail, all interfaces between applications which communicate information. All the stages in the connector view methodology are applicable on all three levels, although Operationalising is a more challenging task on level 3.

In our work with the connector view we have shown that there is no strict procedural order between the tasks which are part of the collaboration, either it is an activity that generates information or it is an act that directly triggers an act of collaboration. By this insight it is easy to understand statements such as "it is often difficult to understand the reasons behind a certain process design and what consequences alternative designs would have" [12 p. 131]. No doubt it is a major step to grasp the logic that is necessary for choreography modeling which assumes the existence of clearly defined process steps in order to combine the different web services. We believe that web service technologies such as WS-BPEL and WS-CDL are well suited to carry out the work necessary on what we called "level 3", i.e. establishing connections between collaborating partner when there exists a clear picture of how the collaborating partner want to act. Before this modeling phase it is necessary to strengthen the analysis and we believe that the connector viewpoint can be helpful in defining the complex web of connections that constitute a collaboration. Using the IRTV-methodology can partly be considered as moving into a modeling on level 3. Our experiences concerning this part of the modeling are:

- Modeling as such had a catalytic effect on collaboration and helped to reach a common understanding between the collaborating partners.
- Modeling executable models is an underestimated task and there are many challenges in future work to manage this successfully.

There are still several open issues that require more work. Our intention is to continue the work we have started with the described use case. Some of these open issues to work further with are:

- How to complete the definition and implementation of the operationalisation stage in the connector viewpoint.
- How to extend the connector view to several collaborating partners,
- How to manage exchange of one partner with another partner,
- How to establish the connection with a suitable partner on level 1,
- How to manage the complexity where a more detailed connector view on level 3 is developed,
- How to reuse existing models between the execution environments at the different partners
- How to deal with information that exist as documents (in a literal sense) versus information that exist as models,
- How to deal with the ownership of the information.

References

1. Johnsen, S., et al.: Model-based adaptive Product and Process Engineering. In: Rabe, M., Mihok, P. (eds.) Ambient Intelligence Technologies for the Product Lifecycle: Results and Perspectives from European Research. Fraunhofer IRB Verlag (2007)
2. Lillehagen, F., Karlsen, D.: Visual Extended Enterprise Engineering embedding Knowledge Management, Systems Engineering and Work Execution. In: IEMC 1999 - IFIP International Enterprise Modeling Conference, Verdal, Norway (1999)
3. Krogstie, J., Jørgensen, H.D.: Interactive Models for Supporting Networked Organizations. In: Persson, A., Stirna, J. (eds.) CAiSE 2004, LNCS, vol. 3084, pp. 550–563. Springer, Heidelberg (2004)
4. Jørgensen, H.D., Krogstie, J.: Active Models for Dynamic Networked Organisations. In: Dittrich, K.R., Geppert, A., Norrie, M.C. (eds.) CAiSE 2001, LNCS, vol. 2068. Springer, Heidelberg (2001)
5. Lillehagen, F.: The Foundations of AKM Technology. In: Proceedings 10th International Conference on Concurrent Engineering (CE) Conference, Madeira, Portugal (2003)
6. Lillehagen, F., Krogstie, J.: Active Knowledge Modeling of Enterprises. Springer, Heidelberg (2008)
7. Krogstie, J., Lillehagen, F., Karlsen, D., Ohren, O., Strømseng, K., Thue Lie, F.: Extended Enterprise Methodology. Deliverable 2 in the EXTERNAL project (2000), http://research.dnv.com/external/deliverables.html
8. Stirna, J., Persson, A., Sandkuhl, K.: Participative Enterprise Modeling: Experiences and Recommendations. In: Krogstie, J., Opdahl, A.L., Sindre, G. (eds.) CAiSE 2007 and WES 2007. LNCS, vol. 4495, pp. 546–560. Springer, Heidelberg (2007)
9. Carstensen, A., Sandkuhl, K., Holmberg, L.: Towards a Methodology for Modeling Interoperability Between Collaborating Enterprises. In: Proceedings from: 10th International Conference on Enterprise Information Systems, Barcelona (2008)
10. ISO/IEC, IEEE Std 1471-2000: Recommended practice for Architectural Description of Software Intensive Systems. ISO/IEC 42010 IEEE:24 (2007)
11. Putman, J.R.: Architecting with RM-ODP. Prentice Hall, Upper Saddle River (2001)

12. Johannesson, P.: The Role of Business Models in Enterprise Modelling. In: Krogstie, J., Opdahl, A.L., Brinkkemper, S. (eds.) Conceptual Modelling in Information Systems Engineering, pp. 123–140. Springer, Heidelberg (2007)
13. OASIS: Web Services Business Process Execution Language version 2.0, Public Review Draft, August 23 (2006), `http://docs.oasis-open.org/wsbpel/2.0/`
14. OMG, Business Process Definition Metamodel (BPDM) Beta 1, OMG Document Number: dtc/07-07-01 (2007), `http://www.omg.org/cgi-bin/doc?dtc/2007-07-01`
15. Dijkman, R., Dumas, M.: Service-Oriented Design: A Multi-Viewpoint Approach. International Journal of Cooperative Information Systems 13(4), 337–368 (2004)
16. Barros, A., Decker, G., Dumas, M.: Multi-staged and Multi-viewpoint Service Choreography Modelling. Technical Report 4668, Queensland University of Technology, Brisbane, Australia (2006)
17. Linthicum, D.S.: Next generation Application Integration: From Simple Information to Web Services (2003) ISBN 0-201-84456-7
18. Vernadat, F.: Enterprise Modelling and Integration: principles and applications. Chapman & Hall, London (1996)

Service-Based Business Network Modelling: Application to Dynamic Logistics

Alexander Smirnov and Nikolay Shilov

Institution of the Russian Academy of Sciences
St.Petersburg Institute for Informatics and Automation RAS (SPIIRAS),
39, 14 Line, St. Petersburg, 19978, Russia
{smir,oleg,nick}@iias.spb.su

Abstract. Appearance of business networks can be considered as a response to changes in global markets. Networks can be seen as a step beyond the linear supply chain topography. The paper proposes an approach to business network modelling based on service networks. Since the centralized control is not always possible, presented approach proposes decentralized communication and ad-hoc decision making based on the current situation state and its possible future development. An approach presented is based on application of such technologies as ontology and context management to knowledge sharing. Ontologies are used for description of knowledge domains. The paper also presents experience of application of the above approach to the area of dynamic logistics. The considered problem takes into account continuously changing problem environment and requires nearly real-time solving.

Keywords: Service networks, business network modelling, ontology, context, dynamic logistics.

1 Introduction

Modern global companies have to build supply network strategies that provide maximum flexibility and can optimally respond to changes in their environment [1-3]. The emergence of business networks is one of the consequences of these changes. The automotive industry is a good example of this phenomenon. Today one of the most important competitive advantages for car makers is their ability to manufacture customised cars with a reduced lead time. At the same time, it is necessary to avoid significant inventory levels in order to keep costs lower. Such a strategy is called Build-to-Order (BTO) and stands for the capability to quickly build customized products upon receipt of customer orders without precise forecasts, inventory, or purchasing delays. In the BTO networks, customer orders are introduced in advance of, or at the start of the production process. An opposing strategy is build-to-stock (BTS), whereby the product is built prior to demand [4].

Complex decision making faces problems of management and sharing of huge amount of information & knowledge from distributed and heterogeneous sources (experts, electronic documents, real-time sensors, etc.) belonging to business network members, personalization, availability of up-to-date and accurate information provided by the dynamic environment. The problems include search of right sources, extraction of content, presentation of results in a personalized way, and other. As a rule, the content of several sources has to be extracted and processed (e.g., fused, converted,

J. Stirna and A. Persson (Eds.): PoEM 2008, LNBIP 15, pp. 127–137, 2008.

checked) to produce required information. Due to such factors as different data formats, interaction protocols and others this leads to a problem of semantic interoperability.

Knowledge sharing and exchange in a business network are highly important and should be achieved at both technical and semantic levels. The interoperability at the technical level is addressed in a number of research efforts. It is usually represented by such approaches as e.g., SOA (service-oriented architecture) [5] and on the appropriate standards like WSDL and SOAP [6]. The semantic level of interoperability in the flexible supply network is also paid significant attention. As an example (probably the most widely known), the Semantic Web initiative is worth mentioning [7]. The main idea is to use ontologies for knowledge and terminology description.

The approach presented in this paper also relies on the ontological knowledge representation for its sharing. Ontologies are widely used for problem domain description in the modern information systems to support semantic interoperability. An ontology is an explicit specification of a structure of a certain domain. It includes a vocabulary for referring to notions of the subject area, and a set of logical statements expressing the constraints existing in the domain and restricting the interpretation of the vocabulary [8]. Ontologies support integration of resources that were developed using different vocabularies and different perspectives of the data. To achieve semantic interoperability, systems must be able to exchange data so that the precise meaning of the data is readily accessible and the data itself can be translated by any system into the form that it understands [9].

Ontologies facilitate information retrieval over collections of distributed and heterogeneous information sources; they help to provide for semantic integration of information and facilitate interoperability between heterogeneous knowledge sources at high level of abstraction [10]. The conceptual model of the proposed ontology-driven knowledge sharing is based on the earlier developed idea of knowledge logistics [11]. It correlates with the conceptual integration developed within the Athena project [12]. The ontology describes common entities of the enterprise systems and relationships between them. As a result, it is possible to treat all available knowledge and competencies as one distributed knowledge base.

Centralized control in complex distributed systems is not always possible: for example, business networks consist of independent companies and do not have a central decision making unit. Thus, decentralized organisation of distributed independent components is a promising architecture for such kind of systems [13-15]. However, in order for the self-organisation to operate it is necessary to solve a number of problems including: (i) registration and cancelling of registration of network elements, (ii) preparation of initial state, (iii) self-configuration: finding appropriate network elements [16], negotiation of conditions and assignment of links, and preparation of alternative configurations. Different research projects are devoted to self-management of such networks: self -contextualization, -optimization, -organization, -configuration, -adaptation, -healing, -protection [17].

The following major requirements to the approach to business network modelling have been selected (some of the decision making processes in business networks have been identified in [18]): (i) intensive information exchange, (ii) distributed architecture, (iii) decentralised control, (iv) semantic-based information processing, (v) ad-hoc decision making support based on the current situation state and its possible future development. The developed methodology proposes integration of environmental information in a certain context. The context is any information that can be used to characterize the situation of an entity where an entity is a person, place, or object that is considered relevant to the interaction between a user and an application, including the user and applications themselves [19]. The context is purposed to represent only relevant information from the large amount of those. Relevance of information is evaluated on a basis how they are related to a modelling of an ad-hoc problem. A number of already solved problems and problems to be solved includes interoperability at both technological and semantic level, situation understanding by the members via information exchange, protocols of ad-hoc decision making for self-organization. Proposed technological framework incorporates such technologies as situation management, knowledge and ontology management, profiling, Web-services, decision support, negotiation protocols.

The proposed methodology is based on the earlier developed concept of knowledge logistics [20] and includes such technologies as situation management, ontology management, profiling and intelligent agents [18]. Standards of information exchange (e.g., Web-service standards), negotiation protocols, decision making rules, etc. are used for information exchange and rapid establishing of ad-hoc partnerships and agreements between the operation members. In the second section of the paper the developed methodology is presented. The application of the approach to a dynamic logistics problem is described in the third section. Some results are summarised in the Conclusion.

2 Proposed Approach

The main idea of the approach is to represent business network members by sets of services provided by them Fig. 1. This makes it possible to replace the interoperability between business network members with that between their services.

At the first stage of the research the lifecycle phases of the service-based network and major requirements to them were defined (Table 1). Based on these requirements the main ideas the approach is based on were formulated:

1. A common shared top-level ontology (application ontology) serves for terminology unification. Each service has a fragment of this ontology corresponding to its capabilities / responsibilities. This fragment is synchronized automatically when necessary (not during the operation).
2. Each service has a profile describing its capabilities, appropriate ontological model.
3. Each service is assigned an intelligent agent, representing it (together they will be called "*agent-based service*"). The agent collects information required for situational understanding by the service, negotiates with other agents to create ad-hoc action plans. The agent has predefined rules to be followed during negotiation processes. These rules depend on the role of the appropriate member.
4. Web-service standards are used for interactions. External sources (e.g., medical databases, transport availability, weather forecasts) should also support these standards and the terminology defined by the application ontology. This is achieved by developing services for each particular source.

The developed methodology proposes a two-level framework of context-driven information integration for decision making. The first level addresses activities over a prestarting procedure of the system as creation of semantic models for its components (Fig. 2); accumulating domain knowledge; linking domain knowledge with the information sources; creation of an application ontology describing a macro-situation; indexing

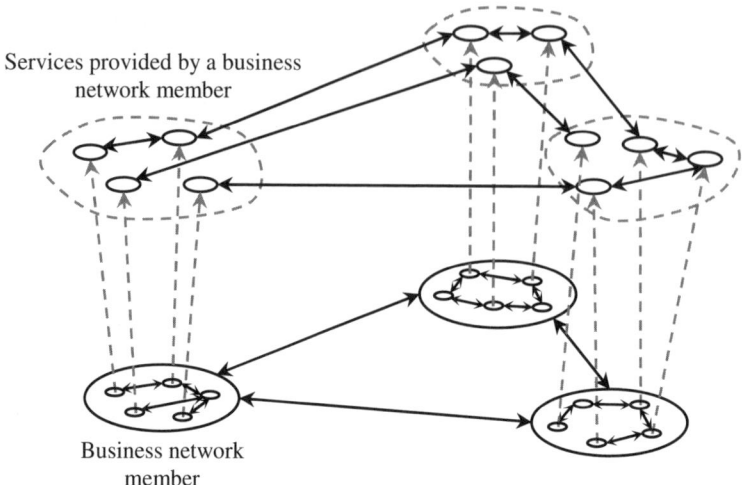

Services provided by a business
network member

Business network
member

Fig. 1. Representation of business network members by sets of services

Table 1. Lifecycle phases for the service network, its needs and services to fulfil them

Life cycle phase	Needs	Services
Community building (once, new members are added on a continuous basis)	Common infrastructure	Modelling goals and objectives
	Common communication standards and protocols	Identification, qualification, registration of members Common knowledge representation Common modelling for community members
Formation (continuous, initiated by the situation, or a task as a part of the situation)	Task definition model (context) Partner selection	Task modelling Rules of partner selection
Operation (continuous)	Coordination and synchronization	Rules of re-negotiation and solution modification if necessary
Discontinuation (continuous, initiated by members)	Termination of the established agreements	Update of the current solution

a set of available e-documents against the application ontology. This level is supported, if required, by the subject experts, knowledge and ontology engineers.

The second level focuses on decision making supported by the system. This level addresses a problem recognition presented by a user request; context creation; identification of relevant knowledge sources; generation of a set of problem solutions; and making a decision by the user.

The internal knowledge representation is supported by the formalism of object-oriented constraint networks (OOCN) [21]. All the system components and contexts are represented

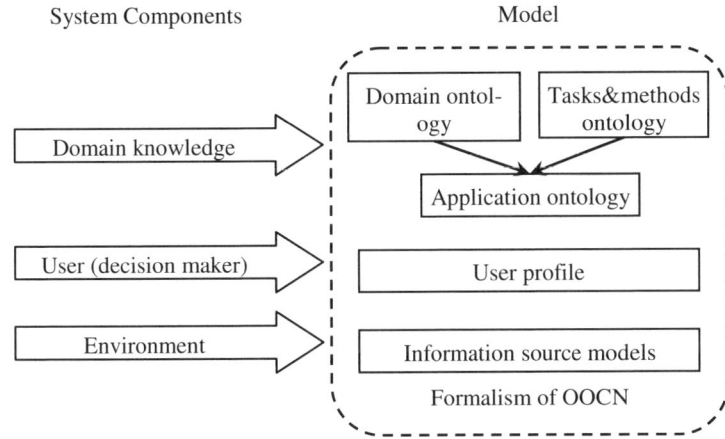

Fig. 2. Models for system components

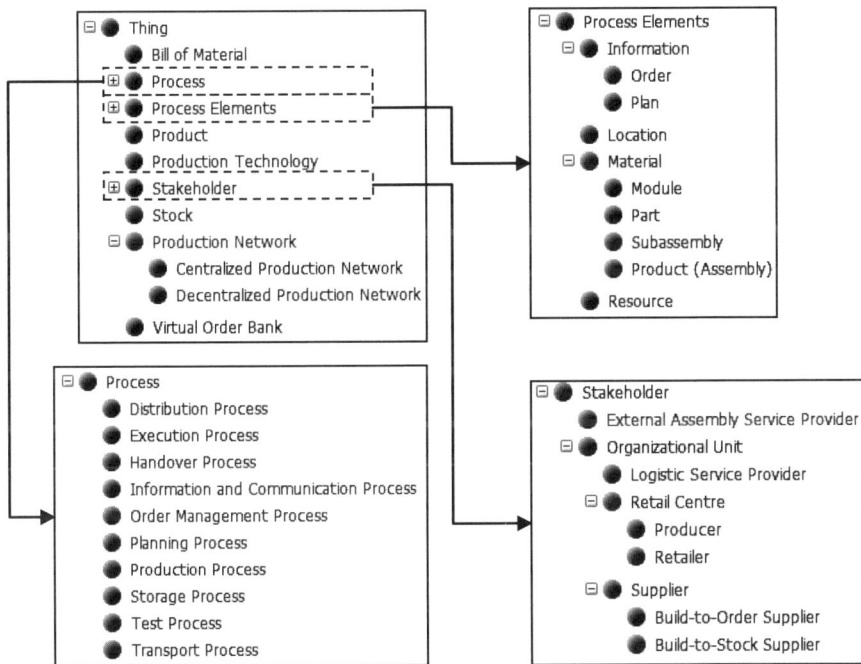

Fig. 3. Taxonomy of the application ontology for a production network

by means of this formalism. According to the formalism, the application ontology is represented as sets of classes, class attributes, attribute domains, and constraints. The set of constrains comprises constraints describing "class, attribute, domain" relation; constraints representing structural relations as hierarchical relationships "part-of" and "is-a", classes compatibility, associative relationships, class cardinality restrictions; and constraints describing functional dependencies. Below examples of some constraints are given:

- "class, attribute, domain" relation: the attribute *costs* belongs to the class *component* and takes *positive values*;
- hierarchical relationship "is-a": the *body production facility* is a *resource*;
- hierarchical relationships "part-of": an instance of the class *component* can be a part of an instance of the class *product*;
- associative relationship: an instance of the class *body* can be connected to an instance of the class *body production facility*;
- classes compatibility: the class *body* is compatible with the class *body production facility*;
- functional dependence: the value of the attribute *cost* of an instance of the class *body production facility* depends on values of the attribute *cost* of instances of the class *component* connected to it and on the number of such instances.

Fig. 3 represents the macro-level taxonomy of the built by domain experts application ontology for a production network as an example of business network. The represented classes are the main concepts for the production network configuration problem.

To demonstrate implementation of the approach in a prototype related to the "Transportation Network Configuration" task is considered. In the case study the knowledge acquired from a number of sources is shared in order to find a feasible solution.

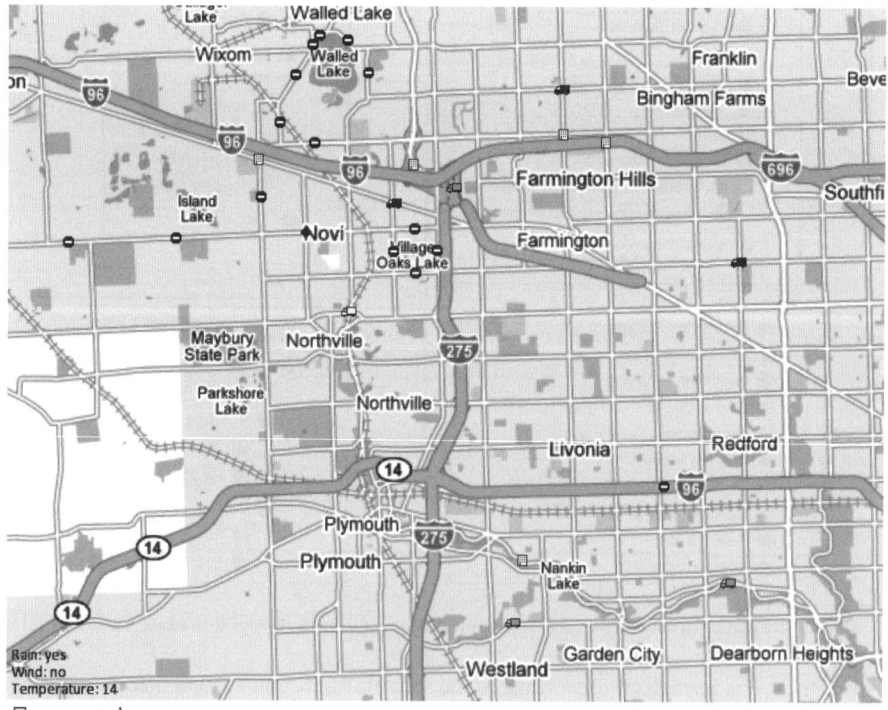

	- warehouses
	- vehicles
	- unavailable roads
	- depot location

Fig. 4. Current situation for the dynamic transportation problem

3   Case Study

Logistics management often involves such problems as creation of routing plans for a given set of vehicles available and goods to be transported. This is quite a common problem that has a number of solving techniques, e.g., [22]. However, in real life situations it is often necessary to take into account continuously changing traffic situation (e.g., to take into account traffic jams, closed roads, etc.) what makes the problem more complex and requires its solving it in real-time. This section presents application of the above described approach to this problem in the form of a Decision Support System (DSS).

In the case study the problem is considered as a dynamic transportation problem. There are several vehicles in different known locations that change in time. There is a central depot with a number of products to be transported (for simplicity containers will be considered instead of products and truck capacity will be one container). Also there exist several warehouses with given capacities where the products (containers) are to be transported. It is necessary to take into account the current situation in the area (traffic jams, closed roads, etc.) to find a feasible solution with possibly minimal time of transportation (Fig. 4). Though the problem seems to be simple it appears to be more complicated than it looks. For example, it can be more reasonable for one vehicle to make two or more rides instead of using two or more vehicles.

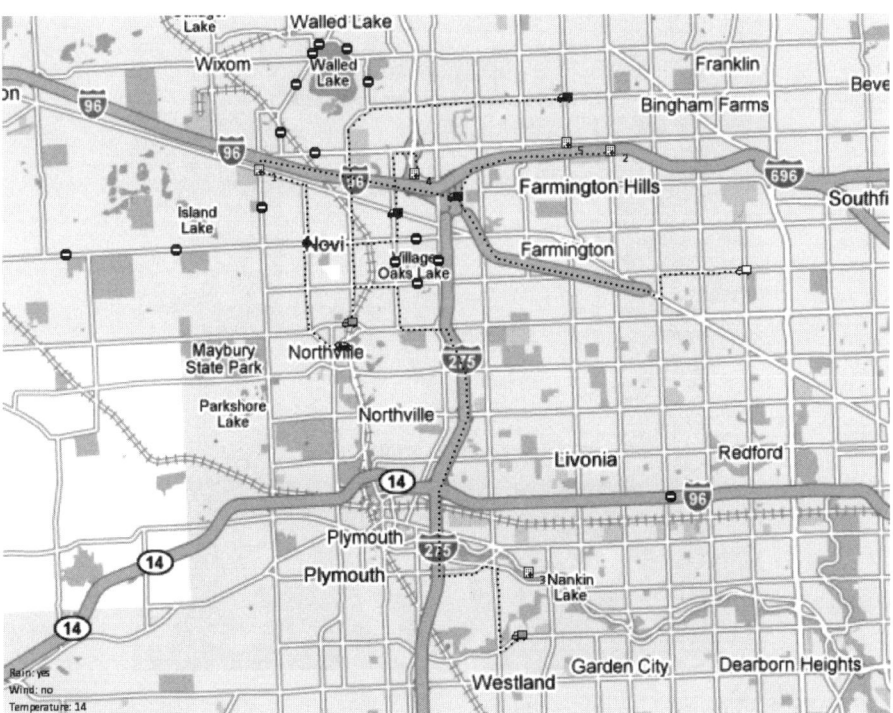

Fig. 5. Example of the solution for the dynamic transportation problem

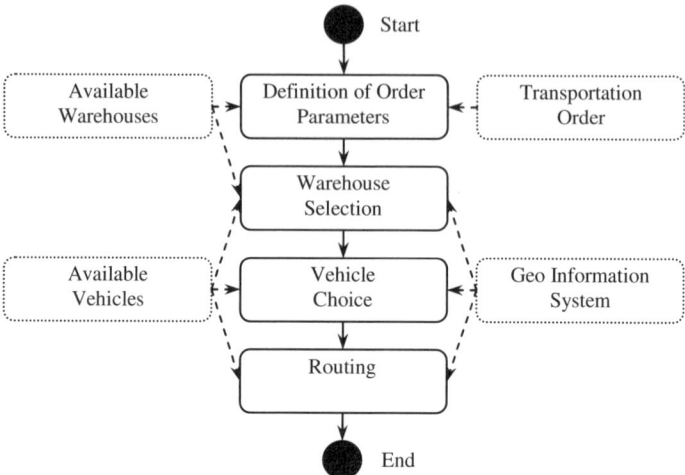

Fig. 6. Sequence of subtasks solving and information sources used

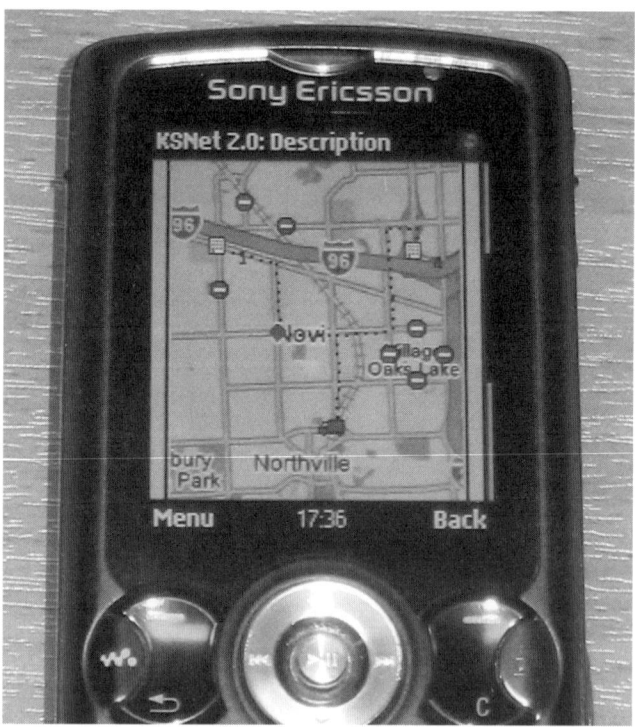

Fig. 7. Example of the vehicle driver assignment on the screen of a mobile phone

An example of generated solution can be seen in Fig. 5.

The problem solving methods have been implemented as a part of a distributed service network. Since information sources are distributed and heterogeneous, Web-services (called wrapper Web-services) have been used for organizing a unified access to them. The proposed architecture makes it possible to use problem solving software modules/services (e.g., the module implementing the described above algorithm) in the same way the sources are used.

Fig. 6 represents a diagram of case study services representing tasks to be solved and information sources used for their solving. Solid rectangles are tasks solved in a sequence. To solve the stated tasks information from heterogeneous sources (dotted rectangles) is used (information flows are indicated by dashed arrows).

The interface of the system is Web-based. This means that regular Web browsers can be used for working with the system. The decision maker can see an interactive map (Fig. 4, Fig. 5) and choose different parameters and criteria for problem solving. The drivers of the vehicles receive their assignments via Internet as well. They can see their routes using PDA or mobile phones (Fig. 7). Presented in the figures example includes 9 containers and 7 vehicles.

4 Conclusions

The paper represents an approach to service-based modeling of business networks. It is proposed that such representation can resolve problems arising from failures of centralized control. Ontologies have been proposed for description of problem domain knowledge. In accordance with the selected model of interoperability, services directly connect and exchange information with one another, but service descriptions (in the paper this is description of the knowledge source content and tasks that can be solved) are mapped to the common shared application ontology. As an example of the approach application the paper presents experience of solving a complex real-life problem from the area of dynamic logistics. The problem considered takes into account continuously changing environment and requires nearly real-time solving.

The further research activities will address development of algorithms for building self-organising service networks and generation and estimation of alternative network configurations. The authors believe that once completed the proposed architecture could efficiently work for a range of the real world problems.

Acknowledgments

The research described in this paper is supported by grants # 06-07-89242 and # 08-07-00264 of the Russian Foundation for Basic Research; projects funded by grants # 16.2.35 of the research program "Mathematical Modelling and Intelligent Systems", and # 1.9 of the research program "Fundamental Basics of Information Technologies and Computer Systems" of the Russian Academy of Sciences (RAS) and project of the scientific program of St.Petersburg Scientific Centre of RAS.

References

1. Gunasekaran, A., Lai, K., Cheng, T.: Responsive supply chain: a competitive strategy in a networked economy. Omega 36, 549–564 (2008)
2. Gunasekaran, A., Ngai, N.: Build-to-order supply chain management: literature review and framework for development. Journal of Operations Management 23(5), 423–451 (2005)
3. Christopher, M., Towill, D.: An integrated model for the design of agile supply chains. International Journal of Physical Distribution and Operations Management 31, 235–244 (2001)
4. Sen, W., Shin, Y.W., Kumar, A., Piplani, R.: Supply chain demand response strategy evaluation and optimization. In: Proceedings of the 2000 IEEE International Conference on Management of Innovation and Technology (ICMIT 2000), vol. 2, pp. 782–787 (2000)
5. SOA: Service-oriented architecture definition (2007),
   `http://www.service-architecture.com/`
   `web-services/articles/service-`
   `oriented_architecture_soa_definition.html`
6. Web Services explained (2007), `http://www.service-architecture.com/`
   `web-services/articles/web_services_explained.html`
7. Semantic Web (2006). Web site, `http://www.semanticweb.org`
8. Foundation for Intelligent Physical Agents (FIPA) Documentation,
   `http://www.fipa.org`
9. Heflin, J., Hendler, J.: Semantic Interoperability on the Web. In: Proceedings of Extreme Markup Languages 2000, pp. 111–120. Graphic Communications Association (2000)
10. Boury-Brisset, A.-C.: Ontology-Based Approach for Information Fusion. In: Proceedings of the Workshop on Ontology and Information Fusion of U.S Army CECOM & the Center for Multisource Information Fusion (2003), `http://www.infofusion.buffalo.`
    `edu/conferences_and_workshops/ontology_wkshop_2/ont_ws2_`
    `working_materials/BouryBrissetOntologyandFusion.PDF`
11. Smirnov, A., Pashkin, M., Chilov, N., Levashova, T.: Knowledge Logistics in Information Grid Environment. International Journal on Future Generation Computer Systems (2004); Zhuge, H. (ed.): The special issue Semantic Grid and Knowledge Grid: The Next-Generation Web, vol. 20(1), pp. 61–79
12. Ruggaber, R.: Interoperability of Enterprise Systems and Applications. Strengthening Competitiveness through Production Networks. In: A perspective from European ICT research projects in the field of Enterprise Networking, pp. 58–70. European Communities (2005)
13. Viana, A.C., Amorim, M.D., Fdida, S., Rezende, J.F.: Self-organization in spontaneous networks: the approach of DHT-based routing protocols. Ad Hoc Networks J., special issue on Data Communications and Topology Control in Ad Hoc Networks 3(5), 589–606 (2005)
14. Hammer, B., Micheli, A., Sperduti, A., Strickert, M.: Recursive self-organizing network models. Neural Networks 17(8-9), 1061–1085 (2004)
15. Nakano, T., Suda, T.: Self-Organizing Network Services with Evolutionary Adaptation. IEEE Transactions on Neural Networks 16(5) (2005)
16. Chandran, R., Hexmoor, H.: Delegation Protocols Founded on Trust. In: KIMAS 2007: Modeling, Exploration, and Engineering (Proceedings of the 2007 International Conference on Integration of Knowledge Intensive Multi-Agent Systems), pp. 328–335. IEEE, Los Alamitos (2007)

17. Baumgarten, M., Bicocchi, N., Curran, K., Mamei, M., Mulvenna, M., Nugent, C., Zam-bonelli, F.: Towards Self-Organizing Knowledge Networks for Smart World Infrastruc-tures. In: Teanfield, H. (ed.) International Transactions on Systems Science and Applica-tions, vol. 2(2), pp. 123–133 (2006) ISSN 1751-1461
18. Smirnov, A., Shilov, N., Kashevnik, A.: Constraint-Driven Negotiation Based on Semantic Interoperability in BTO Production Networks. In: Panetto, H., Boudjlida, N. (eds.) Inter-operability for Enterprise Software and Applications (Proceedings of the Workshops and the Doctoral Symposium of the Second IFAC/IFIP I-ESA International Conference: EI2N, WSI, IS-TSPQ 2006), pp. 175–186. ISTE Ltd. (2006) ISBN-13 978-1-905209-61-3, ISBN-10 1-905209-61-4
19. Dey, A.K., Salber, D., Abowd, G.D.: A Conceptual Framework and a Toolkit for Support-ing the Rapid Prototyping of Context-Aware Applications, Context-Aware Computing. In: Moran, T.P., Dourish, P. (eds.) A Special Triple Issue of Human-Computer Interaction, vol. 16. Lawrence-Erlbaum, Mahwah (2001)
20. Smirnov, A., Pashkin, M., Levashova, T., Chilov, N.: Fusion-Based Knowledge Logistics for Intelligent Decision Support in Network-Centric Environment. George J 34(6), 673–690 (2005)
21. Smirnov, A., Sheremetov, L., Chilov, N., Sanchez-Sanchez, C.: Agent-Based Technologi-cal Framework for Dynamic Configuration of a Cooperative Supply Chain. Multiagent-based supply chain management. In: Chaib-draa, B., Müller, J.P. (eds.) Multiagent-based supply chain management. Series on Studies in Computational Intelligence, vol. 28, pp. 217–246. Springer, Heidelberg (2006)
22. Romero, M., Sheremetov, L., Soriano, A.: A Genetic Algorithm for the Pickup and Deliv-ery Problem: an Application to the Helicopter Offshore Transportation. In: Castillo, O., Melin, P., Montiel-Ross, O., Sepúlveda-Cruz, R., Perdycz, W., Kacprzyk, J. (eds.) Theo-retical Advances and Applications of Fuzzy Logic and Soft Computing, Advances in Soft Computing, vol. 42, pp. 435–444. Springer, Heidelberg (2007)

Quantifying IT Impacts on Organizational Structure and Business Value with Extended Influence Diagrams

Pia Gustafsson, Ulrik Franke, David Höök, and Pontus Johnson

Royal Institute of Technology, Industrial Information and Control Systems,
Osquldas v.12, SE-100 44 Stockholm, Sweden
{piag,ulrikf,davidh,pj101}@ics.kth.se

Abstract. This paper presents a framework for analysis of how IT systems add business value by causally affecting the structure of organizations. The well established theory of organizational behavior developed by Mintzberg combined with more recent research on business value of IT is used to develop a quantitative theoretical framework showing which business values are affected by IT in relation to the organizational structure. This framework, which is based upon a qualitative equivalent developed in an earlier paper, describes relationships in an Extended Influence Diagram for quantified *conditional probability tables* and open up for an empirical appliance. Hence obtained data can be mathematically expressed for more sound assessments. The intention is to create a fully functioning tool for analyses of what kind of IT system should be used by an organization with a given structure to maximize its business value.

Keywords: IT benefits, organizational structure, Mintzberg, business value.

1 Introduction

It has long been discussed in the IT value research area whether IT adds value to an organization or not. Following Brynjolfsson [1], the discussion in the literature increasingly supports the theory that IT can add business value to an organization. For instance, Bergsjö et al [2] have shown that the user satisfaction achieved by functionality, usability, information structure etc. affects the quality, efficiency and innovations of IT users. Researchers (and practitioners) now turn focus to the question of *how* IT adds value to the organization [3]. This problem is approached here by an attempt to combine the traditional theory of organizational structures with more recent research on how aspects of IT affect the structure or the workings of the organization. Dahlgren [4] stresses that organizational structure has a defining role on how information flows within an organization and, as a consequence, how well processes are performed and resources are spent. Other studies of the impact of electronic communication systems on business organizations are Fulk et al., [5], Andersen [6], and Gurbaxani et al. [7].

Traditional organizational theory describes organizations; the behavior of groups of people in them, how strategies and structures influence the groups, how the organizations suit different purposes and how they can be managed to achieve goals. Research on the business value of IT, often within the enterprise architecture research

J. Stirna and A. Persson (Eds.): PoEM 2008, LNBIP 15, pp. 138–152, 2008.

paradigm, tends to focus on the relation between various information systems and business values, not necessarily taking other organizational factors, such as the division of labor, unit size and grouping, training, etc. into account [8]. Our method is directed at the synthesis of traditional theories of organization and management and current research on the business value of IT, as shown in Fig. 1, instead of relating IT to the final business values directly.

Fig. 1. The relationship between IT and business value goes through organizational impact

By including its impact on the organization in the analysis of IT, a more diversified and correct evaluation can be achieved. In [12], a qualitative framework for describing the causal influence of organization and IT on business value is given. In the present article, we aim to make that description quantitative. Using a quantitative, Bayesian, description lets the model be iteratively trained in a non-arbitrary manner as empirical evidence is collected. This enables future research to contribute and be fully integrated into the present framework.

1.1 Outline

The remainder of this paper is structured as follows. Extended influence diagrams used for probabilistic modeling are introduced in section 2, along with the phenomena that are described with the conditional probability tables. Section 3 presents an overview of our use of organizational theory, taxonomy of business values and categorization of IT systems. Section 4 is structured to reflect the organizational theory of Mintzberg [8], but describes in detail the entire causal chain from IT systems, via organization, to business values. The research results are discussed in Section 5 and Section 6 concludes the paper.

2 Related Works

The Influence Diagram approach adopted in the present paper is but one out of several possible formalisms for quantitative Enterprise Architecture analysis. One alternative is Dempster–Shafer theory [9,10]. Dempster–Shafer is designed to represent degrees of belief, something that a pure Bayesian formalism is capable of only to a limited degree. Dempster–Shafer theory, however, cannot represent decisions and goals.

I* (or I-star) is a goal-oriented description framework where actors, their goals and the dependencies between these are modeled [11]. While an I* inspired framweok was used in a previous paper [12], this formalism is unable to deal formally with different kinds uncertainties, and was therefore abandoned in the present paper. Both Dempster–Shafer theory and I* are more thoroughly evaluated against the Bayesian approach in [13]. The notion of leaky probabilistic relationships is described in [14]. The noisy OR-gate was introduced in [15].

Several organizational theories have tried to describe the complexity of organizations from different aspects. The classical organization theory starts with Weber and Fayol presenting the cornerstones of management and bureaucracy. Mintzberg's theories belong to modern structural theories. Later organizational theories are often inspired by adjacent fields, such as system theories [16], ecology [17] and feminist theories [18] but has not yet been able to present a complete theory that describes all areas of the organization.

3 Extended Influence Diagrams

Extended Influence Diagrams (EID) are graphic representations of decision problems coupled with an underlying representation of the conditional probabilities. These diagrams may be used to formally specify enterprise architecture analysis [13]. The diagrams are an extension of influence diagrams, as described by Shachter [16, 20] which in turn are an enhancement of Bayesian networks (cf. Neapolitan [21] and Jensen [22]). In extended influence diagrams, random variables graphically represented as chance nodes may assume values, or states, from a finite domain (cf. Fig. 2). A utility node represents "what is desirable", this could for example be "Organizational performance" as it is in Fig. 2. The utility node could be further described by other nodes that it has a *definitional* relation to. *Causal* relations capture associations of the real world, such as "an automation system affects the process efficiency". In Fig. 2, this is visualized by "Scenario Selection" that causally affects the "Process efficiency" which itself causally affects the "Organizational performance".

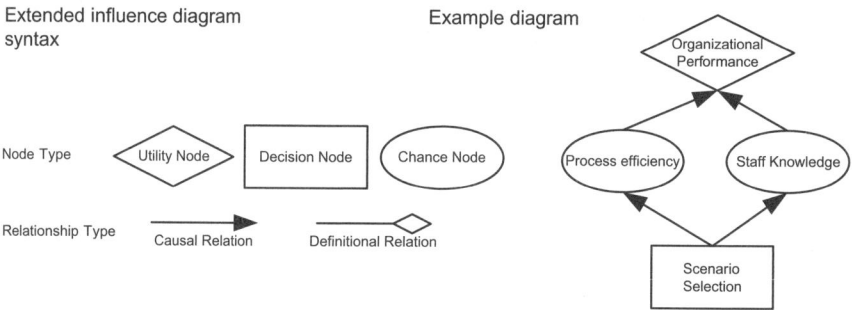

Fig. 2. An extended influence diagram and a simple example

The framework presented here has been developed following the methodology given by Lagerström et al [23]. Extended influence diagrams support probabilistic inference in the same manner as Bayesian networks do; given the value of one node, the values of related nodes can be calculated. With the help of a *conditional probability table* (CPT) for a certain variable *A* and knowledge of the current states of the causally influencing variables *B* and *C*, it is possible to infer the likelihood of node *A* assuming any of its states. With a chosen scenario, the chance nodes will assume different values, thereby influencing the utility node. For more comprehensive treatments on influence diagrams and extended influence diagrams see Johnson et al. [13], Shachter [16, 20], Neapolitan [21], Jensen [22], and Lagerström et al [23].

However powerful a research tool the EID framework is, EID:s cannot be created *ex nihilo*. There exists a lot of research on how to elicit the quantitative estimates of probabilities used to create CPTs, for example Druzdzel et al. [24] and Keeney et al. [25] suggests sources such as; statistical data, literature and human experts to be applied on a network composed of well defined entities (nodes) and relationships covering a properly demarcated domain of interest. The risk of introducing bias into the assessments is of great concern when it comes to these types of sources, specifically when human experts are consulted. By using the formalism of EID:s this can be remedied by taking uncertainty into consideration in the modeling. Keeney et al. acknowledges this in [16] where a formal process of eliciting more rigid probabilistic judgments is outlined.

One important feature is that CPTs can be *updated* in a non-arbitrary fashion, using the well-known learning algorithms of Bayesian networks described for instance by Jensen [22], whenever empirical data is available. Thus, crude conditional probability tables based upon theory only can be fine-tuned as empirical data is collected.

3.1 Parametric CPTs

In [12] the EID formalism was used in a qualitative manner, identifying various relations not given precise CPTs. While allowing for ease and intuition of modeling, this approach is unsuitable for further research and case study validation.

The problem of creating accurate parametric conditional probability distributions is basically a trade-off. On the one hand, (i) there is a need for expressiveness, in the extreme best met by allowing arbitrary distributions satisfying Kolmogorov's axioms. On the other hand, (ii) there is a need for domain specificity, capturing the complex organizational relationships investigated. In particular, three phenomena were taken into account:

1. *Incompleteness.* However thorough a model is, it will inevitably not take all relevant factors into account. A common statistical method to deal with this model incompleteness is to include a "background event"; the conjunction of all factors not explicitly accounted for. This is usually accomplished through "noisy" relations, as described in [22][14][15].
2. *Weighting.* Frequently, the relative importance of different factors influencing a property (such as process specifications and automation systems influencing standardization) can be determined and expressed as weights. This is the lynchpin of the popularly used analytic hierarchy procedure, [26].
3. *Dominance.* Related to weighting is the notion of dominance. If several factors influence a property, they might be ordered in a domination relation, such that if factor A is present, factor B will not affect the outcome, but if factor A is absent, factor B might determine the outcome. A third factor C might determine the outcome if B is absent, etc. This is somewhat similar to the notion of thresholds and squashing functions from artificial neural networks [27].

In the following, we present a number of parametric conditional probability relations that model these phenomena.

Our first relation is the trivial unary relation from A to B, see in Fig. 3 how this is denoted graphically with the incompleteness variable α. By varying the leakage parameter α introduced in Table 1, the incompleteness property is modeled. Weighting and dominance do not exist in this context, of course.

Fig. 3. The unary relation   **Fig. 4.** The weighted leaky relations

Table 1. CPT for unary relation

A		High	Low
B	High	$1-\alpha$	α
	Low	α	$1-\alpha$

As we proceed to consider n-ary relations, however, the need for weighting arises. The weights β introduced in table 2 express the relative weight of factors, such that if A is twice as important as B, then $\beta_A/\beta_B = 2$. The α parameter is retained to express leakage. Thus a leaky weighted sample distribution is created; see Fig. 4 where β is introduced to denote the weighting of the relations.

Table 2. CPT for leaky weighted sample distribution

A		High		Low	
B		High	Low	High	Low
C	High	$\left(\dfrac{\beta_A}{\beta_A+\beta_B}+\dfrac{\beta_B}{\beta_A+\beta_B}\right)-\alpha \equiv$ $\equiv 1-\alpha$	$\left(\dfrac{\beta_A}{\beta_A+\beta_B}\right)-\alpha$	$\left(\dfrac{\beta_B}{\beta_A+\beta_B}\right)+\alpha$	α
	Low	α	$\left(\dfrac{\beta_B}{\beta_A+\beta_B}\right)+\alpha$	$\left(\dfrac{\beta_A}{\beta_A+\beta_B}\right)-\alpha$	$\left(\dfrac{\beta_A}{\beta_A+\beta_B}+\dfrac{\beta_B}{\beta_A+\beta_B}\right)-\alpha \equiv$ $\equiv 1-\alpha$

It should be clear how this distribution is modified for arities greater than 2.

Weighting, however, cannot express the dominance effect, see Fig. 5 where the dominance factors γ are introduced. To cope with this matter, we introduce the distribution of table 3.

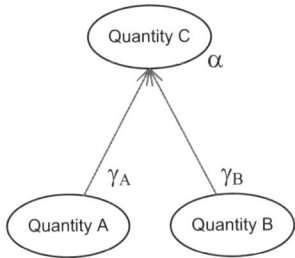

Fig. 5. The leaky dominant relation

Table 3. CPT for leaky dominance relation

A		High				Low			
B		High		Low		High		Low	
C		High	Low	High	Low	High	Low	High	Low
D	High	$1-\gamma_A-\alpha$	$1-\gamma_A-\alpha$	$1-\gamma_A-\alpha$	$1-\gamma_A-\alpha$	$1-\gamma_B-\alpha$	$1-\gamma_B-\alpha$	$1-\gamma_C-\alpha$	0
	Low	$\gamma_A+\alpha$	$\gamma_A+\alpha$	$\gamma_A+\alpha$	$\gamma_A+\alpha$	$\gamma_B+\alpha$	$\gamma_B+\alpha$	$\gamma_C+\alpha$	1

The leaky dominance relation CPT is easily constructed. First, a dominance ordering between the quantities involved is established, e.g. A dominates B, B dominates C. Then, whenever A is high, the probability of D being high is set to $1-\gamma_A-\alpha$. When A is low, B is the dominant factor, and whenever B is high, the probability of D being high is set to $1-\gamma_B-\alpha$. When neither A nor B is high, C is the dominant factor, and the probability of D being high is set to $1-\gamma_C-\alpha$. If none of A, B, and C is high, the probability of D being high is (deterministically) set to 0.

It should be noted, however, that even though the rationale for the dominance relation is to express dominance and saturation phenomena, it has other uses. For instance, by setting all the γ parameters small and equal, a leaky OR-relation is achieved. Sometimes, this is useful.

4 Combining Organizational Theory, IT and Business Values

Business value is a debated subject within the domain's research literature. Several ways to categorize possible IT benefits, differing in scope and granularity, have been suggested. In this work, the categorization of business value dimensions suggested by Gammelgård et al. [28] is used to map the business value to the factors Mintzberg describes [8] to common IT business value categories. The categorization Gammelgård proposes is based on a literature study combining more than 650 business value dimensions from 200 different sources.

Since the research focus here is the organization, only a subset of those IT benefits classified by [28], viz. those related to the organizational structure and the resources within the company were related to the Mintzberg theories. By using a familiar vocabulary the work in this paper can be related to other, previously conducted research within the domain of business value. The business values relevant to this paper are flexibility, efficiency, effectiveness, integration and coordination, decision making, control and follow up and organizational culture. For practical use of the framework, the business values should be weighted against each other to represent the business needs. These business values are visualized in Fig. 6.

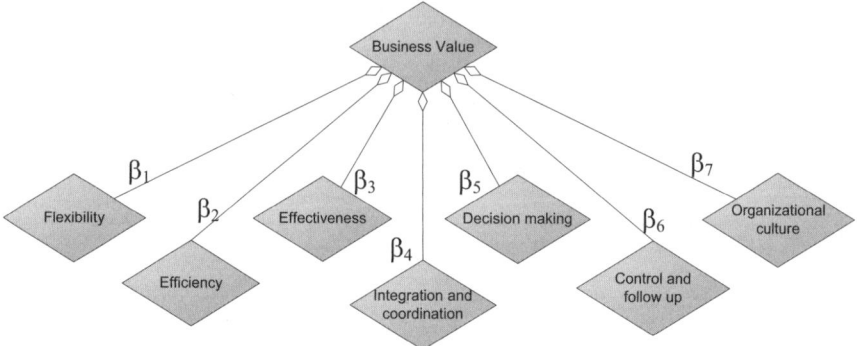

Fig. 6. The business values organizational structure affect, based on Gammelgård et al. [28]

Henry Mintzberg [8] proposes a theory of organization that is now classic within the field. Based upon a synthesis of the literature, Mintzberg attempts to model the form and functioning of organizations by structuring those external and internal factors. Mintzberg's theory is used because it allows for an organization wide view of IT benefits. Furthermore it is readily employed in the research where organizational theories are to be cross fertilized with other associated domains, e.g. in Farbey et. al. [29] it is used to analyze organizational structures and their impact on an IT project.

Focus in this paper is on the internal factors, the design parameters, i.e. those factors that can be consciously affected by management decisions.

Mintzberg [8] presents the following design areas; (i) design of positions, (ii) design of superstructure and (iii) design of lateral linkages. Since the areas are applicable for all organizations, no business specific views can be included in the analysis, such as degree of functional fit. These are the fundamental building blocks that in an overarching manner form the constructed EID. These design areas are further described in chapter 4.

Several concepts used in the literature do not express a clear causality chain, but implies that most concepts are related to each other, sometimes in circular causality. To avoid circular causality chains, and to minimize the complexity of calculations, a small subset of Mintzberg's relations is excluded. The relations that have been excluded are those where no direct causality between two concepts could be identified.

After identifying areas where IT can complement and support the organization, two main system types have been discerned; IT systems that enable communication (vertically and horizontally) between organizational units, and systems that control the processes; either completely (through automation) or partially (through directing the work flow). Hence, we propose the following taxonomy of IT systems, based on the function they fulfill:

1. **Horizontal communication.** This applies to the communication among peers, for example in a project group using a collaboration system. Bidirectional communication is a distinguishing feature.
2. **Vertical communication.** This includes both the upward stream of data that generates decision support for top and middle management (aggregation of information) and the downward stream of data that directs the work of subordinates (dissemination of orders). The unidirectional (either way) communication is a distinguishing feature.
3. **Work flow.** This is the class of systems that standardize work behavior by forcing the user to do things in a certain order or by a certain procedure. This is a semi-automated form of manual labor, where the actual work is still performed by a human, but the process is coordinated by a machine.
4. **Automation.** This represents a further step, as compared to work flow. Work is now fully automatic, performed by a machine. The human operator performs only supervisory tasks.

Below in Fig. 7 the full EID, taking the business values, organizational aspects as well as IT-systems into consideration, is depicted.

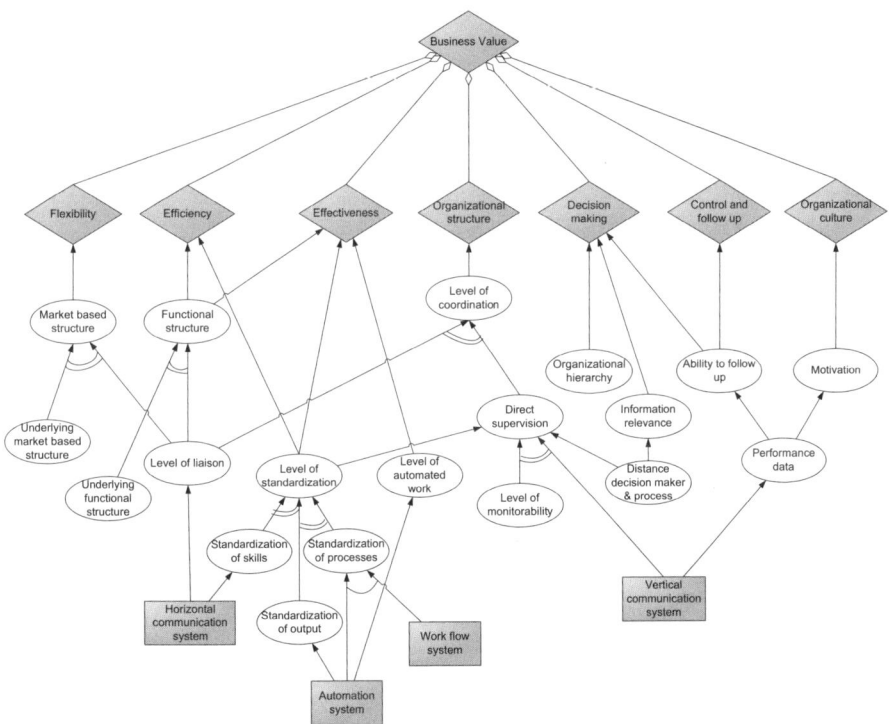

Fig. 7. An EID combining the business values, organizational variables and IT systems

5 Organizational Theory

We purport to describe the entire causal chain from decision variables in the form of IT systems, via a probabilistically modeled organizational structure to the business values sought. Following Mintzberg, this description is split into (i) design of positions, (ii) design of superstructure, and (iii) design of lateral linkages.

5.1 Design of Positions

As defined by Mintzberg, the design of positions within an organization determines (i) the level of specialization of work tasks, (ii) the formalization of behavior, and (iii) the training and indoctrination of workers.

Work can be *specialized* both horizontally and vertically. The horizontal specialization separates work tasks that are of different character from each other. Horizontal specialization is used to increase productivity by streamlining work tasks and lowering switching costs between different tasks. Vertical specialization, on the other hand, is defined as separating "the performance of the work from the administration of it" [8]. The level of horizontally specialized work, in the form of automation, is modeled as one of several factors supporting effectiveness in Fig. 8.

This aspect of specialization clearly connects to the business values of effectiveness and efficiency. Roughly, horizontal specialization increases effectiveness, while vertical specialization increases efficiency. As depicted in Fig. 8, however, the dependencies actually modeled are more complex.

An organization can formalize the behavior of the workers through standardization of the output of the processes or by regulating the work flows. The organization could also use formalization by rules, regulating the limits of the work. This is reflected in Fig. 8

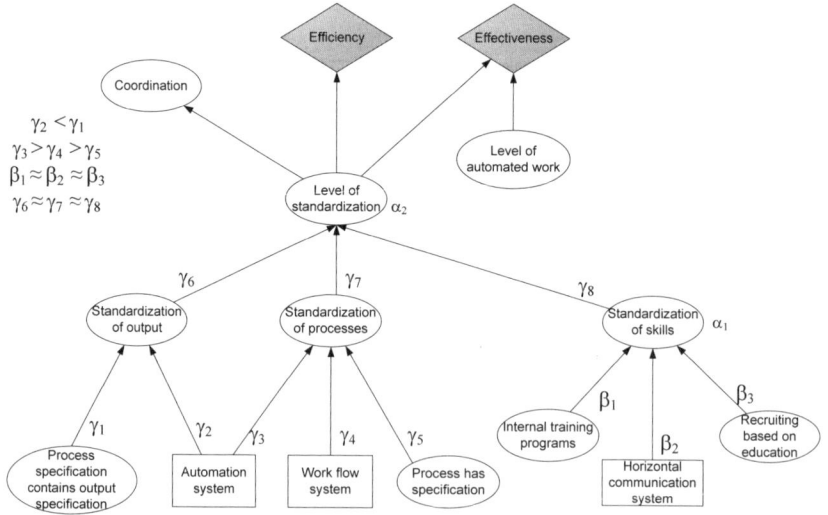

Fig. 8. An EID describing relations between quantities related to design of positions

where a certain overall level of standardization can be achieved either through the standardization of skills, standardization of processes, or through standardization of output. Mintzberg does not make any distinction between the three ways of achieving a high level of standardization, which leads to dominance factors of the same size.

Discussing the standardization of skills, Mintzberg makes the distinction between training and indoctrination. Training refers to the learning of job related skills and knowledge, while indoctrination refers to the internalization of organizational norms. Mintzberg suggests that training and indoctrinations are substitutes: most organizations put more emphasis on either the one or the other. In Fig. 8, these aspects are modeled by having internal training programs and recruiting based on relevant education influence the standardization of skills. A third aspect can make skills more standardized, and that is an IT system that horizontally can spread knowledge. These three aspects are of equal weight, but to achieve full standardization of skills, all of these strategies must be used.

Standardization of output can be achieved either by having a process specification describing the output in detail or if the process itself creates a standardized output, as it will if it is automated by an automation system. An automation system is the most dominant factor here. This is visualized in Fig. 8.

Standardization of processes follows the same argument as standardization of output; a specification for the process affects the standardization, while the automation of the process is the most dominant aspect. If the process is supported by an IT system with work flow functionality, this will also enhance the standardization of the process.

5.2 Design of Superstructure

The superstructure of an organization describes the highest level of its organization diagram; the grouping and size of the constituent units.

Two major types of organizational grouping can be distinguished; viz. (i) grouping by function and (ii) market based grouping. Now, functional grouping is more common when there are significant interdependencies of process and scale, and where standardization works well. Functional grouping allows the functions (e.g. marketing, production, and sales) to develop their very own specialized and streamlined procedures, to benefit as much as possible from the division of labor. Market based grouping, on the other hand, is more common when there are significant interdependencies of workflow, and where standardization works poorly. Market based grouping puts emphasis on processes and work flow, trading cross-functional integration for less specialization. The well-known matrix organization attempts to combine the desirable features of both types of grouping. Such co-existing structure is the rationale for the modeling of Fig. 9, where the market based and functional structures are each separated into (i) an underlying structure and (ii) a resulting, observable, structure. While the model allows at most one of the *underlying* structures to exist at a given time, the other one can get its state raised through the level of liaison. Thus, a high level of liaison will raise the value assigned to the structure not assumed by the underlying structure, i.e. the underlying structure is more dominant then the level of liaison. If both Market based and Functional structures assume high values we have a matrix organization. Roughly, market based grouping leads to higher efficiency while functional grouping leads to higher effectiveness and flexibility. The connection to these business values is modeled by the causal relations in Fig. 9.

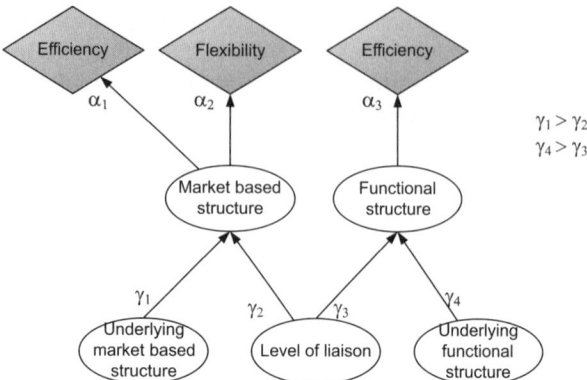

Fig. 9. An EID describing relations between quantities related to the design of superstructure

Mintzberg distinguishes three different basic means of achieving coordination: (i) mutual adjustment, (ii) direct supervision, and (iii) standardization. This is reflected by the weighted relations between these concepts with respect to coordination, as illustrated in Fig. 10. Coordination supports the business value of having a favorable organizational structure. By what means coordination supports the organizational structure is determined by the state of the coordination node.

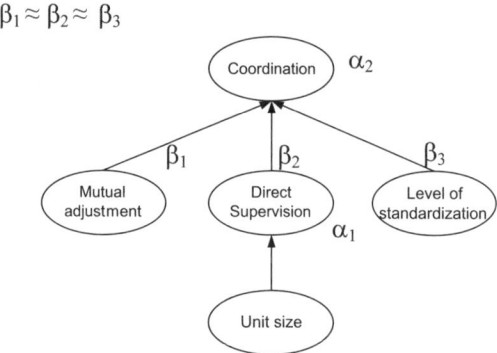

Fig. 10. An EID describing relations between quantities related to coordination

The next parameter relevant to organizational superstructure is the size of units. According to Mintzberg, the primary factor governing feasible unit sizes is the mechanism of coordination employed by the organization. Whenever standardization is used as a means of coordination, the need for supervision decreases and the ability of a single manager to keep track of a larger group of subordinates increases. If direct supervision is used, on the other hand, group sizes cannot grow very large, as is reflected in Fig. 10 where unit size has a unary relation to the level of direct supervision. Mutual adjustment, direct supervision and level of standardization are of equally weights with respect to coordination.

5.3 Design of Lateral Linkages

Two sorts of lateral linkages within an organization are discussed by Mintzberg; (i) liaison devices and (ii) planning and control systems.

Liaison devices, that interconnect distant parts of an organization, are common in modern organizational structures. Their basic rationale is the coordination of complex, interdependent activities. Mintzberg identifies a number of liaison devices that characterizes the spectrum between a purely functional and a purely market oriented organization. Using (i) liaison officers, (ii) task forces or standing committees, and (iii) integrating managers, functional and market based organizations can be blended. The most radical liaison measure is the introduction of the matrix organization, which fully does away with unity of command. All these measures are reflected in Fig. 11, together with the existence of a horizontal communication system which is of a significantly larger weight then the other factors. Performance control is a tool for management to measure the results of a unit, but also a tool that gives feedback to the unit. Some such qualities, taken from Mintzberg, are reflected in Fig. 11, where they are connected to the business values of decision making, control and follow up and organizational culture. The two first are intuitive, and the third business value is achieved through higher motivation of employees who get feedback on how well they meet goals according to Mintzberg [8].

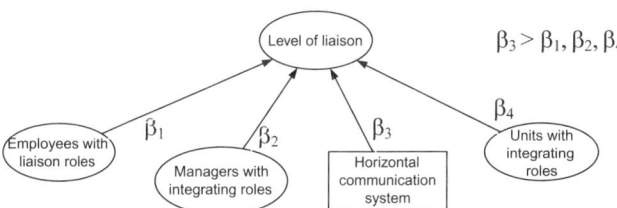

Fig. 11. An EID describing relations between quantities related to level of liaison

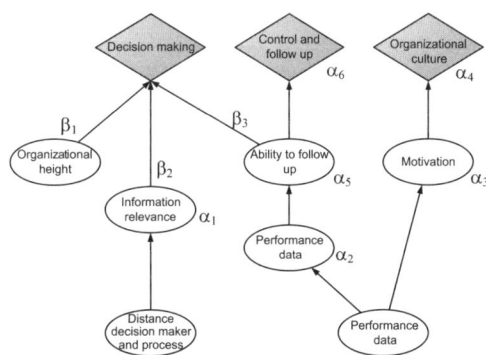

Fig. 12. An EID describing relations between quantities related to planning and control

The hierarchy of the organization is here described as the relation between number of levels, and maximum number of divisions in organigram, i.e. the relation between its height and width. If the ratio is more than one the hierarchy is set to High, otherwise the value is set as Low. This since Mintzberg claims that an organization profits more when it comes to Decision making if the organizational formation is wide [8].

6 Discussion

This paper presents a framework for assessing how IT affects organizations and thus creates business value. The framework is expressed in a quantitative manner to form a foundation for empirical studies. The CPTs in the paper are, at the present state, subjectively defined by the authors as a reflection of our interpretation of Mintzberg's organizational theory. However, the use of Bayesian networks allows the CPTs to be *updated* in a non-arbitrary fashion, using well known learning algorithms. Therefore, case studies and other empirical work can be readily integrated into the framework, thus converging on an ever more precise representation of reality.

Following the quantification given in the present paper, some future directions on the road towards a fully applicable tool for business value assessments can be given. One important goal is the construction of an abstract model/meta-model from which concrete and empirical instantiations can be formed. Furthermore, attention should be drawn to the scales on which empirical data is measured. The latter of these tasks can be seen as implied by the former, i.e. in order to form a domain-specific instantiation the scales have to be considered explicitly. It should be clear, for instance, that the percentage of processes regulated by documents might affect the corresponding business values differently depending on the sort of business conducted within the studied organization.

7 Conclusions

We have seen that the business values of IT can be derived through analysis of the impact IT has on an organization. Using the qualitative framework from [12] as a foundation a quantitative equivalent was constructed by means of defining conditional probability tables, CPTs for all nodes having one or more parent nodes. Three important modeling aspects were identified and expressed in the form of CPTs; incompleteness, weighting and dominance.

By modeling the impact IT has on business value through its organizational impact using Extended Influence Diagrams we have created a platform for quantitative assessments of business value, i.e. the platform enables an investigator to be presented a discrete value on a predefined scale representing the organization's overall fulfillment of the modeled business values. Now, having developed a quantified version of the framework we are one step closer to a complete assessment tool for business value studies. The quantification enables that the framework now can be employed empirically, which in turns enables trimming of the determined CPTs through Bayesian learning algorithms.

References

1. Brynjolfsson, B.: The Productivity Paradox of Information Technology. Communications of the ACM 36(1), 67–77 (1993)
2. Bergsjö, D., Malvius, D.: A Model to Evaluate Efficiency, Quality, and Innovation through User Satisfaction with Information Management Systems. In: Proceedings of CSER 2007, Hoboken, March 14-16 (2007)
3. Sneller, L., Bots, J.: A Review of Quantitative IT Value Research. Nyenrode Business University, The Netherlands (2006)
4. Dahlgren, J.: Real options and Flexibility in Organizational Design. In: Proceedings of CSER 2007, Hoboken, March 14 -16 (2007)
5. Fulk, J., DeSanctis, G.: Electronic Communication and Changing Organizational Forms. Organization Science 6(4), 337–349 (1995)
6. Andersen, T.J.: Information technology, strategic decision making approaches and organizational performance in different industrial settings. The Journal of Strategic Information Systems 10(2), 101–119 (2001)
7. Gurbaxani, V., Whang, S.: The impact of information systems on organizations and markets. Communications of the ACM 34(1), 59–73 (1991)
8. Mintzberg, H.: The Structuring of Organizations. Prentice-Hall, Upper Saddle River (1979)
9. Shafer, G.: A mathematical theory of evidence. Princeton University Press, Princeton (1976)
10. Yang, J.-B.: Rule and utility based evidential reasoning approach for multiattribute decision analysis under uncertainties. European Journal of Operational Research 133, 31–61 (2001)
11. Yu, E.S.K., Mylopoulos, J., Lesp, Y.: Ai models for business process reengineering. IEEE Expert: Intelligent Systems and Their Applications 11(4), 16–23 (1996)
12. Gustafsson, P., Franke, U., Johnson, P., Lilliesköld, J.: Identifying IT impacts on organizational structure and business value. In: Proceedings of the Third International Workshop on Business/IT Alignment and Interoperability, pp. 44–57 (2008)
13. Johnson, P., Lagerström, R., Närman, P., Simonsson, M.: Enterprise Architecture Analysis with Extended Influence Diagrams. Information System Frontiers 9(2-3), 163–180 (2007)
14. Henrion, M.. Some practical issues in constructing belief networks. In: Kanal, L.N., Levitt, T.S., Lemmer, J.F. (eds.) Uncertainty in Artificial Intelligence, vol. 3, pp. 161–173. Elsevier Science Publishers B.V., North Holland (1989)
15. Pearl, J.: Fusion, propagation and structuring in belief networks. Artificial Intelligence 29, 241–288 (1986)
16. Katz, D., Kahn, R.: Organizations and the system concept - Classics of Organization Theory, Thomson Learning (1966)
17. Hannan, M.T., Freeman, J.: The Population Ecology of Organizations - American Journal of Sociology. Chicago Press (1977)
18. Martin, J.: Deconstructing organizational taboos: The suppression of gender conflict in organizations. Organization Science 1, 339–359 (1990)
19. Shachter, R.: Evaluating influence diagrams. Operations Research Institute for Operations Research and the Management Sciences 34(6), 871–882 (1986)
20. Shachter, R.: Probabilistic inference and influence diagrams. Operations Research 36(4), 36–40 (1988)
21. Neapolitan, R.: Learning Bayesian Networks. Prentice-Hall, Inc., Upper Saddle River (2003)

22. Jensen, F.V.: Bayesian Networks and Decision Graphs. Springer, New York (2001)
23. Lagerström, R., Johnson, P., Närman, P.: Extended Influence Diagram Generation. In: Enterprise Interoperability II – New Challenges and Approaches, pp. 599–602. Springer, London (2007)
24. Druzdzel, M., van der Gaag, L.: Building probabilistic networks: Where do the numbers come from? IEEE Transactions on knowledge and data engineering 12(4), 289–299 (2000)
25. Keeney, R., von Winterfeldt, D.: Eliciting Probabilities from Experts in Complex Technical Problems. IEEE Transactions on engineering management 38(3), 191–201 (1991)
26. Saaty, T.L.: Axiomatic Foundation of the Analytic Hierarchy Process. Management Science 32(7), 841–855 (1986)
27. Laurene, V.: Fausett, Fundamentals of Neural Networks. Prentice Hall, Englewood Cliffs (1994)
28. Gammelgård, M., Ekstedt, M., Gustafsson, P.: A Categorization of Benefits From IS/IT Investments. In: Proceedings of the 13th European Conference on Information Technology Evaluation, ECITE (2006)
29. Farbey, B., Land, F., Targett, D.: How to assess your IT investment: A study of methods and practice. Butterworth-Heineman Ltd., Oxford (1993)

Enterprise Modelling for Value Based Service Analysis

Paul Johannesson[1], Birger Andersson[1], Maria Bergholtz[1], and Hans Weigand[2]

[1] Royal Institute of Technology
Department of Computer and Systems Sciences, Sweden
{pajo,ba,maria}@dsv.su.se
[2] Tilburg University, P.O. Box 90153, 5000 LE Tilburg, The Netherlands
H.Weigand@uvt.nl

Abstract. Service oriented architectures are becoming increasingly important as enablers of exchange, coordination, and cooperation between organizations and individuals. Engineering and management of services raise a number of issues concerning the analysis, design, integration, bundling, and maintenance of services. These issues are notoriously difficult to resolve due to the abstractness of services as compared to other kinds of resources. In this paper, we analyze the concept of service based on a number of definitions from the literature and propose a conceptual service model based on the REA ontology. The model relates the service notion to the resource concept and shows how the abstractions offered by services can be represented using an encapsulation relationship. The use of the proposed service model is illustrated by means of an application on marketing oriented representation and design of services.

1 Introduction

Enterprise Modelling is the practice of describing a business enterprise with the dual purposes of maintaining a fit between on the one hand, the enterprise and its IT resources, and on the other hand, the enterprise and its business context. To maintain the fit between the enterprise and its business context methods and frameworks have been developed that typically include notions such as goals, means, and strategies, e.g., [1, 2, 3]. To maintain the fit between the enterprise and its IT resources, a rich body of research stretching from the 80's and onwards is available. This research has mainly focused on information and information systems modelling, together with related methodologies, and on enterprise architectures, e.g., [4, 5, 6].

In recent years the notion of "service" has gained in interest. It was originally conceived as a convenient abstraction for thinking about legacy and other IT-resources within an enterprise, but its scope has widened [7]. According to [8] service science refers to the modeling of service systems and their life cycles ranging from business components and business models to value networks of businesses linked globally. Service engineering is about the design, development, deployment, operations and maintenance of service systems based on IT, knowledge workers and outsourced business components.

The service abstraction has proved useful for the purpose of modelling IT resources of an enterprise, but is, in the context of enterprise modeling, not as commonly used as a

J. Stirna and A. Persson (Eds.): PoEM 2008, LNBIP 15, pp. 153–167, 2008.

business concept. One reason may be the vagueness and abstractness of the concept of service, stemming from many differing and conflicting definitions [9, 10, 11, 12, 13, 14, 15]. Common is that the concept of service is defined from a technical standpoint and then often in SOA terms [16, 17]. We agree with [8, 18] in that the technical standpoint is but one aspect of the concept, and when discussing collaborations leading to resource distribution among economic agents we claim it is not even the most important one. In this context, the concept of service should be explained in social and economic terms.

We believe that enterprise modeling can be an effective instrument for clarifying the service concept and the main purpose of this paper is to propose a conceptual service model. The starting point of this model is not software services, but services that provide value to customers at the business level and that can be offered in an economically viable way. We, therefore, use value oriented notions as the basis of the service model, in particular the REA ontology. Furthermore, we illustrate the use of the proposed service model by showing how it can be applied for describing and designing services from a marketing oriented perspective. The benefit of this work is that services are explained and justified in terms of marketing notions, such as needs, benefits, and transfers of value. Those are notions that are closely aligned with the concepts of business collaborations, and service models of such collaborations become more stable as a result.

The remainder of this paper is structured as follows. In section 2, we recapture the REA ontology that we use in section 3 to ground a conceptual service model. In section 4, we apply and elaborate this service model by showing how it can be used to describe and design services from a marketing perspective; for instance, how do we conceptualize needs and wants? Section 5 provides conclusions and directions for future research.

2 The REA Ontology

The Resource-Event-Agent (REA) ontology was formulated originally in [19] and has been developed further, e.g. [13, 20, 21]. Its conceptual origins can be traced back to traditional business accounting. REA was originally intended as a basis for accounting information systems and focused on representing increases and decreases of value in an organization. REA has been extended to form a foundation for enterprise information systems architectures [21], and it has also been applied to e-commerce frameworks [13].

The following outline of core REA concepts is slightly adapted by adopting some concepts from [21] and [22] that are further emphasized in [23] and [24]. The main adoption is in the usage of rights. When in the following we say that resources are transferred between agents, we mean that different kinds of rights on resources are transferred. We stick to the conventional value modeling terminology while keeping in mind that by this adoption it is more correct to say that value models capture the distribution of rights among agents.

2.1 Resources

The core concepts of the REA ontology are Resource, Event, and Agent (also referred to as Economic Resource, Economic Event and Economic Agent), see Fig. 1. A resource is an object that is viewed as being valuable by some agent. Some concrete

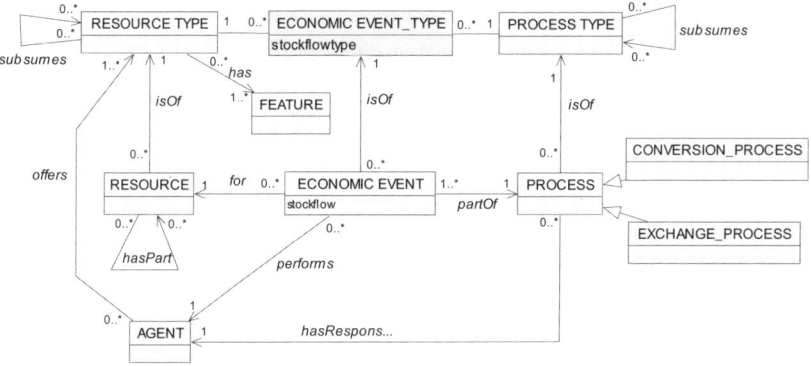

Fig. 1. REA ontology core concepts

examples of resources are books, cars, movies, hair cuts, and medical treatments. However, resources can also be of a more psychological and social nature, such as status, beauty, pleasure, health state, honor, and feeling of safety. To distinguish between these different kinds of resources, we identify two categories of resources, economic resources and internal resources. Intuitively, an *economic resource* is a resource that can be transferred. More precisely, an economic resource is a resource that can be under the control of an agent, in the sense that the agent may have legal rights on the resource. Analyzing economic resources, we have identified the following categories:

- *Goods*, which are physical objects, like cars, refrigerators, and cell phones.
- *Information*, which is data in a certain context, like blueprints, referrals, and customer databases.
- *Labor*, which is physical or intellectual work done by people.
- *Services*, which are economic resources that encapsulate other resources and are used for changing, in some respect, another resource. Examples of services are hair cuts and eye treatments.
- *Vouchers*, which are certificates that can be exchanged for other specific economic resources, e.g. a good or a service. Usually, a voucher can be exchanged only at some pre-specified agent(s). Money can be viewed as the most general form of voucher without any restriction on economic resources and agents.

In addition to economic resources, there are also *internal resources* that cannot be directly transferred between agents. An internal resource is defined as a resource that is not an economic resource. Some straight-forward examples of internal resources are beauty, health state, honor, and glory. It is not meaningful to talk about legal rights on these resources, neither is it possible to transfer any of these resources from one agent to another. Another example of an internal resource is knowledge. At first sight, it might seem that knowledge is possible to transfer from one agent to another. However, knowledge itself cannot be transferred, but only the information that may be used for producing knowledge, e.g. in the form of a book or a lecture. Resources are often desired by people for their own sake, e.g. someone might desire more knowledge without any intention to use it in a particular way. However, someone else might desire knowledge in order to make money through lecturing or other knowledge services, i.e. she uses knowledge as an instrument for producing some other resource. Thus, internal resources can be seen both as ends in themselves and as instruments for other purposes. Economic resources, on the other hand, are only valuable as instruments for producing other resources.

A resource may have properties and associations to other objects, like the nutritional content of a pizza or the number of shops accepting a credit card. Such properties and associations are modeled by means of the class *Feature* [21].

When modeling resources, there is often a need to distinguish between a class *Resource* and a class *ResourceType*, see Fig. 1. A resource type is the abstract classification or definition of a resource. An example of a resource type could be a car model, such as "Volvo V70", while a resource is a specific, concrete car, which can be classified as being of the resource type "Volvo V70". This distinction between two model levels is relevant not only for resources but also for practically any phenomena [25]. The lower level, often called the operational level, models concrete, tangible individuals in a domain. The upper level, often called the knowledge level, models information structures that characterize categories of individuals at the operational level. The Resource type may furthermore model resources on different levels of abstraction and in fig. 1 the relationship between resource types on different levels is captured by means of the association *subsumes*.

2.2 Economic Events and Conversion Processes

As stated in the previous section, resources can be used as instruments to produce or modify other resources. A process that uses some input resources to produce new or modify existing resources is called a conversion process, [Hru06], see the class *ConversionProcess* in Fig. 1. For example, water and flour can be used as input economic resources in a baking conversion process to produce the output economic resource bread. Another example is an eye treatment (input economic resource) that is used to improve the health state (output internal resource) of a patient. In some cases, a conversion process produces a brand new resource (bread), while in other cases the conversion process modifies an existing resource (health state). In other words, a conversion process can have two different results: a new resource or a modified resource. A conversion process consists of atomic actions called economic events, where each economic event either consumes, uses or produces a resource.

2.3 Economic Events and Exchange Processes

An exchange process takes place when two agents exchange resources. To acquire a resource an agent has to give up some other resource. For example, in a goods purchase a buying agent has to give up money in order to receive some goods. The amount of money available to the agent is decreased, while the amount of goods is increased. Conceptually, two economic events are taking place in this exchange process: one where the amount of money is decreased and another where the amount of goods is increased. This combination of economic events is called a duality and is an expression of economic reciprocity – an economic event increasing some resource is always accompanied by an economic event decreasing another resource. A corresponding change of availability of resources takes place at the seller's side. Here the amount of money is increased, while the amount of goods is decreased.

2.4 Processes

A conversion process consists of economic events that change the features of resources, while an exchange process consists of economic events that change the rights agents hold on resources. However, conversion processes and exchange processes are similar in the sense that they both consist of economic events that increase or decrease the value of resources for an agent. Thus, we generalize *ConversionProcess* and *ExchangeProcess* into *Process*, as shown in Fig. 1. Following [21], we introduce a *stockflow* attribute on *EconomicEvent* that shows how the economic event affects a resource; there are five possible stockflows:

- *take* - the economic event results in an increase of the value of some resource within an exchange process
- *give* - the economic event results in a decrease of the value of some resource within an exchange process
- *produce* - the economic event results in an increase of the value of some resource within a conversion process
- *use* - the economic event results in a decrease of the value of some resource within a conversion process
- *consume* - the economic event results in the consumption of some resource within a conversion process

While the take, give, and produce stockflows are straight-forward to understand, the use and consume stockflows may seem difficult to distinguish as both decrease the value of resources. The difference is that a resource subject to use remains after its use and can be reused, while a resource subject to consumption ceases to exist after its consumption.

Just as for resources, we distinguish between an operational and a knowledge level for processes. In a conversion process, concrete resources are used or consumed to produce or modify other resources, while a conversion process type specifies requirements on resource types that play the roles of inputs and outputs. Furthermore, there is an association *subsumes* on process types, analogous to the corresponding one on resource types.

2.5 Agent

Finishing off this outline of core REA concepts, an *Agent* is an individual or organization capable of having control over economic resources, and transferring or receiving the control to or from other individuals or organizations [26].

3 A Conceptual Service Model

In this section, we analyze the notion of a service starting from a number of definitions and characterizations in the literature of business administration, software engineering and service science and engineering. We then identify a number of salient features of services and show how they can be understood and represented using the REA ontology.

There are many definitions of the term "service" in the literature, some representatives being:

W3C: "A service is an abstract resource that represents a capability of performing tasks that represents a coherent functionality from the point of view of provider entities and requester entities. To be used, a service must be realized by a concrete provider agent. A Web service is a software system designed to support interoperable machine-to-machine interaction over a network. It has an interface described in a machine-processable format (specifically WSDL)." [14].

OASIS: "A service is a mechanism to enable access to one or more capabilities, where the access is provided using a prescribed interface and is exercised consistent with constraints and policies as specified by the service description." [11].

WSMO: "A service in contrast is the actual value provided by this invocation. Thereby a Web service might provide different services, such as for example Amazon can be used for acquiring books as well as to find out an ISBN number of a book. A WSMO Web service is a computational entity which is able (by invocation) to achieve a users goal." [15].

Preist: "A service is the provision of something of value, in the context of some domain of application, by one party to another. We need to distinguish between a particular provision of value from the general capability to provide. We refer to the former as a concrete service, and the latter as an abstract service. Hence an abstract service is defined as the capacity to perform something of value, in the context of some domain of application. An agreed service is an abstract service agreed between two parties." [12].

Lusch: "In S-D logic, service is defined as the application of specialized competences (knowledge and skills) for the benefit of another entity, rather than the production of units of output. These benefits are always manifested in the context of the customer, rather than in the production of its offering by the provider. The contextual perspective suggests that what firms provide should not be understood in terms of outputs with value, but rather as resource inputs for a continuing value-creation process." [10].

UN: "Services are heterogeneous outputs produced to order and typically consist of changes in the conditions of the consuming units realized by the activities of producers at the demand of the consumers." [13].

In these definitions, a common view is that a service is an abstraction of activities that once started will achieve some user goal. However, the exact way of defining a service depends on the perspective of a particular source. For example, Preist, UN, and OASIS focus on a business service perspective, while W3C and WSMO have a web (or software) service perspective.

Drawing on an extensive literature study, [27] argues that there are four main characteristics of services: intangibility, inseparability, heterogeneity, and perishability. Intangibility means that services cannot be seen, felt, or touched in the same concrete way as goods can be sensed. Intangibility is often seen as the critical difference between goods and services from which all other differences emerge, [28]. Inseparability is the simultaneous production and consumption of goods. "Whereas goods are first produced, then sold and then consumed, services are first sold, then produced and consumed simultaneously", [27]. Heterogeneity is about the high variability in the performance of services. The quality of a service may vary from provider to provider, from customer to customer, and from time to time. Heterogeneity, however, can also be observed in the production of certain goods and information, such as handicraft objects and newspaper articles. Perishability means that services cannot be saved. If an airline seat is unoccupied, it cannot be saved for future use. However, many kinds of goods are also perishable, such as fresh food.

Based on the above definitions and descriptions of services, it is possible to identify five salient characteristics of services:

1. A service is a resource since it is an object that is considered valuable by agents and that can be transferred from one agent to another.
2. A service is always provided by one agent for the benefit of another agent. An agent will never provide a service to himself, but always to another agent.
3. A service is existence dependent on the processes in which it is produced and consumed, which means that the service exists only when it is consumed and produced. In other words, a service is consumed and produced simultaneously. In contrast to goods and information, a service cannot be stored for later consumption.
4. A service is an intangible and abstract resource in the sense that it encapsulates a set of resources that are provided by one agent to be used by another agent. More precisely, when an agent consumes a service in a process, this means that she uses the resources encapsulated by the service. It should be noted that when an agent acquires a service in an exchange process, she does not get ownership rights on the encapsulated resources, but only use rights.
5. A service is always governed by a policy. This means that when a service is consumed, the resources encapsulated have to be used in compliance with a number of rules formulated in a policy.

Fig. 2 shows how these characteristics of services can be captured using REA notions. The figure shows the REA classes from Fig. 1 in white, while new classes are in grey.

1. We introduce *Service* as a subclass of *Resource* as well as *ServiceType* as a subclass of *ResourceType*.
2. In order to be able to represent that a service is always provided by one agent to another agent, we make use of the association *offers* from *Agent* to *ResourceType* and *consumedBy* from *Service* to *Agent*. The second association is in fact derivable, as the consumer of a service is the agent that performs the economic event that consumes the service.
3. In order to model that a service is existence dependent on the processes in which it is consumed and produced, we include two associations *produces* and *consumes*. These two associations are in fact derivable; a process consumes a service if it contains an economic event with a consume stockflow that is related to that service, and the same holds for production of services.

4. In order to model the fact that a service is an abstract resource encapsulating other resources, we use an association *encapsulates*, which is needed on the operational as well as the knowledge level. An example is that a surgery service could encapsulate hospital facilities, laser instruments, surgeon and nurse labour, and anesthesia. Stating that a resource is encapsulated in the service is not equivalent to stating that it is a part of the service. The *partOf* association is homogenous in the sense that a resource and its parts must be of the same kind, while a service may encapsulate a resource of any kind. For example, a part of a good must be a good, while a service may encapsulate both goods and information as well as other kinds of resources. Furthermore, the *partOf* association is transitive with respect to ownership rights, while *encapsulates* is not. For example, if an agent owns some goods, she also owns all its parts, but if she owns a service, she does not own the encapsulated resources.

5. In order to represent the policy governing a service type, the class *Policy* has been introduced.

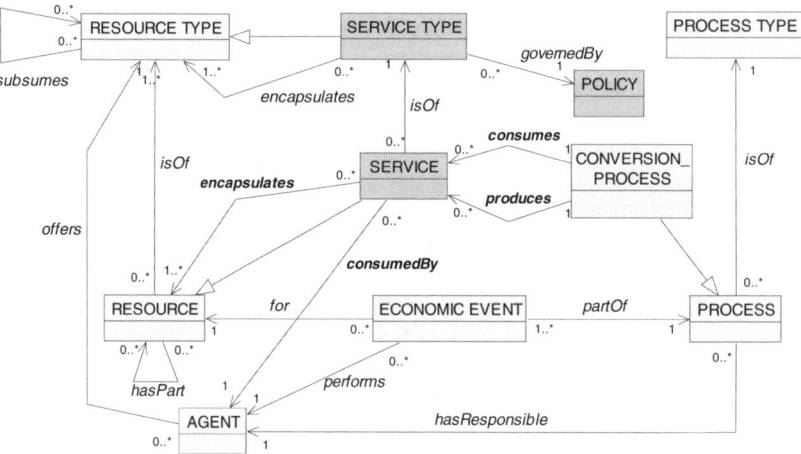

Fig. 2. Conceptual service model with relations to the REA ontology

When describing and advertising a service, it is typically more important to make clear how the service can be used in conversion processes rather than to specify the resources it encapsulates. In other words, it is often immaterial which resources the service encapsulates and sometimes the exact resources to be included when using it can be determined at delivery time. For example, when offering a hair-cut service, the decision whether to use a pair of scissors or a machine can be taken at delivery time. This implies that in describing services using the class *ServiceType*, the specification can often be at a more abstract level omitting the resource types encapsulated. Using the *subsumes* association, a more concrete description of a service can be given that also specifies resources encapsulated.

In summary, the conceptual service model (Fig. 2) is based on the REA ontology with primarily the concept of service and its relations added. We have omitted those parts of REA that have no immediate effect on or connection to the service concept, such as contracts and commitments. In the following section, we will further elaborate on this model by indicating how common marketing concepts, like needs, wants, and benefits, can be related to it.

4 Application to Marketing Oriented Service Design

In this section, we will discuss how the conceptual service model introduced above can be used for describing and designing services based on a marketing perspective. Our starting point will be a small number of well established core concepts in marketing as introduced in [29], in particular needs, wants, demands, and benefits (grey in fig. 3). We will describe these concepts, show how they can be modeled using REA, and suggest a graphical device based on these concepts and the proposed service model that can assist service description and design from a marketing point of view.

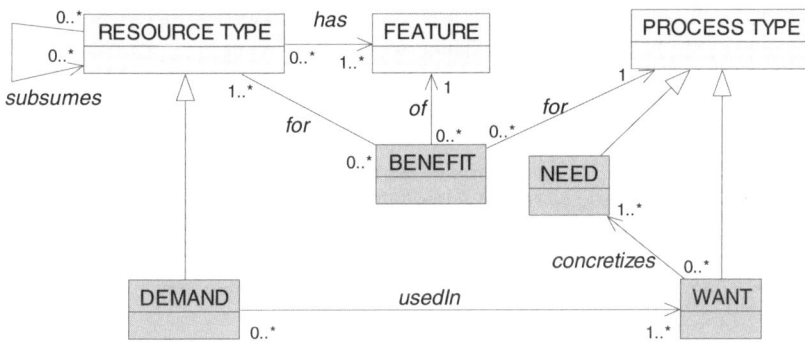

Fig. 3. Conceptual marketing model with relations to the REA ontology

According to [29], needs are basic human requirements, like food, water, rest, and to get shelter. People also have a need to get recreation, entertainment, education as well as other social needs. A well-known framework for classifying and analyzing needs is Maslow's hierarchy of needs, [30], which includes physiological needs, safety needs, and social needs as well as cognitive and aesthetic needs. A need becomes a want when it is directed to resources that can be used to satisfy the need. For example, a person may have a need to reduce his thirst, which can be directed to the want of having a soft drink. A demand is the desire for a particular product that is backed up by the willingness to pay for it. For example, the want of having a soft drink can result in a demand for a Coke, a product offered by a specific supplier. Benefits are properties of products that make them particularly useful for satisfying needs and wants.

It is possible to model needs in several different ways using the REA ontology. A need could be viewed as an internal resource, as a process that is carried out to produce an internal resource, or as an economic resource that is essential for producing some internal resource. In all these cases, the focus is on internal resources as these are objects that have an intrinsic value and are not only means for achieving something else. This is in line with the idea that a need is a basic human requirement concerning something desired for its own sake and not as an instrument. We choose here to model a need as an abstract process type that is related only to economic event types with a produce stockflow concerning internal resource types. Thus, a need is modeled as an activity, e.g. "to take care of my eyes". Furthermore, the need is related to its reasons, why the activity should be carried out, in the form of the internal resource types that the process type produces. For example, the need "to take care of my eyes" is related to the internal resource "eye health", as this activity helps to produce or maintain the eye health. However, a need is abstract in the sense that it does not specify what resource types that are requested as input for the activity. We have chosen to model needs as process types as this enables easy and flexible ways of formulating needs, and it also simplifies the modeling of wants as discussed below.

A need can be made more specific and concretized into a want by specifying what resource types that are needed as input for carrying it out. This means to outline a solution for how to satisfy the need. For example, the need "to take care of my eyes" can be concretized into the wants "to have an eye treatment" or "to take medicine". In the first case, the input resource type is a service type "eye treatment" and in the second case a goods type "medicine". Thus, we model a want as a process type that is related to economic event types with both produce and use/consume stockflows. A *demand* is a supplier specific resource type that is used as input to a want.

When a resource is used in a process, some of its features can be especially useful, beneficial, for that process. For example, the nice taste (feature) of a medicine (good) can be a benefit in a process "to take medicine", in particular for kids. Thus, we define a benefit as a relationship between a feature of a resource type and a process type. As there are many different kinds of benefits, it is helpful to identify a number of benefit categories that can be used to structure and discover benefits.

Table 1. Examples of benefit categories

Speed	Reliability	Low cost	Flexibility
Customizability	Quality	Security	Safety
Convenience	...		

The benefit relationship has been widely explored in management science, e.g. [27, 29, 31] and also in computer science, e.g. [32, 33], but there under different names, like value enhancers or second order values. The consolidated list in Table 1 contains a sample of benefit categories suggested in the literature from those domains. The topic of identifying benefit categories is important as they help in organizing benefits and thereby justify particular processes. However, a deeper investigation of benefit categories is outside the scope of this paper.

Based on the conceptual models in Figs. 2 and 3, we introduce a graphical device that can be used for describing and justifying product and service designs at various levels of abstraction (Figs. 4-6). This graphical device is essentially a set of object diagrams based on the above models, though we use a slightly different notation. The diagrams are in some respects similar to that of [34], but differ in the emphasis on

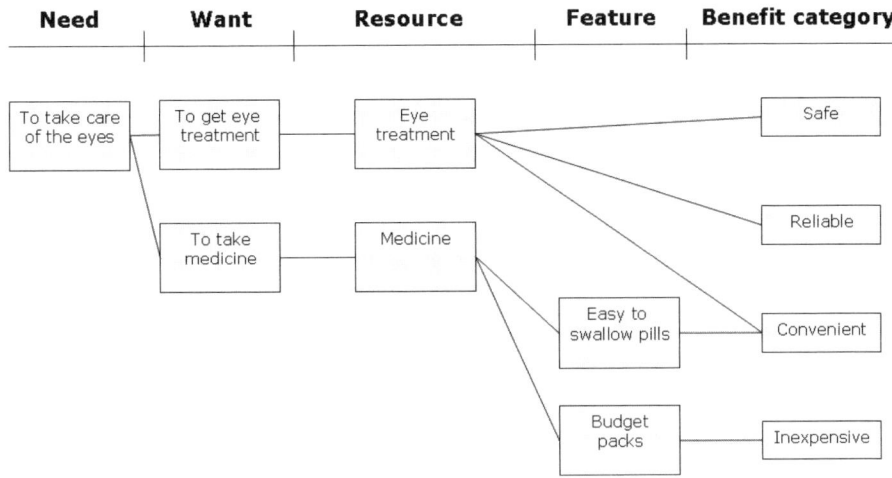

Fig. 4. Object model of a care taking scenario

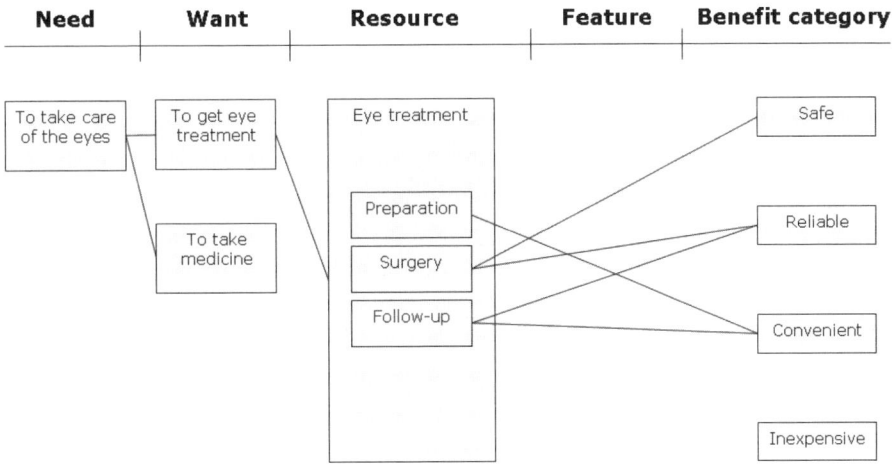

Fig. 5. Expanded object model showing component resources

resources, the introduction of benefit categories, and the omission of offerings. The diagram can be viewed as a table with five columns. The first column contains needs modeled as process types, the second column contains wants concretizing these needs, the third column includes resources used as input in the want processes, the fourth column contains features of these input resources, and the last column is used to specify what kinds of benefit the resources and features bring. An example is shown in Fig. 4, which is about eye health care needs and services.

The diagram in Fig. 4 is at a high level of abstraction displaying services as input resources. However, these services can be exploded on two levels using the *partOf* and *encapsulates* associations, respectively. In this way, it becomes possible to show

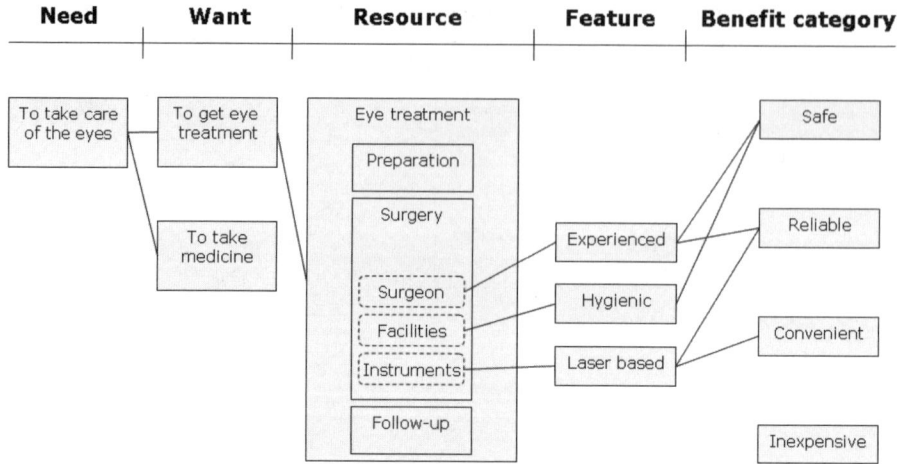

Fig. 6. Expanded object model including features

the subservices that are components of a service as well as the resources used when a service is consumed. An example is given in Figs. 5 and 6 where *partOf* is shown in square rectangles and *encapsulates* in rounded rectangles with dotted lines. Fig. 5 shows how the service "Eye treatment" consists of the component services Preparation, Surgery, and Follow-up. Fig. 6 shows the resources encapsulated by the service Surgery: Surgeon, Facilities, and Instruments.

This type of diagram will assist in describing the value and structure of services by showing the wants and needs a service can fulfill and by making explicit the components and benefits of a service. It can be noted that for services it is often difficult to identify their specific benefits as they are abstract and intangible. Instead, only the benefit category can be identified, as in Fig. 5 where the Eye treatment is characterized as safe, reliable, and convenient. However, when showing the resources encapsulated by a service, it becomes possible to identify specific benefits, e.g. the experience of a surgeon in Fig. 6, and their benefit categories.

5   Concluding Remarks

The notion of service has proved to be a useful abstraction for understanding how IT-resources can be provided for business enterprise but has still to reach its potential as a means for understanding business offerings and collaborations. For enterprise modelling the abstractness, however, contributes to the problem of understanding it as a business concept. This paper has addressed the issue of describing and representing business services. For this purpose, we have introduced a conceptual service model based on value oriented notions, in particular from the comprehensive REA ontology. The model emphasizes that a service is a special case of a resource that it is always provided by one agent to another, that a service is produced and consumed simultaneously, that a service works as an encapsulation of other resources, and that the use of these resources is governed by policies. To illustrate the use of this service model, we have also used the REA ontology to analyze basic notions in marketing, like need, want and benefit, and summarized them in a conceptual marketing model. The proposed models can be used to achieve a number of different goals in service design and description:

- *Clear and uniform representation and formulation.* Modeling services, needs, wants, and benefits by means of REA notions will encourage precise expressions and clarifies the relationships between service and marketing notions. Furthermore, uniformity is supported in the sense that the models assist different designers to formulate themselves in similar ways.
- *Traceability.* The conceptual marketing model supports traceability by making explicit how services contribute to wants and needs and how features of resources can function as benefits.
- *Benefit design.* The models can help in identifying benefits of services. A company could start from a product it currently offers and identify its benefits. For each benefit category, the company can then consider whether it should improve its product offering by including new or improved features of the product, which are benefits in that category.
- *Support of comprehensive service design.* The models can help in designing and visualizing more complete and comprehensive service offerings. A company could start from a product it currently offers and identify all the wants it can be used in. For each want, the company can then determine the other needed input resources and consider whether it would be useful for the company to package these resources and its current product into a new service to be offered.

In the SOA area, there exist several models of services, e.g. [11, 14]. In contrast to the model proposed here, these models focus on software services including their technical aspects such as message transfers and choreography while disregarding economic value aspects. This paper extends previous work presented in [35] by a more detailed analysis of encapsulation, an explicit grounding on the REA ontology, and a novel application.

There are several different directions for future work on the conceptual service model. One is to extend the model by including more service related aspects, such as service functions, service goals, and details on service policies. The present model includes the core notions of services but needs to be expanded in order to improve the applicability. Another direction is to identify other applications of the model, e.g. on service matching, business process design, and the relationship between real-world services and software services.

References

1. Gordijn, J., Akkermans, J.M., van Vliet, J.C.: Business Modeling is not Process Modeling. In: Mayr, H.C., Liddle, S.W., Thalheim, B. (eds.) ER Workshops 2000, vol. 1921, pp. 40–51. Springer, Heidelberg (2000)
2. Yu, E.: Models for supporting the redesign of organizational work. In: Proc. Conference on Organizational Computing Systems (COOCS 1995), Milpitas, California, USA, pp. 226–236. ACM, New York (1995)

3. Business Motivation Model release 1.3. The Business Rules Group (2007), `http://www.businessrulesgroup.org/second_paper/BRG-BMM.pdf`

4. Olle, W., Hagelstein, J., Macdonald, I., Rolland, C., Sol, H., van Assche, F., Verrijn-Stuart, A.: Information Systems Methodologies. A Framework for Understanding. Addison-Wesley, Reading (1988)

5. Sowa, J.F., Zachman, J.A.: Extending and formalizing the frameworkfor information systems architectures. IBM Systems Journal 31(3), 590–616 (1992)

6. IDS Scheer. Enterprise Architectures and ARIS Process Platform, White Papers (Acc. June 30, 2008) (2005), `http://www.changeware.net/doc/wp_ea.pdf`

7. IBM Systems Journal. Service Science, Management and Engineering 47(1) (Acc. March 08, 2008) (2008), `http://www.research.ibm.com/journal/sj47-1.html`

8. Spohrer, J.: Service Science: The next frontier in service innovation, IBM Corporation (2007), `http://www-304.ibm.com/jct09002c/university/scholars/skills/ssme/spohrer07int.pdf`

9. Goldkuhl, G., Röstlinger, A.: Beyond Goods and Services – an Elaborate Product Classification on Pragmatic Grounds. In: Seventh International Research Symposium on Service Quality, QUIS, Karlstad, Sweden, vol. 7 (2000)

10. Lusch, R.F., Vargo, S.L., Wessels, G.: Towards a conceptual foundation for service science: Contributions from service-dominant logic. IBM Systems Journal (January 24, 2008), `http://www.research.ibm.com/journal/sj/471/lusch.html`

11. OASIS. Reference Model for Service Oriented Architecture 1.0 (2006) (Feburary 19, 2008), `http://www.oasis-open.org/committees/download.php/19679/soa-rm-cs.pdf`

12. Preist, C.: A Conceptual Architecture for Semantic Web Services. In: van Harmelen, F., McIlraith, S.A., Plexousakis, D. (eds.) ISWC 2004, LNCS, vol. 3298, pp. 395–409. Springer, Heidelberg (2004)

13. United Nations Centre for Trade Facilitation and Electronic Business UN/CEFACT Modelling Methodology (UMM) User Guide (Acc. November 2007) (2003), `http://www.unece.org/cefact/umm/UMM_userguide_220606.pdf`

14. W3C. Web Services Architecture W3C Working Group (2004), `http://www.w3.orgTRws-arch`

15. Roman, D., et al.: Web Service Modeling Ontology. Applied Ontology 1(1) (2005)

16. Colan, M. Service-Oriented Architecture expands the vision of Web services, Part 1. IBM DeveloperWorks (2004) (March 27, 2008), `http://www.ibm.com/developerworks/library/ws-soaintro.html`

17. Papazoglou, M., van den Heuvel, W.J.A.M.: Service-oriented design and development methodology. Int. Journal of Web Engineering and Technology 2(4), 412–442

18. Chesbrough, H., Spohrer, J.: A Research Manifesto for Service Sciences. Comm. ACM 49(7) (2006)

19. McCarthy, W.E.: The REA Accounting Model: A Generalized Framework for Accounting Systems in a Shared Data Environment. The Accounting Review (1982)

20. Geerts, G., McCarthy, W.: Policy-Level Specifications in REA Enterprise Information Systems. Journal of Information Systems 20(2), 37–63 (2006)

21. Hruby, P.: Model-Driven Design of Software Applications with Business Patterns. Springer, Heidelberg (2006)

22. van der Raadt, B., Gordijn, J., Yu, E.: Exploring Web Services Ideas from a Business Value Perspective. In: Atlee, J., Roland, C. (eds.) Proceedings of the 2005 13th IEEE International Conference on Requirements Engineering (RE 2005), pp. 53–62. IEEE CS, Los Alamitos (2005)

23. Andersson, B., Bergholz, M., Edirisuriya, A., Ilayperuma, T., Johannesson, P., Gordijn, J., Gregoire, B., Schmitt, M., Dubois, E., Abels, S., Hahn, A., Wangler, B., Weigand, H.: Towards a Reference Ontology for Business Models. In: Embley, D.W., Olive, A., Ram, S. (eds.) ER 2006. LNCS, vol. 4215, pp. 482–496. Springer, Heidelberg (2006)

24. Weigand, H., Johannesson, P., Andersson, B., Bergholtz, M., Edirisuriya, A., Ilayperuma, T.: On the Notion of Value Object. In: Dubois, E., Pohl, K. (eds.) CAiSE 2006. LNCS, vol. 4001, pp. 321–335. Springer, Heidelberg (2006)

25. Fowler, M.: Analysis Patterns - Reusable Object Models. Addison-Wesley, Reading (1996)

26. Gailly, F., Poels, G.: Towards Ontology-driven Information Systems: Redesign and Formalization of the REA Ontology. Working paper. Universiteit Gent, Faculteit Economie en Bedrijfskunde, http://www.FEB.UGent.be/fac/research/WP/Papers/wp_07_445.pdf2008-03-27

27. Zeithaml, V.A., Parasuraman, A., Berry, L.L.: Problems and Strategies in Services Marketing. Journal of Marketing 49, 33–46 (1985)

28. Bateson, J.E.G.: Do We Need Service Marketing?, in Marketing Consumer Services: New Insights, Marketing Science Institute, Report #77-115 (December 1977)

29. Kotler, P., Keller, K.L.: Marketing Management, 12th edn. Prentice Hall, Englewood Cliffs (January 1, 2006) ISBN-10: 0131457578, ISBN-13: 978-0131457577

30. Maslow, M.: A Theory of Human Motivation. Psychological Review 50(4), 370–396 (1943)

31. Holbrook, M.B., Hirschman, E.C.: The Experiential Aspects of Consumption: Consumer Fantasies, Feelings, and Fun. The Journal of Consumer Research (1982)

32. Andersson, B., Johannesson, P., Zdravkovic, J.: Aligning goals and services through goal and business modelling. Information Systems and E-Business Management (2008) ISSN:1617-9854, doi:10.1007/s10257-008-0084-2

33. Zarvic, N., Wieringa, R., Daneva, M.: Towards information systems design for value webs. In: Workshop proceedings (BUSITAL 2007) of the 19th Conference on Advanced Information Systems Engineering (CAiSE 2007), vol. 1 (2007) ISBN: 9788251-922456

34. de Kinderen, S., Gordijn, J.: e3 service: An ontological approach for deriving multi-supplier IT-service bundles from consumer needs. In: Proc. HICSS (2008), http://docs.e3value.com/bibtex/pdf/MultiSupplierITServiceBundles2008.pdf2008-03-27

35. Weigand, H., Johannesson, P., Andersson, B., Bergholtz, M., Edirisuriya, A., Ilayperuma, T., Zdravkovic, J.: Value-based Service Design Based On A General Service Architecture. In: Proc. BUSITAL 2008, Montpellier, France (2008)

Bringing Enterprise Business Processes into Information System Products

Naveen Prakash

GCET, 1 Knowledge Park Phase II, Greater NOIDA 201306
praknav@hotmail.com

Abstract. We propose here that enterprise business processes need to be mapped to information systems. Therefore, an information system deliverable is an integration of Enterprise information, Enterprise business rules, and Enterprise processes. Since the process model is built on top of business rules, we propose a uniform representation system that shall explicitly bring out process logic as well as rule logic. As a result, we shall obtain a hierarchy that shall allow smooth movement between process and rule logic. Conceptually, this implies that we shall treat rules as atomic processes. We instantiate the generic method model with concepts of the IS deliverable and thereby represent rule and process logic as dependency graphs. We exemplify our representation with the ATM bank example and show a verification step to ensure that enterprise process needs are indeed met.

Keywords: Enterprise Business Process, Information System etc.

1 Introduction

An enterprise model has been defined [Fox97] as a "computational representation of the structure, activities, processes, information, resources, people, behaviour, goals and constraints of business, government, or other enterprise". The framework of Enterprise Architecture of Zachman [Zac93] provides a structure for classifying and organizing the description of an Enterprise for both, enterprise management and enterprise systems development. Enterprise modelling [Lou95] has been applied in such diverse areas as Computer Integrated Manufacturing, Enterprise Integration, Business Process Re-engineering and Information Systems Engineering. Our interest here is in enterprise modelling from the Information Systems perspective.

Modeling enterprise processes is a well recognized research problem. Keller and Detering [Kel96] have pointed out the essential dilemma faced when using an ERP system, namely, whether to adapt to the software and radically change business practice or to modify the software to suit enterprise needs. Obviously, the latter is ruled out once investments in ERP packages like SAP [ASA99] are made. While highlighting the importance of enterprise processes, Dalal et al [Dal04] pointed out their crucial role in the next generation of ERP systems, christened ERP II.

Loucopoulos and Kavakli [Lou95] establish a relationship between enterprise modeling and requirements engineering and suggest that the enterprise-information

J. Stirna and A. Persson (Eds.): PoEM 2008, LNBIP 15, pp. 168–181, 2008.

systems relationship provides justification criteria and explanations about the information system to be developed. However, Requirements engineering [Myl92] is essentially concerned with functional and non-functional requirements and process model elicitation, has to our knowledge, not been addressed. Thus, it is not possible to deal with enterprise process models in Requirements engineering.

From the foregoing, it can be seen that, in enterprise modelling, we have to represent both, the information/data aspect of enterprises and their process aspects. The completeness principle postulated in [Pra07] provides a basis for this. This principle implies that the deliverables of IS/SW activity are information/data models and associated usage process models. During enactment, the latter produces the former. Notice that the completeness principle gives primacy to the process model over system functionality. Indeed, a process model is built over functionality but the argument is that it is enterprise processes that deliver value and therefore, are paramount.

We refer to the integration of information/data model and process model by the relatively neutral term, information system deliverable or IS deliverable. Essentially, we are dealing with three phenomena that are to be integrated together in the IS deliverable. These are

- Enterprise information,
- Enterprise business rules, and
- Enterprise processes.

A number of techniques, data-oriented, function-oriented, behaviour-oriented and object-oriented, have been developed for representing enterprise information types and business rules. Since the process model is built on top of business rules, we shall look for a uniform representation system that shall explicitly bring out process logic as well as rule logic. As a result, we shall obtain a hierarchy that shall allow smooth movement between process and rule logic. Conceptually, this implies that we shall treat rules as atomic processes.

Once business rules and processes are treated in the same uniform manner, we need to address the question of the level of abstraction of their representation. BPML {Ark02], BPEL [OAS07] and workflow[wfm95] provide features for representing sequence, parallelism and choice in process logic, fault and exception handling, synchronization and other such features. We believe that there is a higher level of abstraction at which enterprise process models should be represented that brings out their essential features and acts as a specification for the low level representation. Thus, synchronization, faults/exceptions are left to be elaborated in subsequent stages.

We choose the generic method model [Pra06] as the basis for instantiation of the IS deliverable. This model has integrated the information and process parts of methods together. For the latter, it produces a dependency graph based on different types of dependency. Thus, the dependency graph captures a range of process situations. We represent the enterprise process model as a dependency graph and shall refer to this representation as the Application Process Model, APM.

The layout of the paper is as follows. In the next section we present the generic method model and highlight the features that we shall use. In section III, we develop a set of concepts to represent the IS deliverable, instantiate the generic model with these and show the use of the dependency graph for representing business rules and process models. In section IV we apply the notions we have developed to model the ATM of a bank. Section V introduces a verification step called matching for ensuring a good fit between the APM and the enterprise business model. It uses the ATM example to show how matching can be done. In section VI we compare our approach with others like workflow, BPML etc.

2 The Generic Method Model

In this section, we provide an overview of the generic method model so as to show its usefulness in building the IS deliverable. The details of the model can be found in [Pra06]. As its name implies, this model was developed to capture the generic notion of a method. One of its stated objectives is to integrate the product and process aspects of methods together. Thus, if we treat an IS deliverable as a method, identify its concepts and instantiate the generic method model with these, then the IS deliverable shall have integrated product and process parts together with all other properties of the generic model.

The generic view treats a method as a triple <M, D, E> where M is the set of method blocks, D is the set of dependencies between method blocks, and E is the enactment mechanism. The notion of a dependency is used to build a dependency graph with method blocks as nodes and dependency types as edges.

A method block has two parts, an argument part and an action part. The action part acts upon the argument part to produce the product. These two parts correspond to product primitive and process primitive respectively of Fig. 1. The product primitive is found in the product model. Therefore, if the product model is the schema of an application, then the concepts of this schema form the product primitives. The process primitives correspond to the operations allowed on the concepts in the schema. For example, <Reservation, Create> is a method block.

Complex method blocks are built out of simpler ones. For example, <Name, Address, Start, End, Room type, Book> is a complex method block, built out of simpler method blocks that create a client, check availability of rooms and reserve a room respectively. Here, Book is the action part and the rest are arguments.

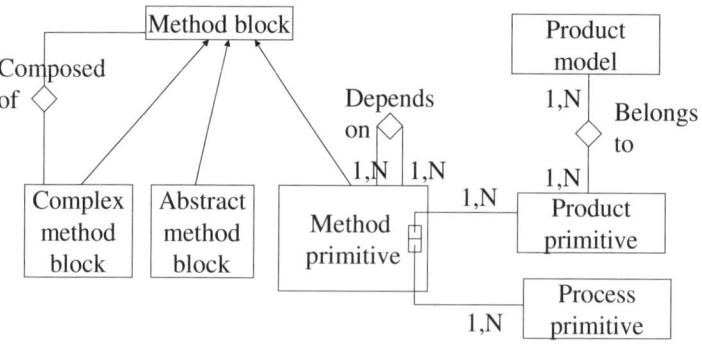

Fig. 1. The Generic Model

Now consider the notion of a dependency. Two attributes, urgency and necessity, are associated with each dependency type. Urgency refers to the time at which the dependent method block, O_2, is to be enacted. If O_2 is to be enacted immediately after O_1 is enacted then this attribute takes on the value *Immediate*. If O_2 can be enacted any time, immediately or at any moment, after O_1 has been enacted, then urgency takes on the value *Deferred*. Necessity refers to whether or not the dependent method block O_2 is necessarily to be enacted after O_1 has been enacted. If it is necessary to enact O_2, then this attribute takes the value *Must* otherwise it has the value *Can*. As discussed earlier, this gives rise to four dependency types displayed in Table 1.

Table 1. Dependency Types

Type	Urgency	Necessity	Abbreviation
1	Immediate	Must	IM
2	Immediate	Can	IC
3	Deferred	Must	DM
4	Deferred	Can	DC

It can be seen that the urgency property of a dependency type supports both instantaneous and long running phenomena. If the dependency between a pair of method blocks has Urgency=Immediate then the two are to be immediately enacted, one following the other. This amounts to a representation of instantaneous phenomena. On the other hand, if Urgency=Deferred then there can be a time interval between the enactment of the two method blocks and one can represent long running phenomena.

The necessity property of a dependency type supports planned, determined action or selection of alternative actions. If the dependency type between O1 and O2 has Necessity=Must, then O2 must be enacted after O1. This corresponds to a planned, determined course of action. On the other hand if Necessity=Can, then O2 represents a choice of action.

Using the notion of a dependency, a method can be organized as a dependency graph. This graph when traversed from its start to stop nodes represents an activity that can be performed by the system and can be seen to be a process model. As a result of process enactment, the system produces an instance of the product model, the product.

We illustrate a dependency graph by considering a method with the set of method primitives $O = \{O_1, O_2, ..., O_{14}\}$. Let there be two dependency types (see Table 1), one of type 1 and the other of type 2. Let the following dependencies be defined:

IM dependencies

$O_1 \rightarrow O_2$	$O_1 \rightarrow O_3$	$O_1 \rightarrow O_4$	$O_1 \rightarrow O_5$
$O_6 \rightarrow O_7$	$O_6 \rightarrow O_8$		
$O_9 \rightarrow O_{10}$	$O_9 \rightarrow O_{11}$	$O_9 \rightarrow O_{11}$	

IC dependencies

$O_1 \rightarrow O_6$	$O_1 \rightarrow O_9$
$O_6 \rightarrow O_{13}$	$O_6 \rightarrow O_{14}$

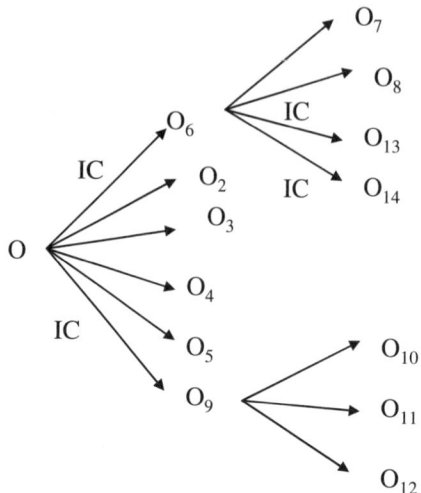

Fig. 2. A Dependency Graph

Using the foregoing dependencies, we arrive at the dependency graph as shown in Fig. 2. In this Figure, only the IC dependencies are labeled and the non-labeled ones are assumed to be IM dependencies.

The dependency graph shows that the entire activity represented in it is instantaneous. Further, there is choice to enact O_6 and O_9 after O as well as O_{13} and O_{14} after O_6.

Enactment Initiation and Termination. A dependency graph has a set of nodes, called START, that have no edges entering them. This implies that enactment can begin from any of the nodes in this set. For example, for Fig. 2, START contains exactly one node, O, and enactment begins from this node.

Now consider termination of enactment. We define a set STOP that contains nodes at which enactment can terminate. The following nodes belong to this set:

1. Nodes that have no edges coming out of them. For example, in Fig 2, O_7, O_8 and O_{10} to O_{14} shall be members of STOP.
2. Nodes that have edges leaving them but all these edges have Necessity = Can. Since the edges identify nodes which are optional and may not be enacted, it is possible for enactment to terminate. Notice that even if one of the edges has Necessity=Must then termination cannot occur since the node determined by such an edge is to be necessarily enacted.

For example, consider the dependency graph shown below. There are no nodes leaving B. Therefore it is a member of STOP. A has two edges leaving it and both have Necessity=Can. Therefore, it is possible that these may never be enacted, and enactment may stop at A. Therefore, A is a member of STOP. Similarly, the edge leaving C has Necessity=Can and B may never be enacted after C. Therefore C is also part of STOP.

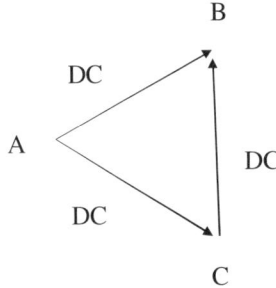

From the foregoing we get STOP = {A, B, C}. That is, enactment may stop at A, after the enactment of AB, of AC, or of ACB.

Let us determine STOP for the dependency graph of Fig. 2. By rule 1 above, we get O_7, O_8 and O_{10} to O_{14}. Further an examination of the graph shows that only two out of the six edges leaving O have Necessity=Can and the rest Must be enacted. Therefore, O is not a member of STOP. All edges coming out of O_9 have Necessity=Must. Therefore, it is not a member of STOP. Similarly, O_6 is not a member of STOP because only two of its four edges have Necessity=Can. Therefore, we get STOP = {O_7, O_8, O_{10}, O_{11}, O_{12}, O_{13}, O_{14}}.

3 The IS Deliverable

As mentioned earlier, our view of an IS deliverable is based on the completeness principle. This completeness principle [Pra07] states that an information system deliverable should be a faithful representation of the product and process models at the required level of conceptualization. In other words, applications can be visualized at different levels of abstraction and at each level the IS deliverable is complete if and only if both the product and process models have been developed. Our interest here is not in the different levels of abstraction but in the representation of the product and process aspects of an IS deliverable.

Looking at the generic method model from this perspective, we notice that the product primitive comes from the product model. We first need to conceptualise product primitives and associated process primitives of an IS deliverable and thereafter, instantiate the generic model.

In information systems, the data part of a deliverable is modelled as a conceptual schema. The conceptual schema contains application specific types of information that we refer to as Application Product (AP) types. The conceptual schema can be populated with instances of AP types by operations of create, delete and modify. We refer to these operations as Operations on AP or OAP for brevity. For example, Student is an AP type and read, create, delete, and modify are OAPs. AP types and OAPs come together to form the basic 'action' capability that leads to product construction. For example, Create Student populates the product with students. We shall refer to this coupling as an application primitive.

Application engineers build system functionality using application primitives. For example, we may have AP types Student and Enrolled_in and build method blocks Create student and Create Enrolled_in. We can define Admit Student over Create student and

Create Enrolled_in. We refer to operations like Admit that provide functional capability as User Operations, UO.

In the next section, we instantiate the generic method model with the concepts, AP type, AOP and UO found in the product model of the IS deliverable.

3.1 Instantiating the Generic Model

The instantiation of the generic model is shown in Table 2. A product primitive is instantiated with AP type, whereas a process primitive is instantiated with OAP. To instantiate a method block we define the notion of an application chunk. An application chunk represents the operations that can be performed on the AP types of the application. It is the mechanism for creation of the product part of the information system deliverable and can be used as a node in the dependency graph.

We instantiate method block with the notion of application chunk. An application chunk represents the capability to build the product. A method primitive is instantiated with application primitive introduced above. An application primitive represents the smallest meaningful product building action that can be performed in the application.

Table 2. Instantiating the Generic Model

Generic Method Concept	Application Method Concept
Product primitive	AP type
Process primitive	Operation on AP (OAP)
Method Block	Application chunk
Method primitive	Application primitive, <AP type list, OAP>
Complex Method Block	Complex application chunk <AP type list, UO>
Abstract Method Blocks	Abstract UOs

A complex method block is instantiated by a complex application chunk, CAC. The CAC is built over other simpler application chunks. The argument list and action of a CAC is useful to represent the coupling <AP type list, UO>. Thus application functionality can be represented as a CAC.

An abstract method block is instantiated with abstract application chunk. Such a chunk abstracts out the common features of application chunks and allows us to look at chunks at different levels to construct an ISA hierarchy of application chunks.

Using the four kinds of dependencies, we can now build an application dependency graph with application chunks as nodes and edges that represent their ordering. Edges are labeled with their dependency types. There are two interesting graphs

1. The Function Graph, FG: The distinguishing feature of a FG is that its nodes are application primitives only. We can treat FG as a complex application chunk of the form <AP type list, UO> by associating a UO with it and determining the AP types involved.
2. The APM graph, APMG, constructed with a mix of the three different types of application chunks. As its name implies, this graph can be used to represent a usage process model.

These two kinds of graphs form a hierarchy of graphs. At the root, is the APMG that captures the global process model, the APM. Nodes in this graph can be decomposed into FGs, possibly through a multi-level decomposition hierarchy of graphs.

3.2 FG for Representing a Business Rule

We show that a function graph can be used to capture a business rule. To illustrate this, consider the business rule for making a reservation, "Obtain full requestor information before doing the reservation". Let the AP types be Requestor, Reservation, and Availability. Upon getting a booking request, we can instantiate these using application primitives, Create Requestor, Create Reservation, Modify Availability. A dependency graph for this is shown in Fig. 3.

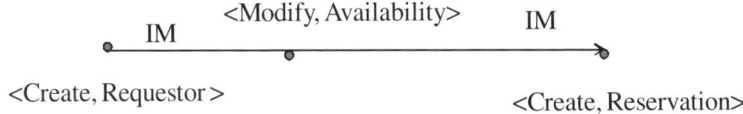

Fig. 3. An FG for a Business Rule

The business rule is instantaneous; the entire execution from the first to the last is done at the same time. Now consider a different business rule that expects the reservation to be carried out before obtaining requestor information. This calls for a different dependency structure among the application primitives as shown in Fig 4.

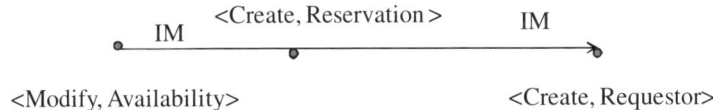

Fig. 4. Representing a Different Business Rule

Again, this is an instantaneous function. Notice that both the dependency graphs can be seen as modelling the business function, Make reservation; both represent instantaneous phenomena, and both will have the same arguments. However, the business rule followed in the two cases is different. Naturally, that dependency structure that best meets the business rules of the enterprise is t be selected. Notice also that Make reservation is a complex application chunk.

As an example of a function graph that captures long-running phenomena consider development of a complex application chunk for admitting a student. Candidates apply for admission and some of these who are prospective students are selected to appear for a test and interview. Based on performance in these, selected students are identified and offered admission. The dependency graph is shown in Fig. 5. Notice that the dependency type between Create Candidate and Create prospective student is Deferred Must. Since the urgency property of this dependency type is deferred, the dependency graph captures a long-running business rule.

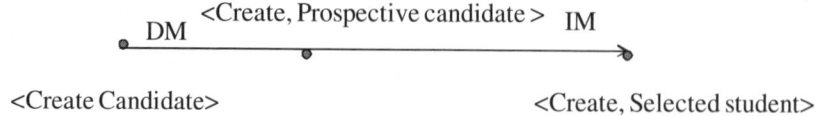

<Create Candidate>   <Create, Selected student>

Fig. 5. Representing a Long running Business Rule

3.3 APMG as Process Model

Having looked at the representation of enterprise business rules, let us now consider the enterprise business process model. The application chunks with UOs are the building blocks of such a model. Consider the set of application chunks

ACset = {Ac1, Ac2, …. Acn}

A number of process models can be built each with a different ordering of ACset. Out of these, only some are feasible. Further, out of the feasible operations only some are compatible with the required enterprise business process of the organisation. To illustrate, consider a simple hotel reservation application having

ACset = {Make Reservation, Cancel Reservation, Postpone reservation}

Out of the different orderings possible, the useful one is that which starts with Make, followed by either Cancel or Postpone.

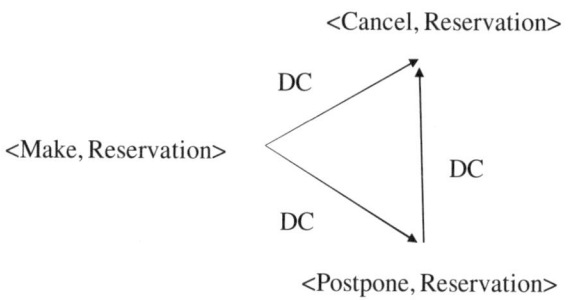

Fig. 6. An APMG for Reservation Process

The dependency graph of Fig. 6 shows that the business process can stop at three nodes, at cancellation, at postponement or at making the reservation. Thus we can have four processes (a) Make reservation, (b) Make reservation, cancel reservation (c) Make reservation, postpone reservation, cancel reservation (d) Make reservation, postpone reservation Further, if it is possible to postpone more than once then the dependency graph needs to be augmented by a self loop from Postpone reservation to itself with the dependency type DC.

The process model represented by the dependency graph is a long running process (Urgency = Deferred). Further, cancellation and postponement of a reservation are choices (Necessity=Can). Notice that as the process model is enacted, the product model of the reservation system is instantiated.

4   The ATM Example

In this section we illustrate our proposals with the help of the example of an ATM of a bank. The information part of the application product model of the ATM is shown in Fig. 7. As shown customers have a name and hold accounts in our bank. Accounts have a number, Acno, and balance. A personal identification number, pin, is associated with each account held by a customer.

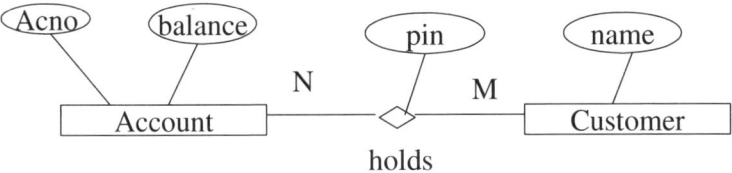

Fig. 7. An IS/SW Product

Now, let us look at the second part, the business rules part, of the IS/SW deliverable. Consider withdrawing money from the ATM. After reading the account number, Acno, and the pin of the customer, withdrawal can be done in either fast or normal mode. In the latter case a statement of the balance and withdrawal details are printed out. The dependency graph is shown in Fig. 8.

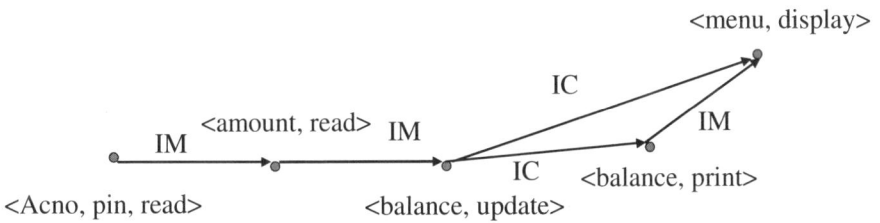

Fig. 8. A Function Graph

The fast and normal alternatives are expressed as IC dependencies. Once the request for withdrawal is satisfied, the main menu of the ATM is displayed again. Fig. 8 can be seen to be a complex application chunk <Acno, pin, amount, withdraw> having AP type list consisting of Acno, pin, and amount whereas the UO is withdraw. It can also be seen as capturing the business rules to withdraw cash from an ATM. In a similar manner, we assume that application chunks to change the pin and check balance respectively have been defined.

We can consider the third part, the process part, now and build a APMG for our ATM example. For this, we assume the set of application chunks consisting of (a) inserting a card into the ATM, <card, insert>, (b) selecting a language, <language, select>, (c) withdrawing amount <Acno, pin, amount, withdraw>, (d) changing the pin <Acno, pin, npin, change>, and (e) checking balance, forming <Acno, pin, check>. These application chunks can be put together in the APMG graph shown in Fig. 9.   First notice that all edges have Urgency=Immediate. This means that the entire APMG is considered instantaneous, to be performed at the same moment. After inserting the ATM card, the language is selected. After that any one of withdraw, check, or change UOs can be performed. One possibility is to exit after performing the chosen UO. The other option is to perform yet another operation from among these. Thus, for example, the sequence of check followed by withdraw could be performed. These alternatives are shown by the IC dependency types associated with edges between application chunks.

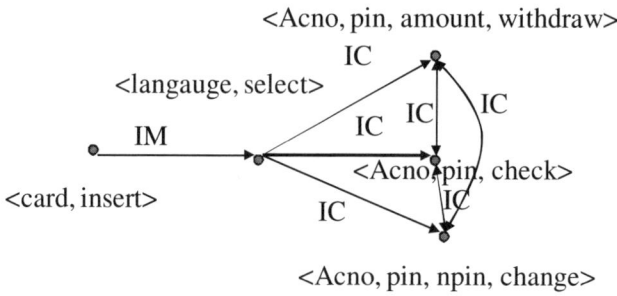

Fig. 9. An Application Process Model Graph

It can be seen that graphs are organized in a hierarchy. In our example, Fig. 9 is the root graph of the hierarchy. One branch of this hierarchy is the graph corresponding to withdraw and the other branches correspond to the graphs for changing pin codes and checking balances (not shown in this paper).

5 Performing Verification by Matching

Once the dependency graphs have been built, we propose that they be verified against enterprise requirements by carrying out a verification activity. Essentially this involves matching enterprise needs against the dependency graphs. We consider this for our ATM example.

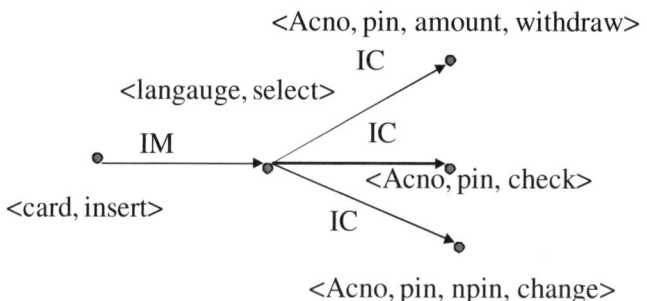

Fig. 10. Selected variants for an Inconvenient ATM Process

There are two strategies that can be followed in enterprises when considering an ATM. One is to offer greater protection to the customer at the expense of convenience. Thus, to protect forgetful customers who may leave their ATM cards in the ATM machine, each operation explicitly requires card insertion. To support such an enterprise process, the APM of Fig. 10 suffices. It requires the removal of three edges in the original APMG of Fig. 9.

The second business strategy could be to assume less forgetful clients and lay greater emphasis on convenience. Then, the APMG of Fig. 9 is accepted as such. Notice that the pin has to be entered for each operation for security purposes but a sequence of UOs can be carried out without having to insert the ATM card many times.

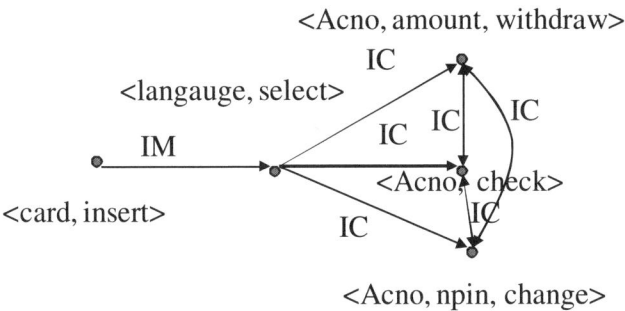

Fig. 11. An Insecure ATM Process

A third strategy could be a variant of the second one. It does away with entering pin each time a UO is to be performed. This leads to an ATM process that is less secure than the one of Fig. 9. Here, it is possible for the client to forget the card in the machine and for somebody else to walk up and use it!! This APMG is represented in Fig. 11 and it requires the modification of nodes. It forces the application engineer to redesign the UOs comprising the APMG to ensure a good fit.

6 Related Work

The workflow approach covers the design, control and execution of business processes. Workflow management systems have been developed to deal with different kinds of workflows, production, administrative, and collaborative. A 3-dimensional framework has been used to bring out the three aspects that go into defining workflows, cases, resources, and tasks. A task-case pair represents a work unit and the logic of this work-unit is the key issue. Workflow logic has been expressed [wfm95] in four basic constructs, sequence, AND-split and join, OR split and join, and iteration. Organization modeling for resource classification and structuring has also been done in the workflow area.

Notice that the 3-dimensional framework does not consider the issue of the output of the workflow, what is the result, the 'information product' produced. Clearly, it deemphasizes the integration of the information product and the process that produces it.

A second approach is business process modeling. BPML [Ark02] has been developed as a means to represent business process models. BPML can be used for expressing abstract and executable processes. Similar to workflows, features for expressing sequences, choice, iteration and parallel execution are available. There is also a full range of facilities for fault/exception handling. Again, the focus is on the representation of business process logic and the result of this logic, the informational products that fall out of these processes are not considered.

A third approach has been developed in the context of web services and their capability to support business processes. WS-BPEL [OAS07] is a language that captures the operational characteristics of business processes. The logic of the process can be implemented and support for execution is provided by an orchestration engine. BPEL code uses constructs similar to those of a general purpose programming language together with full error/exception handling capabilities. BPEL modelling tools have been developed from which BPEL code can be generated. Again notice the lack of emphasis on the information product produced.

Whereas workflow, BPML and BPEL are highly oriented towards enterprise and business process logic, information systems development has de-emphasized it. Early information system products were either data or function oriented, but today a balance between data, function and dynamic aspects of information systems has been found. Consequently, the data aspect of the system being represented is closely coupled with the operational capability that affects the data. Thus, from the point of view of information system developers, the product to be delivered is this combination of data + function. This view ignores the representation of enterprise process models.

It can be seen that whereas information system developers do not pay sufficient attention to enterprise processes, the workflow/business process/web service developers do not pay sufficient attention to modeling the data to be maintained in the system. Our approach can be seen as a way to lay equal emphasis on these twin aspects of enterprises in the design of information system deliverables.

A somewhat different approach is adopted in ERP systems where a cross-module and intra-module process model is assumed. An enterprise using the package must adapt to the prescribed process model. Thus, instead of the system reflecting enterprise process requirements the situation here is the reverse.

7 Conclusion

In this paper we have considered the representation of enterprise business processes in information systems. Information Systems of today provide functionality independent of a process model. This leaves open the possibility of enacting functionality in an undefined order. This problem gets aggravated when the number of functions is high, as it is when doing enterprise modeling, To avoid this, one can build appropriate constraints in the functions but this amounts to 'hard coding' process knowledge. Clearly, this hides process information and makes for change resistance.

Seeing the close relationship between business rules and business processes, we represent these in the same uniform notion of a dependency graph. Thus, we get the same properties for both. For example, it is possible for both, business rules and processes, to be long running.

In order to effectively realize the notion of an information system deliverable we see some open spaces and scope for future

- Requirements engineering techniques need to be augmented to elicit process model needs. This is to be done uniformly both for business rules and enterprise processes.
- Just as notions of product customization and adaptation have become acceptable, we need to develop the notions of process customization and adaptation.
- Information system development methods today have the capacity to support construction of application products, data and functionality only. If methods are to produce the information system deliverable, then method engineering tools and techniques shall have to be extended to produce methods capable of building IS/SW deliverables.

References

[Aal98] van der Aalst, W.M.P.: The Application of Petri Nets to Workflow Management. Journal of Circuits, Systems and Computers 8(1), 21–66

[Ark02] Arkin, A.: Intalio, Business Process Modelling Language (November 2002), http://www.bpml.org

[ASA99] ASAP World Consultancy and Blain, J., et al., Using SAP R/3, Prentice Hall of India (1999)

[OAS07] OASIS Web Services Business Process Execution Language version 2.0, http://oasis-open.org

[Dal04] Dalal, N.K., Kamath, M., Kolarik, W.J., Sivaraman, E.: Towards and Integrated Framework for Modeling Enterprise Processes. CACM 47(3), 83-83-87

[Fox97] Fox, M.S., Gruninger, M.: On Ontologies and Enterprise Modelling. In: International Conferene on Enterprise Integration Modelling Technology, Italy

[Kel96] Keller, G., Detering, S.: Process-oriented Modeling and Analysis of Business processes using the R/3 reference Model. In: Bernus, P., Nemes, L. (eds.) Modeling and Methodologies for Enterprise Integration, pp. 69–87. Chapman & Hall, Boca Raton (1996)

[Lou95] Loucopoulos, P., Kavakli, E.: Enterprise Modelling and the Teleological Approach to Requirements Engineering. Int. J. Cooperative Information Systems 4(1), 45–79

[Myl92] Mylopoulos, J., Chung, L., Nixon, B.: Representing and Using Non-Functional Requirements: A Process-Oriented Approach. IEEETSE 18(6), 483–497 (1992)

[Pra07] Prakash, N.: Complete methods for building complete applications. In: Ralyte, J., Brinkkemper, S., Henederson-Sellers, B. (eds.) IFIP WG8.1 Working Conference on Situational Method Engineering: Fundamentals and Experiences, pp. 207–221. Springer, Heidelberg (2007)

[Pra06] Prakash, N.: On generic method models. Requirements Engineering Journal 11(4), 221–237 (2006)

[wfm95] The workflow Reference Model, http://wfmc.org

[Zac93] Zachman, J.A.: Concepts of the Framework for Enterprise Architecture, Zachman International

Representation of Business Rules in UML&OCL Models for Developing Information Systems

Lina Nemuraite, Lina Ceponiene, and Gediminas Vedrickas

Kaunas University of Technology, Studentu 50-308, LT 51368 Kaunas, Lithuania
{Lina.Nemuraite,Lina.Ceponiene}@ktu.lt, G.Vedrickas@erp.eu

Abstract. Currently Business Rules Approach has attained the great interest in business and software development communities. According to SBVR standard, business rules are the rules under business jurisdiction. Consequently, business rules should be managed by business people. However, acquiring and supporting the correct and reconciled SBVR style rule sets is the difficult problem. In practice, business rules often are managed by software developers and system analysts; more straightforward and safer processes for capturing and modifying business rules are related with visual business process models. In this paper, possibilities of representing business rules by UML&OCL models and their applicability in modern development processes are investigated[1].

Keywords: Business rule, UML, OCL, stereotype, constraint, invariant, event, action, condition.

1 Introduction

Nowadays every complex and long-term information system has to deal with business rules (BR). Business process management, Service Oriented Architecture (SOA), Web Services, Component-based development, Semantic Web and ordinary databases – some day everyone working in these areas will confront with necessity to separate business rules from the rest of the considered domain. Currently business rules-based IS development methods are evolving rapidly; nevertheless the business rules are implemented mainly in the so called business rules engines that are suitable for specific type of business rules (i.e. production rules). Business rules engines are appearing everywhere as a standalone tools (Blaze Advisor, ILOG Rules, Haley systems etc.) as well as components of the middleware, accompanying databases (Microsoft, IBM, Oracle), ERP tools (SAP) etc.

Regardless of these facts, Platform-Independent business rules can be specified in a very limited number of CASE tools (mostly, using informal natural language sentences or OCL); some CASE tools provide limited rule checking functionality; none of the CASE tools provide a full set of business rules management functions.

Business rules techniques are not widely used in the methods of Model Driven Development (MDD); the existing solutions are still of experimental nature. Recently

---

[1] The work is supported by Lithuanian State Science and Studies Foundation according to High Technology Development Program Project "VeTIS" (Reg.No. B-07042).

J. Stirna and A. Persson (Eds.): PoEM 2008, LNBIP 15, pp. 182–196, 2008.

OMG has issued Semantics of Business Vocabulary and Business Rules (SBVR) [26] for documenting and the interchange of business vocabularies and business rules among organizations and software tools. SBVR business rules are based on predicate logic with a small extension in modal logic. They are applicable for linguistic processing and are designed for business people and business purposes, independent of information systems designs.

The core idea of the Business Rules Approach is to take semantic business rule representations and convert them to information system designs. However, this idea is still far from a reality. Business rules in the inputs of business rule engines have the shape of platform-specific representations, i.e. they are very far from SBVR rules. For the present, business rules are entered into IS design process in various phases, mostly – during implementation. This situation may change soon, as OMG already has issued the Production Rule Representation (PRR) standard for platform-independent production rules; RuleML initiative and REWERSE group are working on interchangeable specifications for other kinds of rules, devoted for Semantic Web and Object-Oriented systems; there even are proposals for transformation of SBVR specifications to UML models [11, 21]. Obviously, in the near future we will be able to manage the overall path from business design to implementing software code, inter-relate them and rapidly reflect business changes in supporting information technologies.

While platform-specific representation of business rules is essentially incompatible with requirement of being "designed for business people", semantic SBVR style representation is none the less difficult. Processes for specifying well-formed, reconciled sets of pure declarative business rules, advocated by Ross [22, 23], conformable to the problem domain, are not defined yet. Business rules are better understood and reconciled when they are captured during business modelling by the use of visual modelling tools. Therefore we are discussing the possibilities of using UML diagrams supplemented with Object Constraint Language (OCL) for expressing different types of rules defined in [5, 28, 30] or elsewhere. In UML metamodel, rules can be expressed in OCL or any other language as `OpaqueExpressions`, representing `ValueSpecifications` of constraints, parameters and other elements of UML models. As single UML constraints are not able to describe all known types of business rules, they are suitable to do this together with other UML elements (objects, operations, actions, events etc).

The rest of the paper is organized as follows. In section 2 the related work is analysed. Section 3 presents the life cycle of information systems augmented with business rules solutions. In section 4, applicability of UML&OCL models for representation of business rules is analysed. Sections 5 and 6 shortly present UML constraint extensions and Template-Based Language for representing business rules. Finally, section 9 draws some conclusions and highlights the future work.

2 Related Work

Addressing to the numerous related work, we have raised two questions. The first of them – *how to structure expressions representing business rules*? Business rules are becoming more and more important in information systems. Ontology developers, Business rules community, UML modellers are developing different business rules languages and tools. As business rules are independent from their representation, different business rules systems should be able to communicate and business rules in any language should adhere to a single, unified abstract syntax (metamodel). In SBVR [26] and Ontology Definition Metamodel (ODM) [18] standards such syntax is the Common Logics (CL).

Common Logic (CL) is essentially different from other rule metamodels since it is rather the dialect of first order logic than a modelling language. First order logic is the foundation of knowledge representation models, including relational databases. CL is a modern form of first order logic, oriented to new application domains. For example, CL can represent irregular sentences, required for SBVR modal expressions.

If we look at business rule metamodels related with different business rule modelling languages we would see the very similar but fairly inconsistent pictures. RuleML [30], designed for interchange between different languages and types of rules, is based on the construct common for all types of rules – logical sentence (or logical formula). In SBVR, such construct is called as logical formulation [26], in ODM – logical sentence [18]. The structure of these constructs is slightly different. Such diversities sometimes raise the need to develop own business rule metamodels, similar to OMG and other standards but having own specific properties (e.g. [27]).

OMG has chosen CL over OCL as business rules representation language, because, first, SBVR vocabularies are using natural, but not object-oriented language; secondly, OCL still lacks inference essential for ontological models. OCL is translatable to first order logics [1, 2] and quite capable to represent PIM business rules. As SBVR and ODM standards should be interoperable with other OMG standards it is purposeful to consider them during develment of methodology for modelling PIM business rules. Here comes the REWERSE Rule Markup Language [14, 15, 27] – a format for rule interchange between RuleML, Semantic Web Rule Language (SWRL) and OCL. These languages have rich syntax for representing rules, i.e. they are supporting typed atoms and terms that is unattainable in standard predicate logic. R2ML format retains constructs of different languages by reconstructing them to logical formulas that are suited to access differences between OCL and ontological languages (OWL and RDF) for ensuring lossless transformations. R2ML encompasses integrity, derivation, production and reaction rules (also defined in RuleML).

OMG PRR standard [20] is the UML extension designed for object-oriented PIM level production rules, where production rule extends UML metaclass `NamedElement`; as one of possible implementations, PRR specification is considering rule components as OCL expressions, supplemented by imperative expressions to representing actions (namely, invoke, update state, and assign). In general, the upper PRR structure of production rules is similar to proposed by RuleML and R2ML, but PRR is not explicitly considering correspondence to logical expressions or Semantic Web Languages.

Our approach differs from PRR in two essential points: we are relying on direct usage of UML models with OCL expressions for capturing components of business rules; and we propose constraint stereotypes for aligning OCL expressions with logical expressions of business rules.

URML [13] is the interesting proposal of REWERSE group for visual modelling of derivation and production rules; the approach was implemented in UML CASE tool "Strelka". Rules are represented as the first class entities in class models and have relationship (supplemented with expressions) with concepts involved. Unhappily, this approach differs from practice of expressing business rules in object oriented models and may be inefficient for the large sets of business rules.

The second question – *what process is appropriate for defining "real" business rules*? Current business-driven development, aiming at a tighter alignment of the IT infrastructure with business needs and requirements, centres on business processes when process management software or other artefacts are derived directly from process models [7, 9]. Alternatively, we see the perspective in deriving PIM artefacts from models of interactions and state machines [3]. The Model Driven Enterprise Engineering (MDEE) methodology created by KnowGravity is one of the first efforts to apply OMG SBVR and other standards in the holistic IS development process where information technologies are managed by business needs [25]. MDEE supports the smooth going from SBVR structural and operative rules to PIM Constraints, ECA and CA (Condition-Action) rules (corresponding to production rules). It uses fact diagrams for representing business vocabularies; UML class, use case diagrams and state machines for representing system models; and BPMN for modelling business processes. The final PIM is presented by executable state machines with KnowGravity expressions for business rules that are proprietary solution requiring hard manual efforts; nevertheless, MDEE is an excellent evidence of usefulness and applicability of OMG standards. Finally, a very initial prototype, proposed by Linehan [11] for transformation of limited SBVR rules to OCL preconditions, also is related with business process modelling. Obviously, the desired methodologies for defining Ross's or SBVR business rules do not exist yet and they are the subject of the future research.

The simple, but proven BROOD approach recently published in [12] gives the partial answer[2] to both aforementioned questions by proposing simple templates for specification of restricted typology of business rules, and simple object-oriented development process that augments UML by explicitly considering business rules as an integral part of an object-oriented development. BROOD process is supported by tool developed on top of the Generic Modeling Environment (GME) [10]. This approach (though it is not related with OCL) has many common points with our efforts and represents modern trends in Model Driven Engineering (MDE) [6], i.e. development of modeling environments tailored for specific domains and specific development methodologies.

Considering research related with OCL templates it is worth to mention general OCL templates implemented in Rational Software Architect [31, 32]; our own research in developing stereotypes and templates for integrity constraints [16, 19]; the work [4]; attempts to transform OCL to natural language [1].

3 Model Driven Development Process Incorporating Business Rule Approach

In Model Driven Development the biggest part of the work efforts is put into model development and most of the schemas and program code are generated automatically. Naturally, it becomes more and more vital to computerize and automate the very early

---

[2] BROOD process starts from the analysis phase.

stages of IS development. However, this is not so easy to accomplish. IS developers and business people are still suffering from the absence of a common language that would be understandable for all parties, formal enough to be unambiguous, and not too excessive.

This problem concerns all phases of the IS development life cycle where the collective participation of business people and developers is necessary. Figure 1 shows the vision of the business rule-extended IS development method related with the OMG standards and MDA.

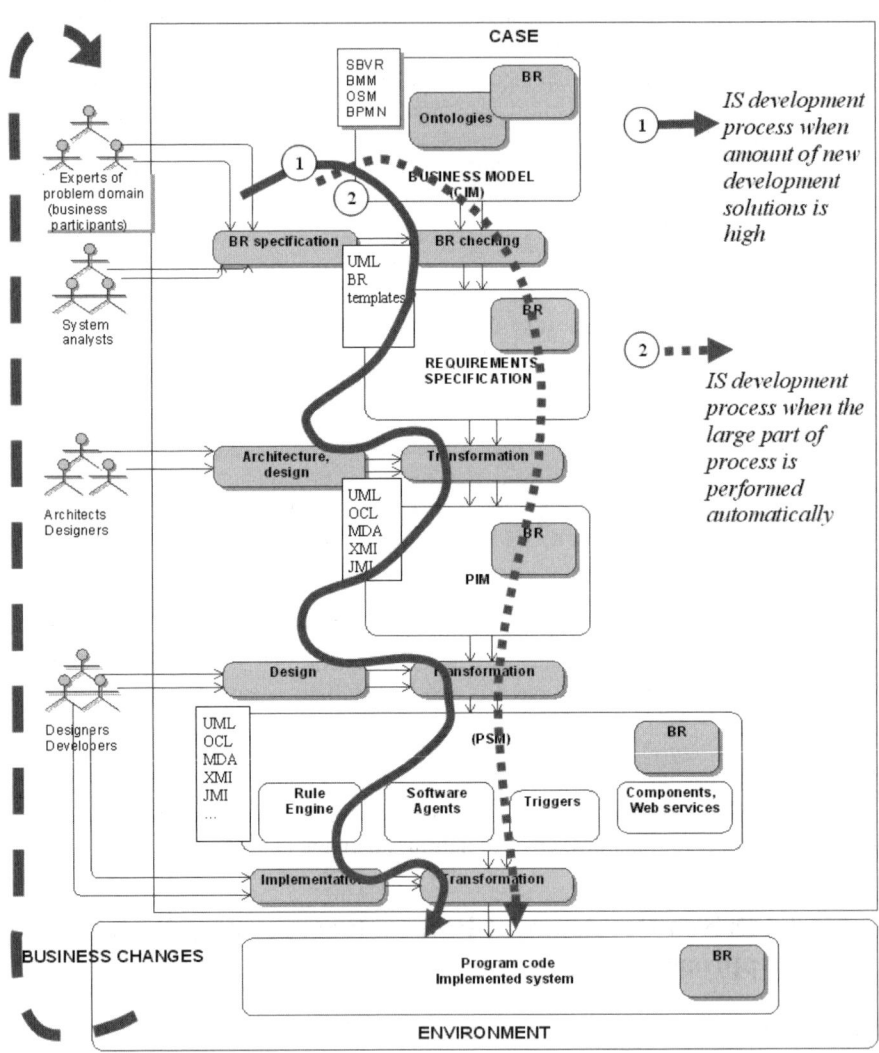

Fig. 1. The life cycle of information systems augmented with business rules solutions

At the beginning of the development process, experts of the problem domain are using the natural language to describe the problem domain. Such descriptions lack precision; they are ambiguous and can be interpreted incorrectly. Later they experience difficulties verifying domain models that were developed by the system analyst. One of the main reasons of this problem are notations (e.g. UML), hardly readable for non-technical people. Business rule specification language could be used as one of the most effective techniques to communicate. This language should be close enough to the natural language and at the same time formal enough to be precise and unambiguous.

Business rules are intensively used during the software development process and should be traceable through the overall IS development life cycle thus linking the program code with problem domain and enabling rapid reflection of changes in business environment to the changes of supporting Information Technology system. Though the ideal Business Rule Approach is to take semantic business rule representations and convert them to information system designs, in many cases these rules would be entered by system analysts during requirements phase. Such rules would have stricter and less end-user friendly form.

The key part of the process is the specification of business rules using natural language based templates, thus preserving their natural form. Such approach allows active participation of the stakeholders in the process of BR specification. The process as well as the ways of the business rules support can have a lot of variations [8, 24, 29]. Figure 1 presents two extreme cases. The first one – when a lot of new design related decisions have to be made and in every stage of the process active participation of analysts, designers and programmers is required. In the second case the main task of IS design is the specification of business rules and requirements, while the subsequent representation of all that in the program code is carried out almost automatically, according to the known, repetitive architectural and implementation solutions. It must be noted that qualified specialists would be required to write the specific code or to set the parameters of the BR templates, but the efficiency of the design process increases dramatically.

Furthermore, developers are relieved of repetitive and uncreative job and the amount of errors decreases. The most important achievement, however, is the strong connection between the business semantics and its implementation. This enables the quicker and more efficient identification of the points influenced by the changes.

4   Applicability of UML&OCL Models for Representation of Business Rules

According RuleML, PRR and R2ML, PIM level business rules may be classified into integrity, derivation, production, event-condition-action (ECA), event-condition-action-postcondition (ECAP) and transformation rules, having condition, action, postcondition, left hand side (LHS), right hand side (RHS) and other expressions as their components (Fig. 2). These components are expressible using UML and OCL constructs. Main UML constructs for business rules representation are *Constrains* that have their context, `constrainedElements` and `ValueSpecifications` [17] (Fig. 6). Value specification may be provided as `OpaqueExpression` using any

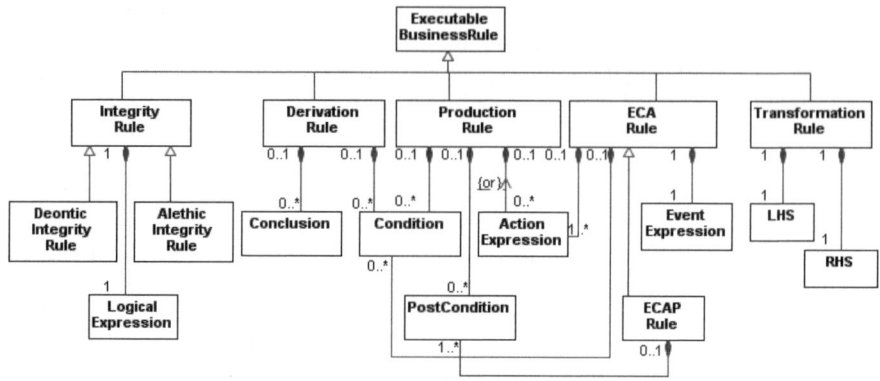

Fig. 2. Classification and composition of executable business rules (adapted from RuleML, R2ML [28, 30])

language un-interpretable in UML. Business rules are represented using logical expressions or sentences such as disjunction, conjunction, negation (strong negation or negation as failure), implication, bi-conditional comparisons ($>$, $<$, $\leq$, $\geq$, ...), quantified sentences (existential and universal), and user defined predicates (i.e. functions or relations).

Integrity rules are represented by OCL invariants. This type of rules is best understandable and supported in several UML CASE tools (e.g. Magic Draw, Rational Software Architect, USE, OCLE etc.). OCL invariants still may represent other types of rules: derivations, transformations and even action expressions (by explicit specification of operations).

State machines are capable to express derivation rules for object states (via state invariants); event and action expressions; conditions and postconditions. Event expressions represent names of called operations, received signals; time and change events and possibly others. For example, `Order` state machine fragment on Figure 3 b is represented by the following OCL expression on Figure 4.

Guards on transitions of state machines should be pure expressions without side effects; they correspond to conditions of PR or ECA rules (Table 1).

Table 1. Correspondence between ECAP rule and UML &OCL model on Figures 3–4

Rule component	UML&OCL element	Example
Event		`Order::approve()`
Condition	Source state[3] and guard	`self.customer.oclInState(Registered)` `self.customer.rating>=0,4`
Action	Effect	`Order::approve()` `Order::verifyCustomer()`
Postcondition	Target state	`self.oclInState(Approved)`

---

[3] Condition implied by a source state often is accepted by default as the condition of existence of operation parameters.

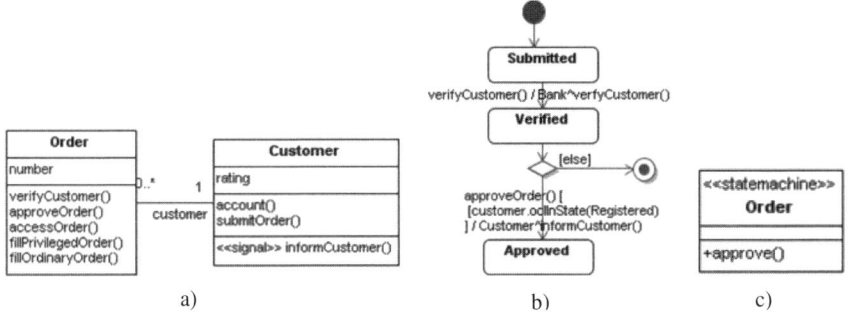

Fig. 3. Fragment of state machine (b) for `Order` (a). Called operations (e.g. `approve()`) may belong to class `Order` (a) or directly to its behaviour (i.e. state machine (c)).

```
context Order::approve():Boolean
pre: self.oclInState(Verified) and
     self.customer.oclInState(Registered) and
         self.customer.rating>=0,4
post: self.oclInState(Approved)
         and self.customer^informCustomer()
```

Fig. 4. OCL constraint for operation `approve()`

Unlike `if-then` constructs in programming languages, production rule languages in BR engines often do not allow `if-then-else` rules, but the action of a PR can represent operation invocation, branching or looping constructs. Similarly, effects of state machine transitions may represent any kind of behavior – state machine, activity, interaction or opaque behavior. Conversely, branching of transitions using decision points and `else` conditions helps avoiding ambiguities and incompleteness, i.e. ensures that for any occurrence of the event only one transition can fire, and an alternative transition exists if event would not occur [17]. As branching transitions may be reconstructed to simple transitions, this factor does not prevent the mapping between state machines and PR, ECA, or ECAP rules. UML protocol state machines directly represent preconditions (subsetting guards) and postconditions (instead of effects) on transitions.

Postconditions often are not needed as postconditions of one rule become the preconditions of another rule(s). Postconditions are important when transition has no event and action. Then we have a derivation rule, i.e. the PR of type `if condition then postcondition`. Postconditions include the target state of the transition (possibly with state invariant). State invariants are derivation rules explicitly stating the meaning of the state.

We can obtain derivation rules from invariants having expressions "`if-then`" and "`implies`". For example, the derivation rule expressing the meaning of `Customer` state `Registered` may be defined as in Figure 5.

However, the implication does not mean a derivation by itself; it may be translated to derivation by making the corresponding methodological solution.

OCL postconditions may include message sending and receiving expressions that in general may represent composite states, activities or interactions. In UML state machine notation, such cases are represented by additional diagrams referenced by an effect. For representation of messages, interactions or sequence diagrams are more suitable. For example, sequence diagram in Figure 6 may be represented by the following OCL expression on Figure 7.

```
Customer inv inv1:
self.oclInState(Registered) implies self.account()=true
or
Customer inv inv1:
   if self.account()=true then self.oclInState(Registered)
      else false endIf
```

Fig. 5. State invariant as a derivation rule

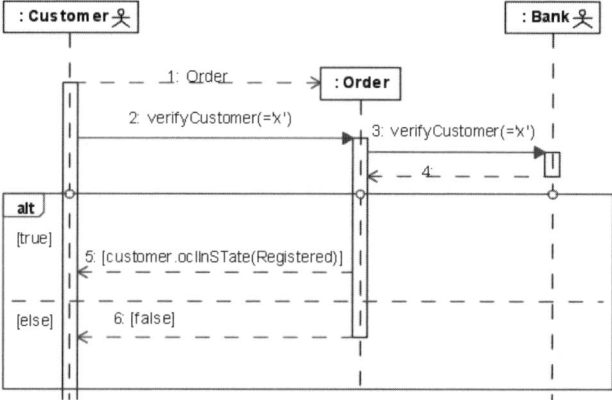

Fig. 6. Sequence diagram for effect `verifyCustomer` (Fig. 3, b)

```
context Order::verifyCustomer(x:Customer):Boolean
post:let message:oclMessage = Bank^verifyCustomer(x:Customer) in
      if message.hasReturned() and message.result=true
      then self.customer.oclInState(Registered) and
      self.customer=x
      else false endIf
```

Fig. 7. OCL expression for operation `VerifyCustomer()` (Fig. 6)

Here we will have ECAP rule with `ElseCondition` (Table 2). Expression `self.customer=x` may be named as "CreationCondition"; such expressions are able to represent bodies of updating or creation operations by assigning values of operation parameters to objects and their properties.

Activity diagrams in some aspects are similar to state machines. For example, we can define operations, corresponding to `callOperation` actions from activity diagram fragment on Figure 8, by the OCL expressions presented on Figure 9.

Table 2. Correspondence between ECAP rule and UML &OCL model on Figures 6–7

Rule component	UML&OCL element	Example
`Event`	`message`	`verifyCustomer(x:Customer)`
`Condition`	`guard`	`message.result=true`
`Action`	`message`	`Bank^verifyCustomer(x:Customer)`
`Postcondition`	`guard`	`self.customer.oclInState(Registered)`
		`self.customer=x`
`ElseCondition`	`guard`	`false`

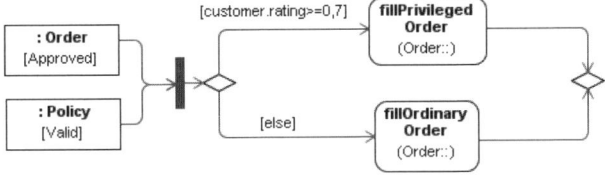

Fig. 8. Activity diagram fragment

```
context Order::fillPrivilegedOrder():Boolean
pre: self.oclInState(Approved) and
      policy.oclInState(Valid) and
          self.customer.rating>=0,7
context Order::fillOrdinaryOrder():Boolean
pre: self.oclInState(Approved) and
      policy.oclInState(Valid) and
          self.customer.rating<0,7
```

Fig. 9. OCL expression for `CallOperation` actions from Figure 8

UML 2 structured activities (conditional activities, loops, sequences), expansion regions, interaction constraints and other also give many possibilities for representing business rules. Generalizing UML possibilities for representing business rules we can conclude:

- Integrity rules are directly represented in class diagrams as invariants;
- Derivations are indirectly represented in class diagrams as invariants; in state machines and interactions – as state invariants or transitions without events and effects;
- Action rules (PR, ECA, ECAP) are indirectly represented in several ways: in class diagrams as preconditions, postconditions or body conditions of operations; guards and other types of constraints on messages, transitions, control and object flows, interaction fragments, structured activities etc in behavioral diagrams (interactions, state machines and activities).
- For explicit representation of business rules it is purposeful to extend UML models reusing existing UML elements as much as possible. In OMG standards semantics of OCL expressions for representing UML constraints is clearly defined

only for invariants and operation constraints in class diagrams. For other diagrams the semantics of OCL expressions is not defined and should be clarified.

5 UML Constraint Extensions for Representing Business Rules

Performed analysis lets us make an assumption that the following extensions (the generalization set is overlapping and incomplete) would be useful for specification of business rules in UML models (Fig. 10).

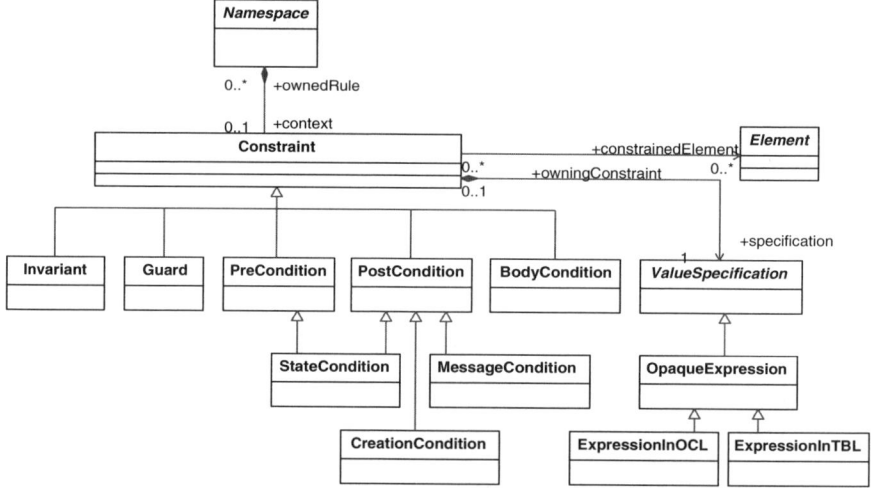

Fig. 10. UML constraint extensions for business rules

Components of business rules represented by UML constraints have value specifications as `OpaqueExpressions` described in OCL (`ExpressionInOCL`) or in any other language, for example, Template Based Language (TBL) as `ExpressionInTBL` (Fig. 10). Example of constraint stereotypes is presented on Figure 11.

```
<<preCondition>><<stateCondition>>: self.oclInState(Submitted)
<<preCondition>><<stateCondition>>self.customer.oclInState(Registered)
<<preCondition>> self.customer.rating>=0,7
<<postCondition>>>><<stateCondition>>: self.oclInState(Approved)
<<postCondition>>>><<messageCondition>>self.customer^verifyCustomer()
```

Fig. 11. Stereotypes for constraints of operation `approve()` (Fig.4)

The greatest obstacle for expansion of business rules approach is the lack of means for supporting the entering of business rules to design models. In the following section we present the prototype of Template Based Language for entering business rules during development of IS.

6   Entering Business Rules Using Template Based Language

Template Based Language currently is a trial language implemented as plug-in of UML CASE tool Magic Draw for input of class invariants into UML class diagrams.

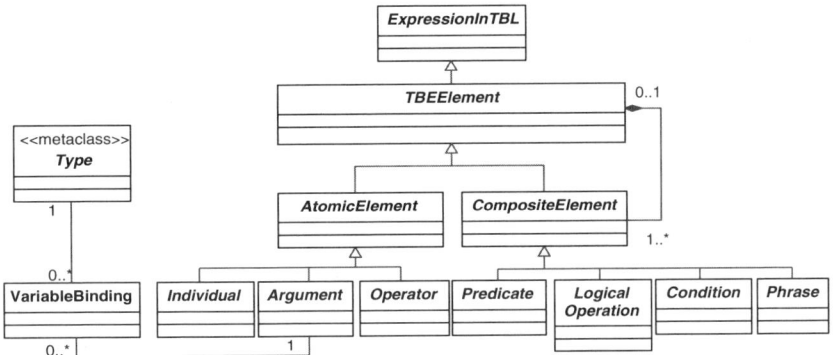

Fig. 12. TBL expressions

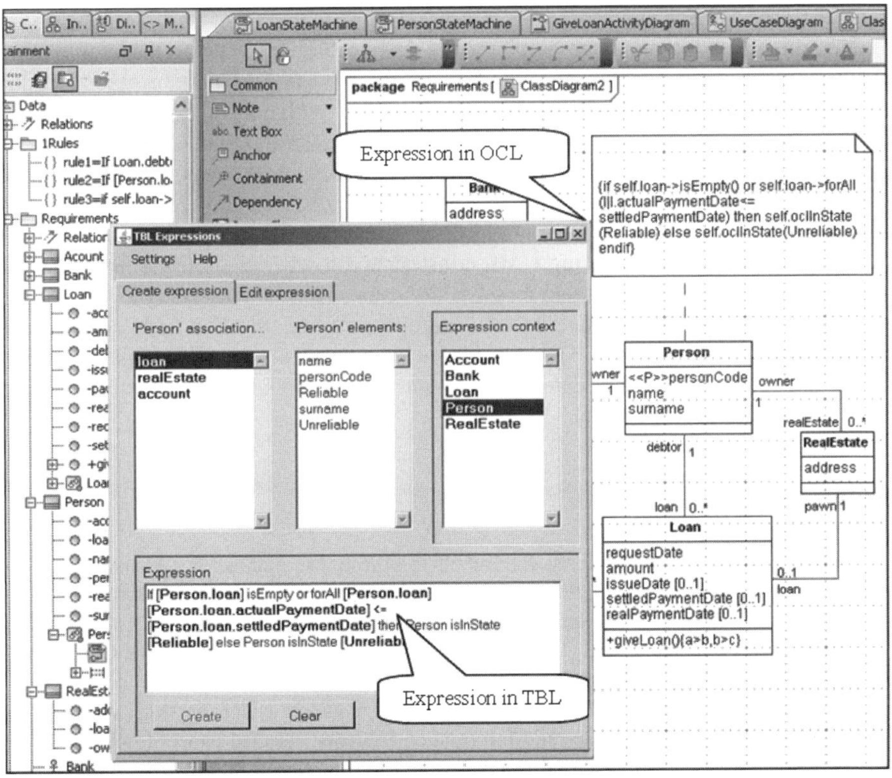

Fig. 13. Interface for entering TBL expressions

Currently this project is under extension for enabling the input of TBL rules into behavioral diagrams – state machines, interactions and activities. TBL rules can be related to classes, properties (attributes, operations and association ends), state machine states and transitions; activity flows and decision points; sequence diagram messages and interaction fragments. Structure of TBL expressions is simple, yet powerful through recursion (Fig. 12) (the similar ExeRule language was implemented in XML [27]). The interface for entering TBL expressions is presented in Figure 13.

Currently TBL expressions are very simple, having a little similarity with natural language. However, they are promising to significantly improve preciseness of IS designs supplementing them with business rules translatable to OCL or rule implementation languages. The most of business rules are simple and mainly require tool support with unambiguous representation and interpretation.

7   Conclusion and Future Work

We have presented the ongoing research that is performed according to High Technology Development Program Project "Business Rules Solutions for Information Systems Development (VeTIS)". In this paper we do not claim to solve all problems related with business rules, or present the overall results of this project. We would rather like to demonstrate our research fragments for discussion about the feasibility and efficiency of such approach.

The raising numbers of research and CASE tool implementations, concerning business rules, natural language and OCL, allow us to hope for the progress in this area. It is also a fact that UML models supplemented with constraints are suitable for the easier representation and implementation of business rules. These direct possibilities of UML may found the broad applicability in practical development of enterprise information systems based on different, specific architectures and development methodologies.

Categorization and structuring UML constraints allows representing them in a limited natural language translatable to OCL and other rule languages. Our very initial prototype for entering template-based constraints is still not the final answer; the future work will extend the TBL for UML behavioral diagrams; translate TBL to OCL, and, of course, investigate transformation of Template Based Expressions to rule implementation languages.

References

1. Ahrendt, W., Baar, T., Beckert, B., Bubel, R., Giese, M., Hähnle, R., Menzel, W., Mostowski, W.: The KeY Tool. Software and Systems Modeling 4(1), 32–54 (2005)
2. Beckert, B., Keller, U., Schmitt, P.H.: Translating the Object Constraint Language into First-order Predicate Logic. In: VERIFY, Workshop at Federated Logic Conferences (FLoC), Copenhagen, Denmark, pp. 1–11 (2002)
3. Ceponiene, L., Nemuraite, L.: Design independent modeling of information systems using UML and OCL. In: Databases and Information Systems: selected papers from the 6th International Baltic Conference on Databases and Information Systems, Riga, Latvia, June 06-09, 2004, pp. 224–237. IOS Press, Amsterdam (2004)

4. Costal, D., Gómez, C., Queralt, A., Raventos, R., Teniente, R.: Improving the definition of general constraints in UML. Software and systems modeling, pp. 1–18 (January 2008)
5. Defining Business Rules ~ What Are They Really? The Business Rules Group, formerly, known as the GUIDE Business Rules Project, Final Report, revision 1.3, pp. 1–77 (July 2000)
6. Deursen, A.V., Visser, E., Warmer, J.: Model-Driven Software Evolution: A Research Agenda. In: Tamzalit, D. (ed.) Proceedings 1st International Workshop on Model-Driven Software Evolution (MoDSE), pp. 41–49. University of Nantes, France (2007)
7. Gudas, S., Skersys, T.: The Enhancement of Class Model Development Using Business Rules. In: Bozanis, P., Houstis, E.N. (eds.) PCI 2005, LNCS, vol. 3746, pp. 480–490. Springer, Heidelberg (2005)
8. Kapocius, K., Butleris, R.: Repository for business rules based IS requirements. Informatica, Vilnius, 17(4), 503–518 (2006)
9. Koehler, J., Hauser, R., Küster, J., Ryndina, K., Vanhatalo, J., Wahler, M.: The Role of Visual Modeling and Model Transformations in Business-driven Development. In: Electronic Notes in Theoretical Computer Science (ENTCS), vol. 211, pp. 5–15. Elsevier Science Publishers, Amsterdam (2008)
10. Ledeczi, A., Maroti, M., Bakay, A., Karsai, G., Garrett, J., Thomason, C., Nordstrom, G., Sprinkle, J., Volgyesi, P.: The Generic Modeling Environment. In: Workshop on Intelligent Signal Processing, Budapest (2001)
11. Linehan, M.H.: Semantics in Model-driven Business Design. In: 2nd International Semantic Web Policy Workshop (SWPW 2006), Athens, GA, USA, pp. 1–8 (2006)
12. Loucopoulos, P., Kadir, W.M.N.W.: BROOD: Business Rules-driven Object Oriented Design. Journal of Database Management 19(1) (2008)
13. Lukichev, S., Wagner, G.: Visual Rules Modeling. In: Virbitskaite, I., Voronkov, A. (eds.) PSI 2006. LNCS, vol. 4378, pp. 467–473. Springer, Heidelberg (2007)
14. Milanović, M., Gašević, D., Giurca, A., Wagner, G., Devedžić, V.: On Interchanging between OWL/SWRL and UML/OCL. In: Proceedings of 6th Workshop on OCL for (Meta-)Models in Multiple Application Domains (OCLApps) at the 9th ACM/IEEE International Conference on Model Driven Engineering Languages and Systems (MoDELS), Genoa, Italy, pp. 81–95 (2006)
15. Milanovic, M., Gasevic, D., Giurca, A., Wagner, G., Devedzic, V.: Sharing OCL Constraints by Using Web Rules. In: Engels, G., Opdyke, B., Schmidt, D.C., Weil, F. (eds.) MODELS 2007. LNCS, vol. 4735, pp. 1–15. Springer, Heidelberg (2007)
16. Miliauskaite, E., Nemuraite, L.: Representation of integrity constraints in conceptual models. Information technology and control 34(4), 355–365 (2005)
17. OMG Unified Modeling Language (OMG UML), Superstructure, V2.1.2. OMG Available Specification formal/2007-11-02 (2007)
18. Ontology Definition Metamodel Specification, OMG Adopted Specification ptc/2007-09-09 (2007)
19. Pakalnickiene, E., Nemuraite, L.: Checking of conceptual models with integrity constraints. Information technology and control 36(3), 285–294 (2007)
20. Production Rule Representation. Submission to Business Modeling and Integration Domain Taskforce. Fair Isaac Corporation, ILOG SA (2007)
21. Raj, A., Prabhakar, T.V., Hendryx, S.: Transformation of SBVR business design to UML models. In: ISEC 2008: Proceedings of the 1st conference on India software engineering conference, pp. 29–38. ACM, Hyderabad (2008)
22. Ross, R.G.: The Business Rule Book: Classifying, Defining an Modeling Rules. Business Rule Solutions, Houston (1997)

23. Ross, R.G.: Principles of the Business Rules Approach. Addison-Wesley, Reading (2003)
24. Ross, R.G., Lam, G.S.W.: The Do's and Don'ts of Expressing Business Rules. Business Rule Solutions,
    http://www.brsolutions.com/rulespeak_download.shtml
25. Schacher, M.: Business Rules from an SBVR and an xUML Perspective (Parts 1–3). Business Rules Journal 7(6-8) (2006)
26. Semantics of Business Vocabulary and Business Rules (SBVR), v1.0. OMG Available Specification formal/2008-01-02 (2008)
27. Vedrickas, G., Nemuraite, L.: Achieving business flexibility by empowering business component system with business rules technology: Executable rules. In: Vasilecas, O., Eder, J., Caplinskas, A. (eds.) Databases and Information Systems: Seventh International Baltic Conference on Databases and Information Systems. Communications, Materials of Doctoral Consortium, Technika, Vilnius, July 3-6, 2006, pp. 193–158 (2006)
28. Wagner, G., Giurca, A., Lukichev, S.: A Usable Interchange Format for Rich Syntax Rules. Integrating OCL, RuleML and SWRL. In: Proceedings of Reasoning on the Web, WWW Workshop, Edinburgh, Scotland (2006)
29. Wagner, G., Lukichev, S., Fuchs, N.E., Spreeuwenber, S.: First-Version Controlled English Rule Language. In: The Rewerse Group, pp. 1–47 (2005)
30. Wagner, G., Tabet, S., Boley, H.: MOF-RuleML: The Abstract Syntax of RuleML as a MOF Model, http://www.ruleml.org
31. Wahler, M., Ackerman, L., Schneider, S.: Using IBM Constraint Patterns and Consistency Analysis. IBM Developer Works (May 2008)
32. Wahler, M., Koehler, J., Brucker, A.D.: Model-driven constraint engineering. In: MoDELS Workshop on OCL for Meta-Models in Multiple Application Domains, Electronic Communications of the EASST, Technische Universität Dresden, Germany, vol. 5, pp. 1–15 (2006)

Laws-Based Ontology for e-Government Services Construction

Case Study: The Specification of Services in Relationship with the Venture Creation in Switzerland

Abdelaziz Khadraoui[1], Wanda Opprecht[1], Christine Aïdonidis[2], and Michel Léonard[1]

[1] University of Geneva, CUI - Batelle, rte de Drize 7, CH-1227 Carouge, Switzerland
Tel.: +41 22- 379 – 0227; Fax: +41 22- 379 – 0233
{abdelaziz.khadraoui,wanda.opprecht,michel.leonard}@unige.ch
[2] Observatoire Technologique, Centre des Technologies de l'Information, État de Genève
64, 66 rue du Grand Pré, 1211 Genève 3
Tel.: +41 22- 388 – 1355
christine.aidonidis@etat.ge.ch

Abstract. In this paper, we present our approach in the field of e-Government services construction. In this work, the ontological level extracted from legal sources is used as means to define and to construct e-Government services. Building Information System (IS) and e-Government services based on legal sources presents many advantages: (i) the services and IS conforms to the legal framework that organize the activities supporting the IS and (ii) the proposed approach allows clarifying the links between legal sources, e-Government services and IS, in particular, the alignment between the amendment of laws and the evolution of e-Government services.

Keywords: Information System, e-Government, service, legal sources, activity.

1 Introduction

The institutional activities are governed by legal sources represented by a set of laws which regulates their execution. The contents of laws are mandatory for the institutional domain and represent a reference for the professionals (managers) as well as for the e-Government designers.

However, the legal sources are not properly considered in most existing approaches for e-Government architectures. Theses approaches lack a systematic framework for the compliance of e-Government services with legal sources. This compliance between legal aspects and e-Government services[1] is a crucial issue for administrations. This

---

[1] We adopt the following definitions of service: From [9]: "In business science, service is defined as any business action or business activity that has a added value result for a person or a system, this action or activity is offered by another person, entities or a system that make benefits from providing this action". From [6] a service is defined as: "Any act or performance that one party can offer to another that is essentially intangible and does not result in the ownership of anything. Its production may or may not be tied to a physical product".

J. Stirna and A. Persson (Eds.): PoEM 2008, LNBIP 15, pp. 197–209, 2008.
© IFIP International Federation for Information Processing 2008

issue becomes more difficult with the fast-evolving dynamics of laws (i.e. the amendment of a law, the abrogation of a law and the introduction of a new law). This paper illustrates two specific problems:

- How to take into account the legal sources in e-Government architecture?
- How to build the e-Government services based on legal sources?

Our goal in this paper is to present our approach to describe and establish the link between e-Government services and legal sources. This link is established by an ontology which is called "Laws based ontology". In other words, this ontology is used to define and construct the e-Government services. The paper is structured as follows. Section 2 introduces our proposed framework for the construction of e-Government services. Section 2.1 describes the method for extracting ontology from legal sources. Section 2.2 presents the conceptual basis for discovering and constructing e-Government services. Section 3 discusses difficulties related to the deployment of the proposed approach in public administration.

2   Framework for the Construction of e-Government Services

Our goal in this paper is to use the ontological level extracted from legal sources as means to define and to construct e-Government services.

We present a method to describe the ontological level for e-Government services construction. This is composed of two steps:

- Step 1: Ontology construction from legal sources.
- Step 2: e-Government services identification.

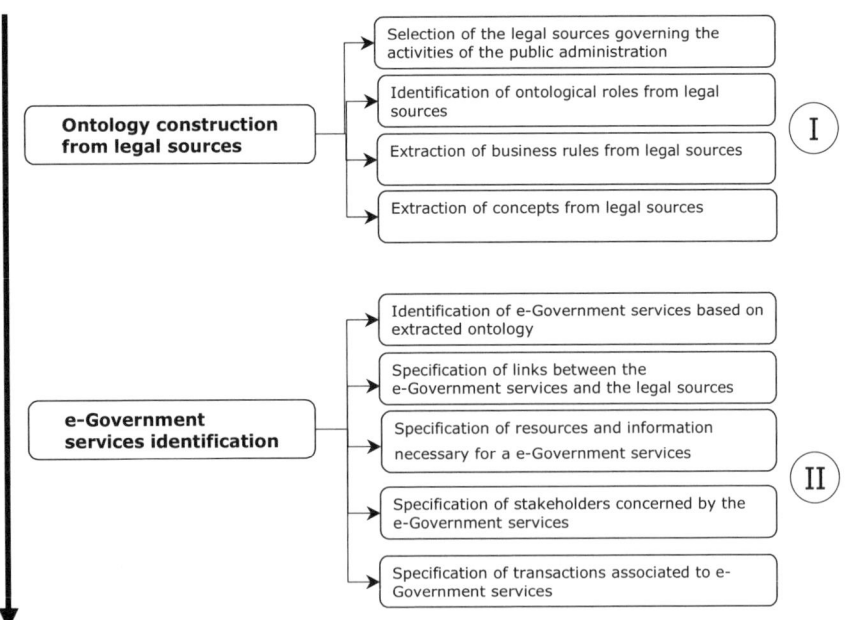

Fig. 1. e-Government services based on legal sources

2.1 Ontology Construction from Legal Sources

In the context of Information System (IS) engineering, we define an ontology as a conceptual information model that describes some specific domain in term of concepts, facts and business rules. An ontology is a reference model which supports information interoperability and shares information: (1) it supports human understanding of the domain under consideration and communication, (2) it facilitates the interoperability across different parts of IS.

The meaning of ontology considerably evolved from its origins in philosophy to its current usage in IS for e-Government. While ontology in the philosophical sense roughly means a categorization of all the entities that exist in the world and the relationships between them, ontology in the IS sense is only considered as a limited universe of discourse [10]. In our research work, laws are considered as a universe of discourse for IS engineering. The concepts and business rules extracted from the appropriate laws are used to build the ontological aspects of the corresponding domain.

Legal texts describe concepts, business rules and roles governing the given institutional domain. The exploitation of these sources of knowledge permits to enhance IS adequacy and compatibility with institution activities and to find stable common information for IS engineering for e-Government in the perspective of sustainable development.

"Laws based ontology" is a new approach for IS engineering that allows establishing and clarifying the links between laws and IS, in particular the alignment between the amendment of laws and the evolution of IS. In other words, we use laws as a source of knowledge to analyze and construct the ontological level of an institutional domain. The exploitation of these sources of knowledge permits to find stable concepts. For us, an ontology contains the stable common information of the IS domain.

In our approach, the "Laws based ontology" is built from one or several hyperconcepts (Hcp) [5]. A Hyperconcept is constructed on a subset of concepts extracted from laws, forming a unity with a precise semantic. It is represented by an oriented graph where nodes are concepts and edges are links between concepts. There are only three types of links: (i) instantiations, (ii) existential dependencies and (iii) generalization-specialization links [5]. Our knowledge representation model to describe the "Laws based ontology" is then an oriented graph.

Several structured languages may be used to describe this ontology. For example, we can employ OWL (Web Ontology Language), OIL (Ontology Inference Layer or Ontology Interchange Language), TELOS language as mean to specify the "Laws based ontology".

The particularity of our knowledge representation model in the context of IS engineering is the ability to establish the link between legal sources and IS specification. More precisely, our aim with this model is to specify the business rules, the organizational roles and the fundamental concepts dedicated to develop an IS and to specify e-Government services.

The hyperconcept schema must satisfy a set of conformity rules including connectivity and concept completeness. The connectivity guarantees that each concept of a hyperconcept is related to at least one other concept from the same hyperconcept. In this case, the hyperconcept represents a homogeneous zone and not a discontinuous unit. If the concept C_1 belongs to the hyperconcept *Hcp* and is linked to the concept C_2, then C_2 also belongs to *Hcp*.

The process model of the construction of an ontology from laws is expressed as a map (i.e. strategic guideline) [8]. The nodes represent the intentions and the links between the nodes represent the strategies. An intention indicates the goal to reach and a strategy specifies the manner with which the intention can be carried out.

Figure 2 specifies the processes of the proposed method for extracting an ontology from laws. This map comprises five intentions called:

- Select the laws governing the IS domain and e-Government services.
- Define the ontological roles.
- Define a hyperconcept.
- Build a hyperconcept.
- Validate a hyperconcept.

In [5], we proposed guidelines and method components for the extraction of the laws based ontology. Each guideline can be composed of a set of more detailed sub-guidelines or on the contrary be a part of some more complex guideline.

For a given domain, we propose firstly to identify the set of legal texts such as laws, application regulation which formalize the IS domain (figure 2). The study of each of these texts should be made only in the perspective of IS engineering. The laws contain information and knowledge of purely legal nature, which cannot be considered in the IS. Only the key concepts of the domain and business rules are identified and retained. The analysis and interpretation of certain laws is a complex process. An important effort is required to carry out this process. Collaboration with an expert in legislation is necessary.

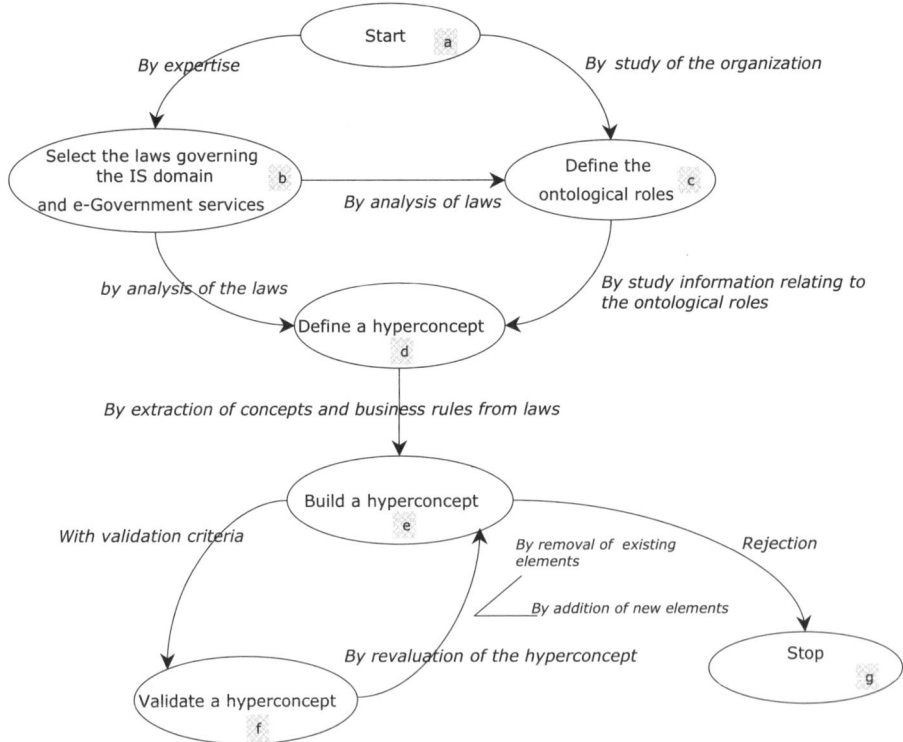

Fig. 2. The process of construction of an ontology from laws

Table 1. Example extracted from the Swiss federal law "Ordonnance sur le Registre du Commercial".

---

4. Associations
Art. 97
The registration of an association indicates:
   a.   the statutes date;
   b.   the name;
   c.   the head office;
   d.   the objective;
   e.   the resources;
   f.   the organisation, the representation and the signature mode.

Art. 98
The registration query is signed by the association's manager. It comes together with:

   a.   a legal abstract of the General Assembly minutes which adopted the statutes
        and designed the bodies, as well as the indication of the authorised people to
        sign and the signature mode (if necessary).
   b.   a copy of the statutes (art. 28, al 4^{110}).

10. Examination by the commercial register office
Art 111a
        a.   … the associations registered at the commercial register receives an iden-
   tification number.

Figure 2 illustrates two strategies for the definition of the ontological roles. The first strategy is based on the analysis of the domain of the corresponding IS and the second is based on the analysis of the laws which formalize the IS domain.

The map (figure 2) proposes two strategies to define a hyperconcept. The first strategy is based on the analysis of the texts of laws and the second is based on the study of the information related to ontological roles.

The construction of a hyperconcept is carried out by the extraction of concepts and business rules from laws. The validation of a hyperconcept is carried out by the application of validation criteria. A hyperconcept can be rejected, which causes its revaluation. This revaluation is expressed by the addition of new elements to the hyperconcept or by the removal of existing elements belonging to the hyperconcept.

The proposed method is illustrated with one case study: the specification of services in relationship with the venture creation in Switzerland and in the State of Geneva. We have selected the Commercial Register area which mainly encompasses the registration of a new company and the modification of its registration. This case study includes services about company registration, raising finance, taxes payment, employees hiring, social insurances and business premises.

With this case, our main goal is to exemplify our methodology, that is, to define and to build e-Government services by the extraction of key concepts from laws. We consider legal sources as prominent, as an absolute referential.

In order to select the most appropriate legal sources at the federal level regarding the Commercial Register and the related services which may be offered, we have used a Swiss doctrinal source[2] which is considered as a reference by legal experts.

---

[2] Fiches juridiques suisses. http://www.fjs.ch

The main law regarding the Commercial Register is the "Ordonnance sur le Registre du Commerce"[3.] We have thus begun to analyse this legal source.

We have then extracted the most significant concepts from the select laws. Here is an example of hyperconcept "Examination of the registration of an association" based on the articles 97-98-111a regarding the registration of an association to the Commercial Register. An association is one out of the fifteen legal forms of organisation concerned by the Swiss Commercial Register.

The following ontological business rules can be extracted from this law fragments:

- the registration of an association to the Commercial Register must indicate the statutes date, the association name, the head office, the objective, the resources, the organisation, the representation and the signature mode.
- the registration query must be signed by the association's manager.
- the registration query must come together with a legal abstract of the General Assembly minutes, the indication of the authorised people to sign, the signature mode, and a copy of the statutes.

The figure 3 illustrates the hyperconcept schema.

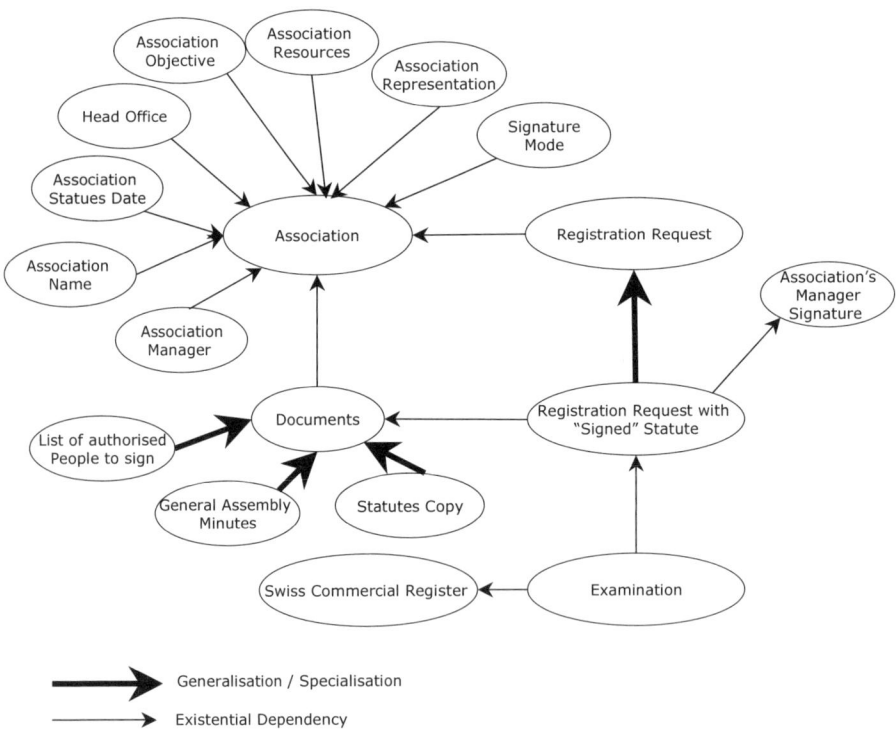

Fig. 3. Hyperconcept "Examination of the registration of an association"

---

[3] Ordonnance du 7 juin 1937 sur le registre du commerce (ORC), RS 221.411. http://www.admin.ch/ch/f/rs/c221_411.html

The following ontological roles can be extracted from this law fragments:

- Association.
- Association's manager.
- Commercial Register Office (cantonal administration).

2.2 Public Administration Services Identification

The model presented below could serve as the conceptual basis for identifying public administration services.

2.2.1 Hyperconcepts and e-Government Services

e-Government services are subject to government regulation. As we said previously, we used the legal framework to define public administration services. More precisely, the constructed hyperconcepts are used as means to define and build e-Government services. The key element of the proposed model is the entity "Service".

A service is defined by a name, a description, a type, and a goal. A subset of services can be defined and proposed based on the established ontology. This task is carried out by analysing the semantics of the constructed hyperconcepts. This analysis requires the validation of the business actors who are concerned by e-Government.

The Entity "Hyperconcept – Service" in the figure 4 expresses a many-to-many relationship between the Entity "Hyperconcept" and the Entity "Service". This relationship expresses the fact that one hyperconcept can be used to define one or several services. A service can be defined on one or several hyperconcepts. A service may need the invocation of other services.

In our example, the semantic of the hyperconcept «Examination of the registration of an association» allows us to define two services:

- The first service allows getting information about the registration conditions.
- The second service permits the validation and the examination of the registration request by the Swiss commercial register.

These two services are clearly identifiable in the hyperconcept.

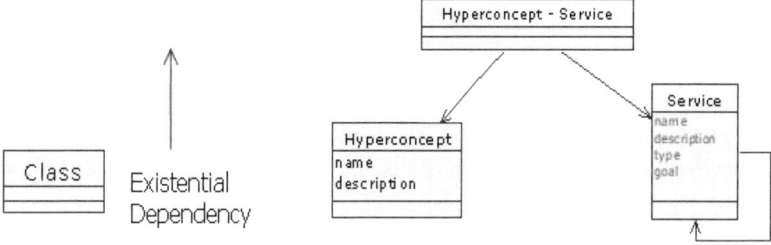

Fig. 4. Link between hyperconcepts and services

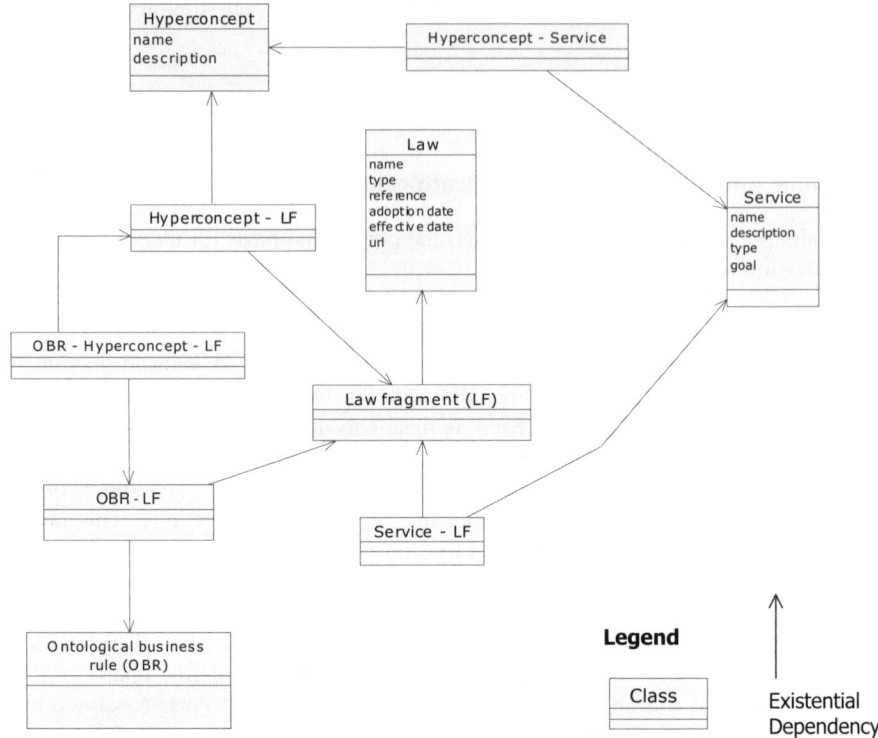

Fig. 5. Link between services, hyperconcepts, laws fragment and ontological business rules

A hyperconcept is defined on the basis of one or several laws fragments (see figure 5). A law fragment can contribute to the definition and the construction of one or more hyperconcepts. We express this semantic relationship by the introduction of the entity "Hyperconcept - LF". An ontological business rule is extracted from one or several laws fragments and a law fragment can contain several ontological business rules. We express this relationship by the introduction of the entity "OBR - LF" in the model. We express the link between services and laws fragment by the entity "Service – LF".

A stakeholder can be concerned by one or more services. A service for its execution can involve one or more stakeholder. There are three categories of stakeholders: Enterprise, Public administration and Person (citizens). The public administration is the entity that provides the service to the enterprise, the citizen or to itself internally. In others words, the enterprise or the citizen interact with the administration to get all relevant information about services. The entity "Public admin.", in the proposed model, specifies the departments, divisions and branches in which public administration services are performed.

The relationship between the "Stakeholder" entity and the "Ontological role" entity expresses the facts that a part of defined stakeholders can be found in an ontological role described in laws. An ontological role represents a set of necessary responsibilities, authorities and capabilities, expressed in laws, to perform the execution of the

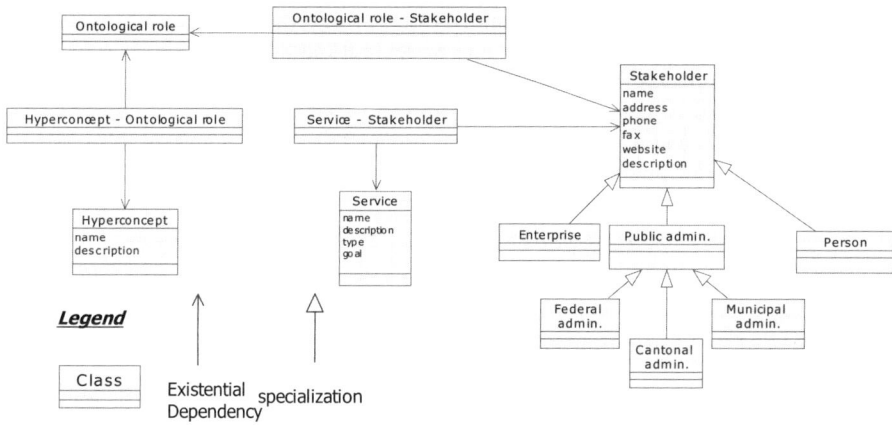

Fig. 6. Link between services, stakeholder and ontological roles

activities of the development process or to watch the execution of activities performed by the other roles.

In our example, the following ontological roles are considered as stakeholders:
- Association.
- Association's manager.
- Commercial Register Office (cantonal administration).

E-Government services are governed by preconditions which are expressed in our model (figure 7) by the entity "Resource and Information" (usually specified as an ontological business rule which is extracted from laws).

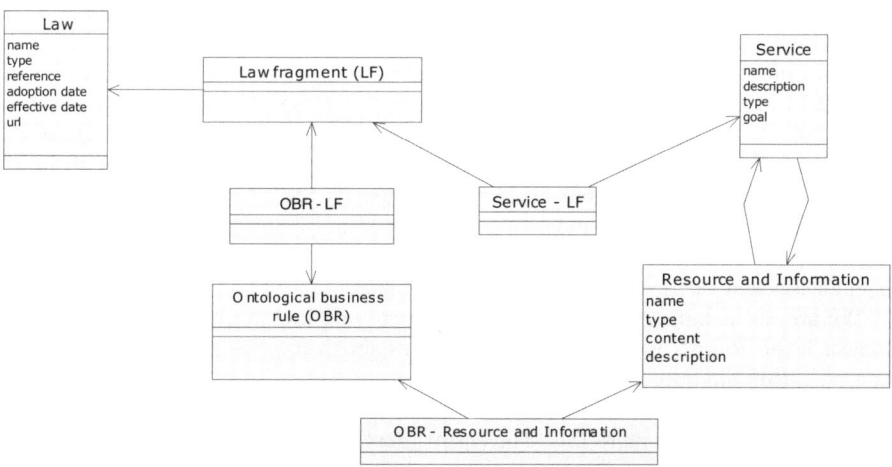

Fig. 7. Link between service, resource and information and ontological business rule

An ontological business rule can specify one or several resource /information. A resource/information is concerned by one or several ontological business rules. This relationship is expressed by the "OBR – Resource and Information" entity. The business rules are used to help the administration to better achieve goals, communicate between principals and agents, between the organization and interested third parties, demonstrate the fulfillment of legal obligations, operate more efficiently, perform analysis on current practices. Consequently, business rules are very significant because they guarantee the conformity of services with the legal framework.

In our example, Resource/Information which governs the "Validation and Examination of the registration request" service are:

- The registration of an association to the Commercial Register must indicate the statutes date, the association name, the head office, the objective, the resources, the organisation, the representation and the signature mode.
- The registration query must be signed by the association's manager.
- The registration query must come together with a legal abstract of the General Assembly minutes, the indication of the authorised people to sign, the signature mode, and a copy of the statutes.

Resource/Information is clearly expressed, at the ontological level, in terms of ontological business rule associated to the hyperconcept «Examination of the registration of an association».

2.2.2 Information System Component (ISC) and e-Government Services

The aim of this paragraph is to specify how the e-Government services are descried and expressed in IS. We propose the concept of ISC to enable to work with a part of an IS as a component.

In other words, we consider that it is a need to work with a part of an IS, in particular with a unique and a coherent set of conceptual specifications. Consequently, we adopt the ISC concept as a solution for the implementation and the deployment of IS and e-Government services.

In our proposed approach, once the ontological level is built, we are able to derive a set of ISC from the ontological level. Three types of aspects constitute the contents of the ISC, as follows: (i) the static aspects which specify the data structure of the IS, (ii) the dynamic aspects which express the behaviour of different elements of the IS and (iii) the integrity constraints aspects which specify the rules governing the behaviour of the IS elements. The integrity constraints of an IS generally represent the business rules of an organisation. An integrity constraint is a logical condition defined over classes and verified by transactions or methods.

We are not detailing in this chapter the process of ISC derivation from the ontological level. Below, we propose a model to establish link between services, hyperconcepts, ISC and transactions.

As we see in figure 8, one hyperconcept then corresponds to one or more services, and a service to one or more ISC. The entity "Service – Transaction – ISC" expresses the direct link between service, transaction and ISC.

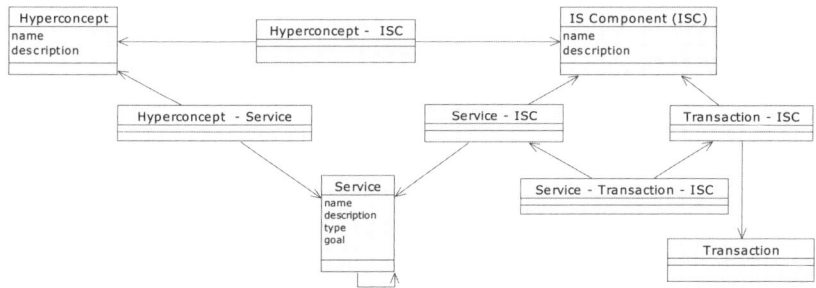

Fig. 8. Link between service, hyperconcept, ISC and transaction

2.2.3 Implementation of the Proposed Model

We have implemented our proposed model to define and construct e-Government services based on legal sources with the Protégé[4] ontology editor. Each hyperconcept which is identified through laws analysis is stored in the same ontological classes' structure, referenced above as our proposed model. We populate the classes one by one, beginning with the class "concept". Protégé allows us to easily navigate through the interrelated concepts of our hyperconcepts (either through the Protégé Frames instances forms or through graph representations such as the ones offered by the On-toviz Protégé plug-in). In the near future, we envision to build a core IS model from a Protégé ontology with a link to an Oracle DB instance (through RFD data store).

3 Discussion about Difficulties Related to the Deployment of the Proposed Approach

Implementing this approach in the public administration certainly creates strong reactions and raises several issues. In this context, we suggest to base the creation of institutional IS engineering and online services on the existing laws, because these legal texts are the unquestionable source of information for the public administration.

One of the main advantages of such an approach is to explicitly match the legal framework, which provides the basis of the activities of a public administration, to the provided services, especially online services. Although not written to build IS, laws nonetheless contain relevant and potentially very valuable information to build IS.

The laws studied in our research - Swiss federal laws, but also cantonal laws and their application regulations - supply information, business rules. Moreover, this analysis also reveals the roles and functions that the public administration (in our case the State of Geneva) has to perform. These elements in the laws have to be transposed in the institutional IS of the State of Geneva, either through software applications and databases, or through other specific organisational functions.

The wealth of information contained in the legal framework is therefore processed to build an ontology of the IS.

---

[4] http://protege.stanford.edu

3.1 What about the Inconsistencies in the Laws?

The complexity of the Swiss legal framework, which encompasses federal, state and local levels, makes reaching a perfect consistency of the laws unlikely. Our approach permits to reveal the inconsistencies included in the legal framework. This raises the broad issue of the means allocated in the public administration in order to solve these inconsistencies. The ideal answer would be to bring this to the attention of the parliament at the political level. However, this ideal way of dealing with the problem is hardly practical. The observed business implementation of the laws and regulations sometimes offers an empirical way of bypassing these formal inconsistencies.

3.2 What Skills Are Required to Implement This Approach?

The hierarchical structure of the laws and the specific legal terms are certainly essential elements to be taken into account when modelling the IS from the laws.

This brings the following questions:

- Should this analysis be performed by the legal experts who write the laws? In this case, should these experts be able to model IS? This analysis could broaden perspectives as far as conceiving and writing the laws, while verifying their consistency. This would raise awareness about consistency issues and offer means of dealing with the problem.
- Should this analysis only be performed by IS designers? In this case, should they take into account the laws as their source for modelling? In order to clarify the legal texts and resolve ambiguities, collaboration with a legal expert is essential.

3.3 The Law Doesn't Correspond to Business Practice

One of the difficulties we have encountered with this approach is in the assessment of the correspondence between legal fragments and the existing practice. Indeed, there are three possible cases where a legal fragment does not correspond to the practice. To begin with, there is the case where the law is incomplete to cover a business practice. Then, there is the case where the law is incoherent with the practice. Finally, there is the case where there is a legal vacuum. These three cases require to be handled by legal expert.

3.4 Is the Legal Framework Sufficient to Describe All the Online Services?

This approach allows the identification of a first set of services. It may not be exhaustive, but it is nonetheless based upon an unquestionable source of information, the laws themselves. This constitutes a strong basis in order to help develop a sound e-Government project.

References

1. Akkermans, H.: Value webs: using ontologies to bundle real-world services. In: IEEE Intelligent Systems, July-August 2004, pp. 57–66 (2004)
2. Apostolou, D.: The ontogov (FP6 - IST) project experience. Technical report, IST Call 4 Infoday (2005)

3. Bench-Capon, T.J.M., Visser, P.R.S.: Ontologies in legal information systems; the need for explicit specifications of domain conceptualisations. In: International Conference on Artificial Intelligence and Law, 0-89791-924-6, Melbourne, Australia, pp. 132–141. ACM Press, New York (1997)
4. Grönroos, C.: Service Management and Marketing: A Customer Relationship Management Approach, 2nd edn. John Wiley & Sons, Chichester (2000)
5. Khadraoui, A.: Method Components for institutional Information System Engineering, Phd Thesis, University of Geneva (2007)
6. Kotler, P.: Marketing Management: Analysis, Planning, Implementation and Control, 6th edn. Prentice Hall, Englewood Cliffs (1988)
7. Lenk, K., Traunmüller, R., Wimmer, M.: Electronic Government - Design, Applications and Management. In: The Significance of Law and Knowledge for Electronic Government, Idea Group Publishing, Hershey (2002)
8. Rolland, C., Prakash, N., Benjamin, A.: A multi-model view of process modelling. Requirement Engineering J4(4), 169–187
9. Zeithaml, V., Bitner., M.J.: Services Marketing. McGraw-Hill, New York (1996)
10. Zúñiga, G.L.: Ontology: Its transformation from philosophy to information systems. In: Welty, C., Smith, B. (eds.) Proceedings of the International Conference on Formal Ontology in Information Systems (FOIS 2001), pp. 187–197. ACM Press, Ogunquit (2001)

Business Process Modelling Perspectives Analysis

Renate Strazdina and Marite Kirikova

Riga Technical University
Kalku iela 1, Riga, LV-1010
{Renate.Strazdina,Marite.Kirikova}@cs.rtu.lv

Abstract. Business process modelling has long been important both for IS development and organization performance optimization. In addition, as demonstrated by practical experience derived from cooperation with organizations it is necessary to design an approach allowing the translation of business processes modelled in a particular perspective to other perspectives – which is not always possible under the existing modelling approaches. This paper brings together business process modelling perspectives that have found their reflection in various existing enterprise architectures. The existing business process modelling perspectives are grouped based on the underlying semantic meaning and analysed from the following viewpoints – the modelling scale and possible values and interrelation between different business process modelling perspectives.

Keywords: business process modelling, enterprise architecture, multidimensional modelling.

1 Introduction

Business process modelling has long been important both for IS development and organization performance optimization. In many cases business process modelling has been developing as part of the enterprise architecture realm. In addition, an analysis of the existing enterprise architectures shows that business process modelling is presented from different perspectives in different enterprise architectures, thus evidencing the correlation between business process modelling perspectives and the final goal and future use of the model. However, as demonstrated by practical experience derived from cooperation with organizations, it is necessary to design an approach allowing the translation of business processes modelled in a particular perspective to other perspectives – provided such a transformation is semantically possible. This is also confirmed by assorted research [1] Besides this, in an organizational context business processes are performed and constructed by people "owning" different business perspectives, therefore it is reasonable to consider the possibility of constructing a multidimensional business process model in a multidimensional business process modelling space where one modelling dimension can consist of a set of different business perspectives.

This article brings together business process modelling perspectives (business perspectives) that have found their reflection in various existing enterprise architectures,

J. Stirna and A. Persson (Eds.): PoEM 2008, LNBIP 15, pp. 210–216, 2008.

thus enabling one to grasp the scope of requirements organizations pose towards business process models. The existing business process modelling perspectives are grouped based on their underlying semantic meaning and analyzed from the following viewpoints: modelling scale and possible values and interrelation between different business process modelling perspectives.

The paper is structured as follows: The overview of business process modelling perspectives selected from related works is presented in Section 2; the analysis of the existing business process perspectives is presented in Section 3; and Section 4 consists of conclusions and points to directions of future work.

2 Enterprise Architectures and Business Process Modelling Perspectives

"'Architecture', in a broad sense, is the synergy of art and science in designing complex structures, such that functionality and complexity are controlled... architecture, hence, is concerned with understanding and defining the relationship between the users of the system and the system being designed itself" [2]. With respect to enterprise architectures, the notion of a business process model frequently appears in definitions of the architectures [3] or enterprise architecture frameworks [4, 5].

By analyzing different enterprise architectures' products it was found that there are many different business perspectives embedded in these architectures and the sets of perspectives used in different architectures are different. The existing business process modelling perspectives are presented in Table 1. The first column reflects all business process modelling perspectives obtained from the analysis; the following columns show the enterprise architectures' products analysed (denoted by Roman numerals which are explained below the table). The plus signs in the cells of the table present the enterprise architecture products which include the particular perspective.

Multiple interrelated terms are used in this article that are known in the business process modelling discipline – perspective, dimension, modelling scale and values. An analysis of assorted research results [1, 4, 5] showed that different terms are used in business process modelling to describe the same artefacts; it was also noted that the definitions of these terms are not always unambiguous.

The following term definitions are used for the purposes of this research: *Business process modelling perspective* – a business process parameter that can be included in a model but cannot be placed in a separate swimlane, where a swimlane is a visual mechanism of organizing different activities into categories of the same functionality. *Business process modelling dimension* is notion derived from mathematics where the dimension of a space is roughly defined as the minimum number of coordinates needed to specify every point within it [6]. In case of business process modelling it can be applied as well – dimension is a set of parameters or one particular parameter associated with the particular business process and these parameters allow reflecting the real world in models. A necessary condition is the possibility of placing a dimension in a separate swimlane. Two categories of dimensions are specified in this research: Simple dimensions consisting of one parameter, e.g. time, and structural dimensions consisting of a multitude of parameters. *Scale* is a concept related to *business process modelling dimension*; this concept determines what swimlanes are required. As an example, a time dimension scale can be a month or a minute. The scale of a structural dimension is expressed as the granularity of the elements reflected by the dimension or the number of decomposition / abstraction levels. It is necessary to note that structural dimensions can be decomposed into subdimensions with different scales. *Value* is also a *business process modelling dimension*-related concept that determines the denominations on the swimlanes created; these could be the names of the days of the week or months for the time dimension.

Table 1. Business process perspectives revealed from enterprise architecture frameworks

Perspectives	I	II	III	IV	V	VI	VII	VIII	IX
Mission, vision, strategy	+		+	+	+	+			+
Business goals	+			+		+		+	+
Organizational structure (process performers, owners, planners, designers, etc) and roles	+	+	+	+	+	+	+	+	
Knowledge, information, data	+	+	+	+	+	+	+	+	+
Geographical space	+		+		+				
Time	+	+				+	+		
Event	+	+		+	+		+	+	
State		+		+		+			
Function	+	+	+	+			+	+	+
Services		+			+	+			+
Rules		+				+*	+	+	
System controls	+			+		+			+
System performance parameters/ resource capability				+	+			+	+
System requirements		+	+		+		+		+
Standards (compliance)		+		+	+				+
Interface with business process support system (software and hardware)	+	+	+	+	+	+	+	+	+
Business process support system (software and hardware)	+	+	+	+	+	+	+	+	+

* cultural

I - Zachman's Matrix of Architectural Views [7], II – The Department of Defense Architecture framework (DODAF) [4], III – Federal Enterprise Architecture Framework (FEAF) [8, 9], IV – Treasury Enterprise Architecture Framework (TEAF) [9], V – Microsoft Enterprise Architecture [10], VI – Extended Current Enterprise Architecture [11], VII – The Extreme Architecture Framework [12], VIII – CIMOSA Application server project architecture [13], IX – TOGAF [4]

An analysis of the existing business process modelling perspectives shows that some of these are semantically similar and thus can be grouped together. This gives rise to the perspectives classification presented in Table 2. By using expert evaluation six different groups were defined based on semantic similarities: 1) Strategic level perspectives; 2) Information system requirements level perspectives; 3) Structure level perspectives; 4) Event level perspectives; 5) Function level perspectives; and 6) Data level perspectives.

Based on the defined groups it is possible to find the source / sources of each group – i.e., where the information necessary for developing the model can be found in the organization or its external environment. In addition, further research could help answer whether perspectives belonging to one group and the corresponding dimensions have any other common features – e.g., how detailed the model can be / is worth creating, what links exist with other perspectives or dimensions and who are the users of the model created in a particular dimension.

Table 2. Groups of business process modelling perspectives

Perspectives	Group
Mission, vision, stratety	Group 1
Business goals	Group 1
Organizational structure (process performers, owners, planners, designers, etc) and roles	Group 3
Knowledge, information, data	Group 6
Geographical space	Group 3
Time	Group 4
Event	Group 4
State	Group 5
Function	Group 5
Services	Group 5
Rules	Group 2
System controls	Group 2
System performance parameters/ resource capability	Group 2
Systems requirements	Group 2
Standards (compliance)	Group 2
Interface with business process support system (software and hardware)	Group 2
Business process support system (software and hardware)	Group 2

The individual business process modelling perspectives from the Group 2 were analyzed to determine whether each of them can be treated as a business process modelling dimension – i.e. whether it can be depicted as a separate swimlane in a business process model (see Section 3). The swimlane in a business process model was taken as the main criteria because of the fact that swimlane is a visual mechanism of organizing different activities into categories of the same functionality.

3   Analysis of Business Process Modelling Perspectives

As it was stated in the previous section the following definition of dimension is adopted for the purposes of this paper - *dimension* is a set of related parameters associated with the process where the parameters refer to particular business process modelling perspectives, e.g time dimension (sequence, execution time, start time, end time), standards dimension (rules, system controls, standards compliance) – defined for enterprise architectures that where analysed in the previous section.

To determine the split by dimension of the parameters mentioned in the previous section an analysis based on the perspectives' business essence was carried out. The

Table 3. Business process modelling perspectives and associated dimensions

Perspectives	Dimension	Scale	Values
Rules	Standards dimension	Standards main requirements (vertically)	Depends on the particular standard
System controls		Controls associated with process (described in the process)	Performance parameters (time, sequence, speed, duration, volume), resource capability, input/output controls
Standards compliance		Compliance maturity level (like maturity level in Capability maturity model) (horizontally)	0-5 (if we use for example Capability maturity model approach)
System performance parameters/resource capability (if we are in the process of system requirements definition then it could be associated with the systems requirements dimension, otherwise it could be the standards dimension (e.g. if we are developing workflow model (executable)))	System requirements dimension or Standards dimension	Types of system requirements according to standards (e.g. IEEE)	
Systems requirements (we assume that one particular requirement of the system is a parameter of a process, so system requirements combined are a set of parameters or dimension)	Systems requirements dimension	Types of system requirements according to standards (e.g. IEEE)	Functional; non-functional requirements, performance requirements, security requirements etc.
Interface with business process support system (software and hardware) (if we are in the process of system requirements definition then it could be associated with the systems requirements dimension, otherwise it could be the integration dimension)	Systems requirements dimension or integration dimension	Reason of integration (integration dimension only)	Input/Output/Support
Business process support system (software and hardware)	Integration dimension	Reason of integration	Input/Output/Support

analysis was based on the following principles: The source of the perspectives that belong to the perspectives group (see Table 2) was defined based on empirical evidence and an analysis of relevant literature. If the source coincided for multiple perspectives and the perspectives were semantically close, and if they could also be presented in a single swimlane, a dimension was defined. For example, the source of rules, system controls, and standards compliance is standards (which, of course, can be very different). As such, this forms a structural dimension that can have up to three parameters (see Table 3). The scale was derived from an analysis of realistic business process models where the respective perspective was modelled. The values followed from the defined scale.

As an example of the results of the analysis done regarding the perspectives of the Group 2 are presented in the Table 3.

As the analysis of business process modelling perspectives shows not all of them are separate business process modelling dimensions, however one perspective can be associated with different dimensions – this depends on the objective of the modelling process. Every dimension has a modelling scale associated with it and a possible range of values.

The results of this analysis show that when analyzing business processes it is crucial to include all the information necessary for building a model that would allow transforming modelling results from one modelling dimension to other(s) as well as demonstrate the connection and interdependence of the modelling dimensions.

4 Conclusions

This paper reflects an early stage of a research on business process modelling in different perspectives. The paper contains analysis of business process modelling perspectives that are a part of the existing enterprise architectures' products. These perspectives have been analyzed to determine if each of them can be viewed as a separate business process modelling dimension. Where this was not possible perspectives were combined to make up a dimension.

Further research will test the dimensions outlined in this paper by modelling real-life situations. Further research will also be made into the interdependence of the dimensions and perspectives in order to assess the feasibility of transforming business process models modelled in one dimension to other dimensions.

References

1. Dreiling, A., et al.: From conceptual process models to running systems: A holistic approach for the configuration of enterprise system processes, Decision Support Systems (2007)
2. Vissers, C.A.: A preface for Lankhorst M. et al., Enterprise Architecture at work: Modelling, Communication, and Analysis. Springer, Heidelberg (2005)
3. Lankhorst, M., et al.: Enterprise Architecture at work: Modelling, Communication, and Analysis. Springer, Berlin (2005)
4. Goikoetxea, A.: Enterprise Architecture and Digital Administration: Planning Design and Assessment. World Scientific Publishing Co. Pvt. Ltd., Singapore (2007)

5. Saha, P.: Handbook of Enterprise Systems Architecture in Practice, IGI Global (2007)
6. WolframMathWorld, http://mathworld.wolfram.com/Dimension.html
7. Zachman, J.: A Framework for Information Systems Architecture. IBM Systems Journal 26(3) (1987)
8. Goethals, F.: An Overview of Enterprise Architecture Deliverables, http://www.cioindex.com/nm/articlefiles/64015-GoethalsOverviewexistingframeworks.pdf
9. Diehl, M.: FEAF level IV matrix, http://www.markdiehl.com/FEAF/feaf_matrix.htm
10. Enterprise Architecture Space Organizing Table, http://download.microsoft.com/download/0/C/4/0C44F7EB-893F-4048-B2C6-C1C889E06DF1/MOAG_F02.pdf
11. Zacarias, M., Caetano, A., Magalhaes, R., Pinto, H.S., Tribolet, J.: Adding a human perspective to enterprise architectures. In: 18th International workshop on database and Expert systems applications, Italy, pp. 840–844 (2007)
12. Robinson, P., Gout, F.I.: Extreme Architecture Framework: A minimalist framework for modern times. In: Saha, P. (ed.) Handbook of Enterprise Systems Architecture in Practice, IGI Global, pp. 18–36 (2007)
13. Spadoni, M., Abdomoleh, A.: Information Systems Architecture for business process modeling. In: Saha, P. (ed.) Handbook of Enterprise Systems Architecture in Practice, IGI Global, pp. 366–380 (2007)

A Research Model for Enterprise Modeling in ICT-Enabled Process Change

Anniken Karlsen

Aalesund University College,
Department of Engineering and Maritime Studies, Norway

Abstract. There are few empirical studies and accompanying models of enterprise modeling (EM) practice in information and communication technology (ICT) enabled process change. This paper presents a research model to be used in a project investigating the use of EM in ICT-enabled process change in Norwegian west coast enterprises. Building on categories and sub-categories from the field of process modeling, the model constitutes a wide array of propositions concerning EM practice, thereby evoking various directions of further inquiery.

Keywords: ICT-enabled process change, enterprise modeling practice, the PMP study.

1 Introduction

According to Persson and Stirna [1], research concerning enterprise modeling practice has been more or less neglected by the research community. Focus has instead been placed on the development of enterprise modeling methods. This matches the situation concerning research into process modeling practice, as emphasized in relation to a study by Eikebrokk et al. [2,3] named the Process Modelling Practice (PMP) study.

In this paper an enterprise modeling practice (EMP) research model is presented, showing possible categories influencing or being influenced by enterprise modeling. Besides being a research model for this particular project, the EMP model exhibits key factors of importance and interest to anyone engaged in practical ICT enabled process change. The model will be applied in a study of enterprise modeling use in ICT enabled process change. Empirical evidence will be gained through cases concerning enterprises on the west coast of Norway. The EMP study is initiated to supplement the PMP study in an effort to contribute towards a theory of model-based process change. Through reviewing literature on the field, the EMP model is derived from compiling different views and findings from a variety of sources. Since most sources relate their work especially to process modeling practice and not the broader scope of enterprise modeling, it becomes essential to emphasize that the categories and relationships of the EMP model constitute a set of propositions/hypotheses in future enterprise modeling practice research where it is inititally assumed that what yields for process modelling yields for enterprise modeling practice also.

J. Stirna and A. Persson (Eds.): PoEM 2008, LNBIP 15, pp. 217–230, 2008.

One faces challenges both in the ICT industry and in and between enterprises implementing new ICT systems to facilitate processes [4,5,6,7,8,9]. Statements emphasize that a large part of implementation failures are related to insufficient alignment between various aspects or parts of an organization and the new technology [10,11]. Henderson [12, page xiii] says that emphasis on modeling is well chosen because it is shared models of systems that will lead to the common understanding on which rapid progress can be made. The acknowledgement of this view can be seen through the development of different enterprise architectures that has emerged over the past decade; the Zachman Framework for Enterprise Architecture, DoDAF, PERA, CIMOSA, ARIS and GERAM, to mention just a few. In addition, several commercial computer tools have come into the marketplace in recent years to assist with architecture visualization and modeling.

2   Theory

2.1   Enterprise Modeling

Enterprise modeling (EM) is concerned with representing the structure, organization and behavior of a business entity [13], i.e., a part of an enterprise, a group of enterprises cooperating, the whole enterprise or just single processes in the value chain, to evaluate its performances or reengineer its material, information or control flows in order to make it more efficient [13,14].

Vernadat [15] defines EM as the set of activities or processes used to develop the various parts of an enterprise model to address some modeling finality, whereas an enterprise model is a consistent set of special-purpose and complementary models describing the various facets of an enterprise to satisfy some purpose of some business users. In this way an enterprise model is not one monolithic model, but an assembly of models [14], for example organization models, process models, data models, configuration models and plant layout models [13].

According to Vernadat [15] an enterprise model already exists in any company, be it small or large. The problem is that in nearly all cases it is poorly formalized. It exists in the form of organization charts established by management, documented operational procedures, regulation texts, and to a large extent in the vast amount of enterprise data (either in databases, knowledge bases, or simply data files) and code of application programs. However, a large part remains in the mind of enterprise people and is not formalized or even documented at all. [15, page 70]. Supporting this view, Kalpic & Bernus [16] say that it is a well known fact that much of the existing extremely valuable information and knowledge in enterprises is not made explicit, externalized or formalized and is consequently not available for use by other individuals, and sometimes even can be lost for the enterprises.

According to Miller & Berger [10], enterprise views such as the executive leadership view, the processes view and resources view relate to each other in general, thus giving rise to questions concerning the who, what, where, when, why and how of enterprise which must be answered simultaneously; all views act as constraints on the others. The making of different enterprise models gives us the possibility to see and discuss how the different parts (the ICT system, the processes, etc.) are interconnected and interplay. Understanding means not only knowing what elements the enterprise consists of and how they are related from different aspects, but also how the elements work together in the enterprise as a whole [17]. Trying to answer all of the questions from a single viewpoint is like trying to explain what an entire house and its contents are by looking through a single window. It seldom provides a complete and accurate answer [10, page 52]. Following this, when using EM in relation to ICT-enabled process change, different stakeholders like ICT specialists, managers, users etc. have a tool, a set of models that might enable them to discuss status quo and future possibilities concerning process changes and their technological implications in a more holistic way. For example they can see how changes in a business process might imply necessary changes in the enterprise ICT systems or how the implementation of an enterprise resource planning (ERP) solution likely results in the need for major changes in business processes. Combining this insight with information about the enterprise vision, values, mission and goals, the different stakeholders get broader perspectives and knowledge about how the parts relate to each other and which framework one has to work within when planning or doing structural changes in processes enabled by ICT. The latter is connected to the special role of the executive leadership view whereby all activities and organizations in the enterprise must somehow align to and sustain.

2.2   ICT-Enabled Process Change

Today, we see both localized exploitation and internal integration of ICT, together with business process redesign, business network redesign, and business scope redefinition. The consequences of ICT on the design of processes can be summarized as [18,19]:

- elimination of human work from the structured process through automation
- change of the sequence of activities and simultaneous working
- gathering of process information
- integration of tasks leading to the coordination of parts and tasks
- object orientation with the effect of tracking the status of process and work
- optimized analysis increasing the possibilities of analyzing information and decision making
- elimination of interfaces with the effect of reducing critical interdependences in processes
- the overcoming of geographic distances resulting in wide area coordination of processes

Information system (IS) development methodologies are largely dominated by a functionalist perspective, that is, how to produce functionally correct and efficient user requirements, as a basis for system specifications. ICT-enabled process change calls for IS development methodologies whereby the development of computer systems is perceived as an organizational issue, in the tradition of sosio-technical systems thinking if one follows Munkvold [20] stating that the development and implementation of information systems can be seen as a special form of organizational change activity and that the mutual relationship between organizations and information technology makes this process sosio-technical by nature. The goal according to the socio-technical perspective is joint optimization of the social and technical systems in an organization [20]. Optimization of one of the systems at the expense of the other will only result in sub-optimal solutions. Therefore all organizational design processes should also focus on the quality of work life of the employees, the latter making it important that different stakeholders participate in the design process since it is believed that decisions regarding the specification of work are best made by those who actually perform the tasks [20].

The MUST method [20] for participatory design is an example of a methodological development that has clear link to the socio-technical perspective which speaks for itself concerning enterprise models as 'natural ingredients when developing an IS. It is based on the principles of participation, close links to project management, design as a communication process, combining ethnography and intervention, co-development of ICT, work organization and users qualifications and sustainability . The method includes management issues in relation to design processes in an organizational context; something that should be highly valuable considering McAfee's reality description: "'Managers I've worked with admit privately that success with ICT requires their commitment, but they're not clear where, when, and how they should get involved. That's partly because executives usually operate without a comprehensive model of what ICT does for companies, how it can affect organizations, and what managers must do to ensure that ICT initiatives succeed" [7, page 142].

2.3   The PMP Model

Iden, Eikebrokk, Olsen & Opdahl [2,21] emphasize that process change, in various incarnations, has been a central topic in the IS field for several decades. Their study, named the process-modeling practice (PMP) study, give insight into Norwegian model-supported process-change practice, focusing especially on process modeling. As part of their study they introduce The a priori PMP model [22], figure 1, and The Revised PMP model [23], figure 2.

The a priori PMP model indicates that characteristics of the organization (process and modeling maturity) have influence on the modeling process. Furthermore, the model shows that the purpose of modeling as well as the artifacts available influence on the modeling process. Particularly interesting is the suggestion that the modeling process has an outcome not only relevant for the process per se, but influence the organization as a whole in form of eventual process maturity and modeling maturity.

The revised PMP model focuses on how Modelling processes and Process competence are related to the Outcome of model-based process change projects, where Process Modeling competence corresponds to Initial process-modelling maturity in the a priori model and Process-orientation competence corresponds

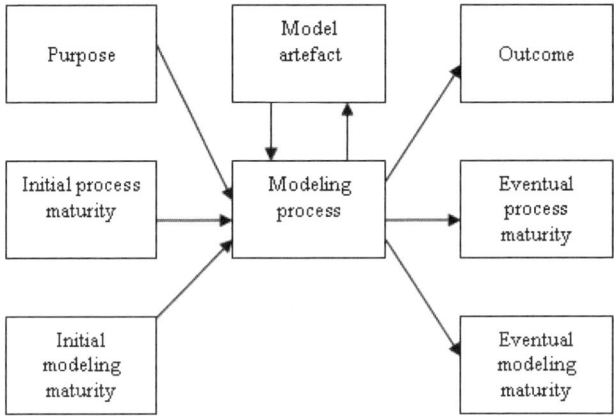

Fig. 1. The a priori PMP model

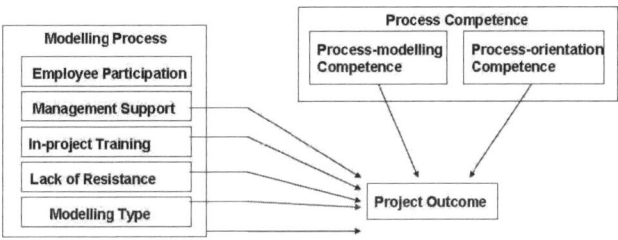

Fig. 2. The revised PMP model

to Initial process maturity in the initial model. The revised model has retained the Modeling process construct in the a priori model; defined as the "activities carried out within the project to improve the organization's processes" [23].

From the initial study the following constructs are kept as dimentions of the modeling process: Employee participation, Management support, In-project training, Lack of resistance and Model type. In the revised model Project outcome is brought in as an main variable decomposed into the dimensions: Goal achievement, Organizational impact, Process-orientation learning and Process-modeling learning [23].

Eikebrokk et al. [23] states that a central hypothesis is confirmed in their study: There is a positive relationship between modeling processes in terms of management support, lack of resistance, in-project training, model types and project outcome.

For short one can sum up that their analysis indicates that a combination of technological (i.e. Model type), social (i.e. Lack of resistance) and organisational factors (i.e. Management support) explain the outcome of model-based process-change projects, being aware that their present study cannot exclude the importance of additional dimensions of Modeling process [23].

A motivation for being occupied with modeling in projects is that quantitative and qualitative analysis in the PMP study [3] shows that high-outcome projects tend to have highly complex modeling processes, whereas middle- and low-outcome projects follow simpler processes. Qualitative analysis also indicates that high-outcome projects use more complex model artifacts than middle- and low-outcome projects.

3   The EMP Research Model

To conduct a study especially related to ICT-enabled process change projects the EMP model has been developed to be used as a tool in further work. In this section the EMP model is presented. The model incorporates and builds upon the categories and subcategories found in the PMP model [2,3], findings from the PMP study, aspects found in literature, especially in relation to the writings of Davenport [19] and Sedera et al. [24], and a pilot study of a corporate merger case[25]. Concerning the EMP model the merger case indicated that the categories project resources, project purpose and systems development methodology might influence on the modelling process, and that outcome of a "'well-conducted"' modeling process might improve user satisfaction through a better match between organizational needs and ICT solution but also through user participation. The findings from the pilot study, which will be further examined, can be found under Context, table 4, in the EMP model. In section 4 the PMP and the EMP study are compared and discussed.

Figure 3 shows the enterprise-modeling practice (EMP) model that has been developed.

The three main categories in the model are Enterprise modeling (EM), Context and Outcome.

Enterprise modeling (EM). EM is defined as the set of activities or processes used to develop the various parts of an enterprise model to address some modeling finality in accordance with Vernadat [15]. This category is the focal point of study; it addresses both the development of new models and the additional usage of existing models in relation to the ICT-enabled process change project. It includes both the usage and making of formalized and non-formalized models, this latter being of interest in accordance with Vernadat [15] saying that to a large extent, models are in the mind of the enterprise people; not being formalized or documented at all. In cases where the enterprise models are just part of the individuals' minds, one should expect that the ability to share insight is reduced, thus giving rise to a sub-optimal ICT-enabled process change solution. EM is further elaborated by sub-categories as shown in table 1, where the column named 'Motivation/Sources' gives references to the sources that motivates the categories and relationships of the EMP model.

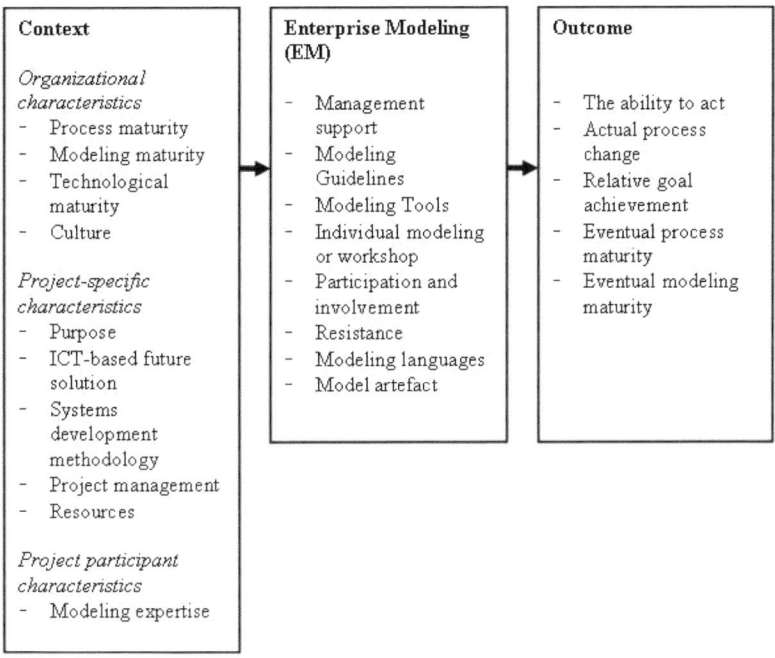

Fig. 3. The EMP model

The sub-categories of the main category Enterprise Modeling are mainly linked to findings from the PMP study, where quantitative analyses [2] show that:

- management support is significantly correlated with outcome
- individual modeling or workshop is correlated with eventual process maturity
- participation and involvement are correlated with outcome
- modeling languages are correlated with modeling framework
- resistance is negatively correlated with model artefact

Sedera et al. [24] among others emphasize the relevance of Modeling Guidelines and Modeling Tools.

Context. Context is defined as the setting of the project comprising organizational characteristics, project specific characteristics and project participant characteristics.

Organizational characteristics is a collective term of those organizational categories that might influence the modeling process. The a priori PMP model points to process maturity and modeling maturity as possible relevant categories.

Project-specific characteristics is a collective term of those categories specific to the project that possibly influence the modeling process. In this category one find sub-categories like ICT-based future solution, Systems development methodology

Table 1. Enterprise modeling practice; Enterprise Modeling.

Category	Definition	Motivation/Sources
Management Support	The level of commitment by management in the organization to the modeling project, in terms of their own involvement and their allocation of valuable organizational resources. (Adapted from Sedera et al. [24])	Eikebrokk et al. [3]; Davenport[19], Sedera et al. [24]
Modeling Guidelines	A detailed set of instructions that describes and guides the process of modeling. (Based on Sedera et al. [24])	Sedera et al. [24]
Modeling Tools	Software that facilitates the design, maintenance and distribution of models. (Based on Sedera et al. [24])	Sedera et al. [24], Sommar [26], Eikebrokk et al. [3]
Individual modeling or workshop	To what extent EM is done as a team-work or on an individual basis. (Based on Davenport [19])	Davenport [19] and Eikebrokk [2]
Participation and involvement	The degree of input from stakeholders, for the design and approval of the models. (Based on Sedera et al. [24])	Eikebrokk et al. [3], Sedera et al. [24]
Model artefact	A man-made representation of parts of an enterprise, for example of a process. (Adapted from Eikebrokk et al. [2])	Eikebrokk et al. [2]
Resistance	A state of mind reflecting unwillingness or unreceptiveness. (Adapted from Hultman [27])	Eikebrokk et al. [3]
Modeling languages	The grammar or the syntactic rules of the selected modeling techniques.	Eikebrokk et al. [3]

and Project Management, among others. The possible relevance of project-specific characteristics to EM might be indicated by the research of Sedera, Gable, Rosemann and Smyth [24], where Project Management was the most cited success factor in relation to process modeling across all three case studies.

Project participant characteristics are characteristics of those involved in the ICT-enabled process change project. It is singled out as a special category in the research model. In contrast, research on the PMP model does not have this perspective as an embedded unit of analysis. In conjunction with this category it can be mentioned that findings from the research of Sedera et al. [24] suggest that experiences with conceptual modeling is related to success in process modeling, indicating a possible relationship in the EMP model.

Each (sub-) category is further elaborated by sub-categories as shown in table 2, 3 and 4, where table 2 shows sub-categories of organizational characteristics in Context, table 3 shows sub-categories of project participant characteristics in

Context, and table 4 shows sub-categories of project-specific characteristics in Context.

The sub-categories of the main category Context can be linked to different sources. For example are Process maturity and Modeling Maturity known from the PMP study, where qualitative analysis indicates weak patterns between high initial process maturity and modeling maturity, and weak patterns between high initial process maturity and modeling maturity. Sedera et al. [24] make clear the importance of culture, modeling expertise, and project management in their work, whilst for example technological maturity is associated with Davenport [19] stating that knowledge of existing solutions implies possible restrictions on the process design and that knowledge of possible future solutions might influence how processes are shaped.

Outcome. Outcome is defined as the phenomena that follow and are caused by EM, including attainment of purpose and the effect of EM on the ICT-enabled process change project solution. This category relates to the outcomes expected

Table 2. Enterprise modeling practice; Context; Organizational characteristics

Category	Definition	Motivation/Sources
Process maturity	An organization's capability for process management and operation, including available competence and current practice. (Adapted from Eikebrokk et al. [2])	Eikebrokk et al. [2]
Modeling maturity	An organizations capability for EM, including available competence and current practice. (Adapted from Eikebrokk et al. [2])	Eikebrokk et al. [2]
Technological maturity	An organizations capability within the field of ICT; knowledge of existing solutions and knowledge of possible future or other enterprises solutions. (Based on Davenport [19])	Davenport [19]
Culture	The organizational readiness to accept and participate in a modeling initiative. (Based on Sedera et al. [24])	Sedera et al. [24]

Table 3. Enterprise modeling practice; Context; Project participant characteristics

Category	Definition	Motivation/Sources
Modeling expertise	The experiences of the project participants in terms of conceptual modeling in general. (Adapted from Sedera [24])	Sedera et al. [24], RAE [28]

Table 4. Enterprise modeling practice; Context; Project-specific characteristics Category Definition Motivation

Category	Definition	Motivation/Sources
Purpose	The purpose of the ICT-enabled process change project	Pilot study of corporate merger
ICT-based future solution	Mean to enable process change. (Based on Davenport [19])	Davenport [19]
Systems development methodology	A standard process followed in an organization to conduct all the steps necessary to analyze, design, implement and maintain information systems [29].	Pilot study of corporate merger
Project management	A controlled process of initiating, planning, executing and closing down a project [29].	Sedera et al. [24]
Resources	Available time, money and people to initiate, plan, execute and close down a project [29].	Pilot study of corporate merger

Table 5. Enterprise modeling practice; Outcome

Category	Definition	Motivation/Sources
The ability to act	Knowledge; ones capacity to set something in motion. Nico Stehr [30]	Henderson [12, page xiii]
Actual process change[1]	The effect of EM on processes. (Adapted from Eikebrokk et al.[3])	Miller and Berger [10] and Vernadat [15]
Relative goal achievement	The result of the project seen in accordance with overarching business objectives (cost reduction, time elimination and so forth). (Based on Davenport [19])	Eikebrokk et al. [3]
Eventual process maturity	Changes in an organizations capability for process management and operation, including available competence and current practice after the modeling process. (Based on the PMP study [2,21,3]	Eikebrokk et al. [3]
Eventual modeling maturity	Changes in an organizations capability for EM including available competence and current practice after the modeling process. (Adapted from Eikebrokk[2])	Eikebrokk et al. [3]

as a result of EM; building upon the PMP project which suggests that the modeling process has an outcome not only relevant for the process per se, but influences the organization as a whole in form of eventual process maturity and modeling maturity. Outcome is further elaborated by sub-categories as shown in table 5. These sub-categories are mainly linked to the PMP model revised. Concerning the term "The ability to act" it is chosen after being inspired by Nico Stehr [30]. In itself the term points to one of the most important reasons for making enterprise models in the first place.

4   Discussion

The EMP study is initiated to supplement the PMP study looking into model-supported process-change practice. Based on this it seems sensible to let the EMP model build extensively on the PMP model, concerning categories, definitions and motivations, thereby making findings from the two studies comparable. At the same time there are fundamental differences concerning the model build-up and scope of modeling practice research between the PMP and the EMP study.

First of all, the PMP study focuses on process modeling in process change. The EMP study has a wider perspective; looking into the making of enterprise models in general in conjunction with process change enabled by ICT. This broader scope is the result of a specific interest in ICT projects and why they fail. It is not enough to just look into the alteration of job practices when involved in ICT projects; it is important to have a holistic view of business and the processes concerned if the ICT system is to achieve the intended outcome [28]. Whilst the EMP model to a large degree incorporates the categories of the PMP model, it additionally incorporates elements from literature and the pilot study that has not been a matter of concern in the PMP study, thereby widen the scope of the model. This especially relates to project-specific characteristics, but other sub-categories can also be found, for example technological maturity in organizational characteristics.

The EMP study is in addition focused on gaining information from different stakeholders involved in the same projects, for example in projects related to supply chain management (SCM); where ICT impacts on the interrelationship between flows of goods and flows of information, as well as interrelationships between different business units.

Whereas the PMP project selected process change projects within an array of different sectors from all over Norway, the EMP study will mainly look into the furniture, the marine, and the maritime sector. These are clusters that to a large degree are situated on the west coast of Norway, far from their markets, and that compete on a global basis. Focusing on these three clusters might very well turn out to be valuable to the EM practice study. For example, there might be sector differences that turn out to influence degree of modeling and there might also turn up some cultural factors that are interesting.

While the PMP study focuses on projects where it is known or highly expected to have been conducted modeling, the EMP study will open up for cases where modeling is weakly present or even completely omitted. As seen from the corporate merger case these instances might also reveal interesting relationships.

In general one can say that the scope of further work on EM in ICT-enabled process change directs the EMP research project to focus on potentially complex change processes, with a high degree of organizational impact, cross functional and cross organizational implications and involvement. Persson [31] e.g. emphasizes a wide array of situational factors influencing the quality of enterprise models that moderate the final outcome of an EM process.

5   Concluding Remarks and Further Work

The overall research question for this EMP study is: "How is enterprise modeling used and how can it be used as a technique for IT enabled process change in Norwegian West Coast enterprises?"

The EMP research model constitutes a wide array of propositions/hypotheses concerning EM practice, thereby evoking various directions of inquiery. Examples of relevant questions that can be drawn from the model are:

- For what purposes are EM used in ICT-enabled process change?
- How does the purpose of the modeling affect how the modeling process is carried out?
- How is the modeling process affected by the level of initial process-, and modeling maturity?
- Does more elaborate modelling processes tend to produce and use more complex model artefacts and vice versa?

Having developed a reseach model, I will now turn to current practice in companies on the west coast of Norway, focusing on what is modeled and why, when and how modeling is done during the ICT-enabled process change project. Herein it is interesting to see to what extent complexity and uncertainty associated with model-making in general influence to what extent enterprise models are used and where they are used within ICT -enabled process change.

References

1. Persson, A., Stirna, J.: Why Enterprise Modelling? An Explorative Study into Current Practice. In: Dittrich, K.R., Geppert, A., Norrie, M.C. (eds.) CAiSE 2001, vol. 2068, p. 465. Springer, Heidelberg (2001)
2. Eikebrokk, T., Iden, J., Olsen, D., Opdahl, A.: In Process Modelling Practice: Theory Formulation and Preliminary Results, NOKOBIT, Molde, Norway (2006)
3. Eikebrokk, T.R., Iden, J., Olsen, D., Opdahl, A.L.: Exploring process-modelling practice: Towards a conceptual model. In: Proceedings of the 41st Hawaii International Conference on System Sciences (2008)
4. Carr, N.: IT Doesn't Matter, May 2003, pp. 41–49. Harvard Business Review (2003)
5. Davenport, T., Short, J.: The New Industrial Engineering: Information Technology and Business Process Redesign, pp. 11–27. Sloan Management Review (Summer 1990)
6. Hammer, M.: Reenginering Work: Don't Automate, Obliterate. Harvard Business Review, pp. 104–112 (July-August 1990)

7. McAfee, A.: Mastering the Three Worlds of Information Technology, pp. 141–149. Harvard Business Review (November 2006)
8. Smith, H., Fingar, P.: Business Process Management: The Third Wave. Meghan-Kiffer Press, FL, USA (2003)
9. Smith, H., Fingar, P.: IT Doesn't Matter - Business Processes Do: A Critical Analysis of Nicholas Carr's I.T. Article in the Harvard Business Review. Meghan-Kiffer Press, FL, USA (2003)
10. Miller, T., Berger, D.: Totally Integrated Enterprises: A Framework and Methodology for Business and Technology Improvement. In: Raytheon Professional Services LLC, St. Lucie Press (2001)
11. Wognum, N.: Editorial/Enterprise modelling and system support. Advanced Engineering Informatics 18, 191–192 (2004)
12. Bustard, D., Kawalek, P., Norris, M.: Systems Modeling for Business Process Improvement. Artech House Publishers, Boston (2000)
13. Berio, G., Vernadat, F.: Enterprise modelling with CIMOSA: functional and organizational aspects. Production Planning and Control 12(2), 128–136 (2001)
14. Vernadat, F.: Enterprise Modelling: Objectives, constructs & ontologies. In: Tutorial held at the EMOI-CAiSE Workshop, Riga, Latvia (June 2004)
15. Vernadat, F.B.: Enterprise Modeling and Integrations, principles and applications. Chapman & Hall, London (1996)
16. Kalpic, B., Bernus, P.: Business process modelling in industry – the powerful tool in enterprise management. Computers in Industry 47, 299–318 (2001)
17. Kirikova, M.: Explanatory capability of enterprise models. Data and Knowledge Engineering 33, 119–136 (2000)
18. Seidlmeier, H.: Process Modeling With ARIS: A practical Introduction. GWV-Vieweg (2004)
19. Davenport, T.: Process innovation: reenginering work through information technology. Harvard Business School Press, Boston (1993)
20. Munkvold, B.: Tracing the Roots: The Influence of Socio-Technical Priciples on Modern Organisational Change Practices. In: Coakes, E., Willis, D., Lloyd-Jones, R. (eds), Springer, London (2000)
21. Iden, J., Eikebrokk, T., Olsen, D., Opdahl, A.: In Prosessforbedring - en vurdering av nasjonal praksis, Universitetet i Bergen, Institutt for informasjons- og medievitenskap, Publikasjon, NOKOBIT, vol. 61, pp. 147–164 (2005)
22. Iden, J., Olsen, D., Eikebrokk, T., Opdahl, A.L.: Process change projects: a study of Norwegian practice. In: Proceedings of ECIS, Gotenburg, Sweden, pp. 1671–1682 (2006)
23. Eikebrokk, T., Iden, J., Olsen, D., Opdahl, A.L.: Toward a model of process-modelling practice: Quantitative validation and results. In: Proceedings of ECIS (2008)
24. Sedera, W., Gable, G., Rosemann, M., Smyth, R.: A success model for business process modeling: findings from a multiple case study. In: Proceedings Eight Pacific Asia Conference on Information Systems, Shanghai, China, pp. 485–498 (2004)
25. Karlsen, A., Engelseth, P.: Corporate merger and developing information connectivity in a pelagic fish network – a case study. In: Proceedings of the 8th International Conference on Management in Agri-Food Chains and Networks, Ede, The Netherlands (2008)
26. Sommar, R.: Business process modelling introduction, tutorial, developed by KTH (2006)

27. Hultman, K.: Managing Resistance to Change. Encyclopedia of Information Systems, USA, vol. 3. Elsevier Science, Amsterdam (2003)
28. RAE, BCS: The Royal Academy of Engineering and the British Computer Society, The Challenges of Complex IT Projects (2004)
29. Hoffer, J., George, J., Valacich, J.: Modern Systems Analysis and Design. Pearson Education, Inc., US (2005)
30. Stehr, N.: The Fragility of Modern Societies: Knowledge and Risk in the Information Age. SAGE Publications, London (2001)
31. Persson, A.: Enterprise modelling in practice: Situational factors and their influence on adopting a participative approach, Ph.D. Thesis. Stockholm University, Report series no. 01-020 (2001); ISSN 1101-8526

Author Index

Printing: Mercedes-Druck, Berlin
Binding: Stein+Lehmann, Berlin